Abstracts
of
HENRY COUNTY VIRGINIA
Deeds
(Books 5 *and* 6)

- 1792-1805 -

Compiled by:
Lela C. Adams

Southern Historical Press, Inc.
Greenville, South Carolina

Copyright 1979
By: Lela C. Adams

Copyright Transferred 1983
To: Southern Historical Press, Inc.

All rights reserved. No part of this publication may be reproduced, stored in a retrieval system, transmitted in any form, posted on to the web in any form or by any means without the prior written permission of the publisher.

Please direct all correspondence and orders to:

www.southernhistoricalpress.com
or
SOUTHERN HISTORICAL PRESS, Inc.
PO BOX 1267
Greenville, SC   29601
southernhistoricalpress@gmail.com

ISBN #0-89308-360-7

Printed in the United States of America

CONTENTS

Deed Book V - Oct. 1792 - Aug. 1797	1
Deed Book VI - Sept. 1797 - Dec. 1805	48
Name Index	149
Water Features	
Land Features	
Counties and States	
Miscellaneous	
Slave Index and Slave Owners	

Henry County, Virginia
Deed Book V

Pages 1-2.   27 Oct. 1792.   WILLIAM ALEXANDER of the county of Pittsylvania to WALTER KING COLE of Henry County conveys a tract of land located on Little Marrowbone Creek containing by estimate 25 acres being of a tract of land sold by CHARLES FARRIS, SENR., beginning at an Old Ford on Little Marrowbone Creek to JAMES REA'S..for the consideration of Twenty Five pounds. Wit: JOHN MCALEXANDER, JOHN KING, INGRAM ALEXANDER. Signed: WILLIAM ALEXANDER.

Pages 2-3.   30 Oct. 1792.   JOHN KING of the county of Henry to GEORGE HAIRSTON of the same for the sum of One hundred pounds, sells and conveys 147 acres on the east side of Marrowbone Creek adjoining the line of ROBERT CHANDLER. Signed: No signature. Proved: 30 Oct. 1792.

Pages 4-5.   17 Aug. 1792.   PETER HAIRSTON of Stokes County, North Carolina to REUBEN PAYNE of the county of Henry, state of Virginia, in fee simple 100 acres more or less..located on the south side of Little Marrowbone Creek, it being part of a tract PETER HAIRSTON purchased of THOMAS BUSH..beginning on Little Marrowbone Creek where the old line crosses the creek just below the Main Road..to include the plantation whereon the said REUBEN PAYNE now lives, and has been in peaceful possession for sometime. Consideration: One hundred fifty pounds. Wit: MICHAEL ROWLAND, JOHN SMITH, THOMAS ADAMS, JR., JOHN EAST. Signed: PETER HAIRSTON. Proved 29 Oct. 1792. Payment rec'd: 17 Aug. 1792.

Pages 5-6.   30 ...., 1792.   SAMUEL JOHNSON and ELIZABETH JOHNSON, and his wife of Henry County to JAMES HAILEY of the same, for the consideration of Fifteen pounds sells 100 acres of land located on both sides of the Grasey Fork of Leatherwood Creek, crosses Camp Branch. No wit. Signed: SAMUEL JOHNSON, BETSY JOHNSON.

Page 7.   29 Dec. 1792.   Power of Attorney. We, MARY OLDHAM, JOHN OLDHAM and THOMAS OLDHAM of Henry County and WINFORD NEVILLS and MARY OLDHAM of Pendleton County, South Carolina have a negro named GEORGE, left to us by JOHN OLDHAM, SENR. late of Northumberland County, Va. by his last will and as the said GEORGE is now living in Fauquire Co., Va., we appoint SAMUEL ELLIOTT of Henry Co., Va. attorney to act in our behalf to sell or receive the said GEORGE. Wit: MARTHA MARROW, ELIZABETH (X) OLDHAM. Signed: MARY OLDHAM, JOHN OLDHAM, THOMAS OLDHAM, WINIFORD _____, MARY OLDHAM, JR. Proved: 30 Apr. 1792.

Page 8. 6 Oct. 1792. Bill of Sale. THOMAS NUNN of Henry County for the sum of One hundred Two pounds, 13 shillings and 4 pence, the amount I am indebted to HENRY LYNE of Henry Co. do sell to the said HENRY LYNE one negro woman named PEGG about 50 years old branded on the shoulder, 1 dark bay horse, 1 eyed, 1 wagon and 4 horses, 11 head of cattle, 14 large hoggs, wt. 2500#, 6,000 wt. tobacco, 50 bbls indian corn, 2 feather beds and furniture. Signed: THOMAS NUNN.

Pages 9-10. 22 Dec. 1792. Deed of Trust. AUGUSTINE LAWLESS of Henry County to HENRY DILLON, SENR. of the same, said LAWLESS being indebted in the amount of Fifty pounds. 60 gal. copper pot, iron oven, 1 skillet, 6 pewter plates, 2 dishes, 3 ewes of Doctor WATSON'S mark, 2 hoes and 2 axes. After the last day of Oct. 1794, should this not be paid, items to be sold. Wit: WILLIAM SHELTON, JOHN SALMON, JOHN SALMON, JR. Signed: AUSTAN LAWLESS.

Pages 10-11. 6 Jan. 1793. WILLIAM DILLEN of Henry County to JOHN BURGESS of the same for Twenty pounds sells 28 acres on the south side of Smith River...joins his own line. Signed: WILLIAM DILLEN.

Pages 11-12. 18 Jan. 1793. JOSEPH MARTIN of Henry County to WILLIAM HOLT of the same for the sum of Sixty pounds sells and conveys 50 acres on the north side of Smith River..more fully appears in a deed of STARKEY BROWN to JOSEPH MARTIN dated 31 Oct. 1791. Lines: below field formerly occupied by CHRISTOPHER BOLLING, SENR. and line of GEORGE HAIRSTON...possession day and date mentioned. Signed: JOSEPH MARTIN.

Pages 13-14. 28 Jan. 1793. JOSEPH MARTIN of Henry County to WILLIAM HOLT of the same for the sum of Sixty pounds sells and conveys 126 acres on Smith River. ..see deed from STARK, BROWN, joins JAMES ANTHONY'S line. Possession date above. Signed: JOSEPH MARTIN.

Pages 14-15. 21 Jan. 1793. JESSE CHANDLER of South Carolina to the heirs of JAMES SPENCER, dec'd..for the sum of One hundred fifty pounds sells and conveys 100 acres, beginning at TAYLOR'S old line and on TAYLOR'S line to Marrowbone Creek to ALEXANDER MOORE'S. Wit: JAMES TAYLOR, DANIEL TAYLOR, JOHN MAY, CHARITY MAY, JAMES LARIMORE. Signed: JESSE CHANDLER. Proved: 28 Jan. 1793. Possession: 21 Jan. 1793.

Pages 15-16. 7 Aug. 1792. JOHN JONYKIN of Hawkins County, (Tenn.????) to BELLEROPHAN SMITH of Henry Co., Va. for the sum of Fifty pounds sells 150 acres on a creek joining the land of SHERED MAYSE. Wit: DRURY SMITH, BENJAMIN MOORE, THOMAS JAMISON, WILLIAM HAYSE. Signed: JOHN (X) JONNYKIN.

Pages 16-17. 4 Jan. 1793. BRICE MARTIN of Henry County to JOSEPH MARTIN for the sum of One hundred pounds sells all that part of land lying north of Smith River, being the survey whereon the said JOSEPH MARTIN now lives. This land was conveyed to BRICE MARTIN from MORDECAI HORD. Wit: JACOB MC-CRAW, JOHN REDD, MARY REDD. Signed: BRICE MARTIN. Proved: 26 March 1793.

Pages 17-18. 24 Mar. 1793. MARKHAM LOVELL of Henry County to JOHN REDD of the same, for and in consideration of One hundred and fifty pounds sells land on Little Beaver Creek by estimate 300 acres with lines of GEORGE HAIRSTON and BENJAMIN JONES. Signed: MARKHAM LOVELL.

Pages 18-19. 26 Mar. 1793. JOHN SMITH of Henry County to JOHN REED of the same for the sum of Twenty pounds sells land on the waters of Fall Creek being 125 acres, joins: PHILIP ANGLIN, LITTLE B. MAYS, THOMAS SMITH and WILLIAM SMITH. Signed: JOHN SMITH.

Pages 19-20. 25 Mar. 1793. Bond of GEORGE WALLER, sheriff. Bondsmen: ROBERT STOCKTON, HENRY JONES, JAMES BAKER, JOHN ROWLAND.

Pages 20-21. 25 1793. Deed of Trust. WILLIAM THOMPSON indebted to ROBERT WILLIAMSON in the amount of Thirty pounds, secures with: 280 acres on Rock Run joins: THOMAS NUNN, JOHN BARKSDALE, JOHN DILLON. To be in effect after 25 Dec. 1793. Wit: WILLIAM STOKES, THOMAS ALEXANDER, P. GARLAND. Signed: WILLIAM THOMPSON, ROBERT WILLIAMSON.

Page 22,23. 10 Apr. 1793. HENRY LYNE of Henry County to GEORGE WALLER of the same, for Twenty two pounds sells land on the waters of Smith River 90 acres..to the old Wagon Ford to WILLIAM COX'S road, JOHN SALMON'S, COL. WALLERS. Wit: ROBERT WILLIAMSON, JOHN WALLER, ROBERT ROWAN, GEORGE WALLER, JR. Signed: HENRY LYNE.

Pages 23-25. 5 Sept. 1792. WILLIAM ROBERTSON of Prince William County, Va. to JAMES REA of Henry Co. for the sum of Two hundred pounds, sells and conveys 400 acres it being part of that messuge tenement tract containing 1142 acres of which 400 ac. is laid off...part of a survey made in the name of JAMES REA...line: to a branch known as the Baptizing Place near the meeting house to REA'S plantation.. RANDOLPH and HARMER'S line now called Dr. G. GILMORE'S land above REUBEN PAYNE'S plantation to the old road that leads to HALL'S old field. Wit: GEORGE HAIRSTON, THOMAS GRAVES, ABSALOM REA, ABNER REA. Signed: WILLIAM ROBERTSON. Pr. & Rec.: 29 Apr. 1793.

MEM: NATHAN HALL claims a part of the 400 acres, should HALL'S right be valid, JAMES REA is not to have recourse against WILLIAM ROBERTSON.

Pages 25-26. 30 Apr. 1793. WILLIAM BROWN of Henry County to ARCHELAUS REYNOLDS of the same for Forty pounds sells land on the waters of Leatherwood Creek containing 80 acres..lines: HALEY'S Mill and PEDIGO. Wit: EDWARD PHILLIPS, WILLIAM THOMAS, RUFFIN BROWN. Signed: WILLIAM BROWN, MARGET BROWN.

Pages 26-27. 29 Apr. 1793. ANDREW REA of Henry County to PHILLIP ANGLIN of the same for Eighty pounds sells 125 acres of land on the north side of the North Mayo River joins lands of REA and ANGLIN, begins at the mouth of ANGLIN'S spring branch, HARBOUR'S line and the line that was formerly GOOLDSBY. Signed: ANDREW REA. Proved: 29 Apr. 1793. . .Payment rec'd and possession given date above.

Pages 27-28. 1 Sept. 1792. JOHN RICHARDSON of Wilks Co., Georgia to JESSE STITH of Henry Co., Va. for the sum of Twenty pounds sells land on Marrowbone Creek being the place the said JOHN RICH-ARDSON last moved from, containing 193 acres, line: formerly JOHN HARDMAN and WASH. LANIER. Wit: JESSE WITT, DANIEL GOLDSBY, STEPHEN ATKISSON. Signed: JOHN RICHARDSON. Proved: 1 Sept. 1792.

Pages 29-30. 30 Apr. 1793. Power of Attorney. JAMES LYON of Patrick Co., Va. appoints his friend THOMAS MITCHELL of Patrick Co. to recover and receive of JOHN HENDERSON of the said county and BARNA WELLS of Henry County, money and tabacco of the said WELLS and HENDERSON that is owing as Deputy Sheriffs, under me for the years 1786-1787. Signed: JAMES LYON. Acknowledged and received: 30 Apr. 1793.

Page 30. 21 Nov. 1792. Bill of Sale. JOHN W. HUNTER of Henry County sold to WILLIAMSON & GARLAND 1 gray horse for Eighteen pounds that was due them. Wit: WALTER SHELTON. Signed: JOHN W. HUNTER.

Pages 30-31. 16 May 1793. Deed of Trust. JOHN FORSSIE of Henry County to GEORGE HAIRSTON. Said FORSSIE is indebted to HAIRSTON in amount of One hundred Ninety seven pounds. GEORGE HAIRSTON signed a bond as security for said JOHN FORSSIE..bond was to ZACHERIAH BURNLY executor of JOHN BURNLY, dec'd of Orange County and has released my property from said BURNLY, execution of which property I have sold to GEORGE HAIRSTON..6 negros, HARRY, CATE, HALL, JUDA, MILLY and PETER, 8 horses, 16 head of cattle, 2 feather beds and furniture..to be in effect 25 Dec. 1793. Wit: ROBERT LAUTON, WILLIAM WATSON, WILLIAM KING, CATY (X) ZACKERY. Signed: JOHN FORSSIE. Rec: 24 June 1793.

Pages 32-33. 1 Nov. 1790. WALTER BERNARD of Franklin County to JOSEPH RAY JOHNSON of Henry County for the sum of Two hundred pounds sells and conveys land on both sides of Lovings Creek of the Yadkin River it being 235 acres that was granted said WALTER BERNARD 23 Apr. 1788 and being on the east side of the Creek. Wit: GEORGE HANCOCK, R. WILLIAMS, JOHN CALL, RICHARD W. VENABLE. Signed: WALTER BERNARD. Proved: 31 Jan. 1791. Rec.: 27 May 1793.

Pages 34-35. 7 Nov. 1792. SAMUEL JOHNSON and WILLIAM LAWRANCE of Henry County to HENRY LAWRANCE of the same for the amount of One hundred pounds sells a tract it being the same tract conveyed from SAMUEL JOHNSON to the said HENRY LAWRENCE and WILLIAM LAWRENCE and received 27 April 1789..it is requested by SAMUEL JOHNSON that deed is to be taken off records and the above to be recorded in its place. The land is 126 acres on both sides of Turkey Cock Creek adjoins the land of JOHN CUNNINGHAM. Wit: JAMES JOHNSON, SAMUEL (X) HUGHES, ALIJAH (X) HUGHES. Signed: SAMUEL JOHNSON, WILLIAM (X) LAWRENCE. Possession: date above.

Page 36.   20 May 1793.   Bond.   We, THOMAS EAST and
                  THOMAS ADAMS, JR. of Henry County, bond in
the amount of Two hundred pounds, whereas THOMAS EAST
has undertaken and agreed with THOMAS JAMISON, RUEBEN
PAYNE and THOMAS STOVALL, commissioners to build a
bridge across Marrowbone Creek near the road ford below HARISTON'S lower Mill..completion date by 1 October.
Wit: RANDOLPH ADAMS, THOMAS RLJ. ADAMS.   Signed:
THOMAS EAST, THOMAS ADAMS, JR.

Pages 36-37.   5 Mar. 1792.   RICHARD CORNWELL of Rock-
                  ingham County, North Carolina to GEORGE
HAIRSTON of Henry Co., Va. for the sum of Twenty
pounds sells and conveys land on both sides of Reed
Creek containing 57 acres.   Wit: JOHN NORTON, JOSEPH
STOVALL, WILLIAM COLLINS REA, JESSE (X) ROACH.   Sign-
ed: RICHARD (X) CORNWELL.   Proved 30 Apr. 1793 & 29
July 1793.

Pages 38-41.   30 Nov. 1791.   CHARLES FINCH of Georgia
                  to GEORGE HAIRSTON of Henry County for
the sum of Fifty pounds sells 90 acres which will
more fully appear by the patent of ABRAHAM PENN eschea-
tor to the said FINCH...on the branches of Marrowbone
Creek.   Also another tract by patent 203 acres granted
FINCH 1 Sept. 1780 it being also the branches of
Marrowbone Creek on Warf Mtn. 58 acres.   Wit: M.
ANTHONY, WILLIAM NEELEY, CHARLES JONES.   Signed:
CHARLES FINCH.   Proved: 21 Dec. 1791 & 29 July 1793.

Pages 41-42.   13 Dec. 1792.   JOSEPH CHANDLER of Rock-
                  ingham County, North Caroline to THOMAS
OAKLEY of Henry County for the sum of One hundred
fifty pounds sells land that JOSEPH CHANDLER bought
of GEORGE HAIRSTON on Marrowbone Creek, joins HENRY
MAYSE and MCKEANS, contains 250 acres.   Wit: WILLIAM
COLLINS REA, JOHN (X) PHILLIPS.   Signed: JOSEPH (X)
CHANDLER.   Proved: July Ct. 1793.

Page 43.   26 Jan. 1793.   Deed of Gift.   DAVID QUARLES
               of Henry County to his son WILLIAM QUARLES
of the same 50 acres adjoins WALTER KING COLE, SANFORD
RAMEY, NEWSOM PACE, DAVID QUARLES and JAMES QUARLES.
The said WILLIAM QUARLES is never to traid the land
out of the family during the life of his father and
mother, except by their leave.   Wit: ROBERT LAUTON,
JOHN (X) QUARLES, JAMES (X) QUARLES.   Signed: DAVID
(X) QUARLES.

Pages 44-45.   20 Nov. 1792.   WILLIAM BRETHART and
                  ELIZABETH BRETHART, his wife, of Henry

County to ZACKARIAH PHILPOTT of the same for the sum of One hundred fifty pounds sells and conveys 1,000 acres of land on Beaver Creek joins AMBROSE JONES and JOSEPH COOPER. Wit: SHADRICK DENT, JAMES MURPHEY, CHARLES T. PHILPOTT. Signed: WILLIAM BRETHETT, ELIZABETH (X) BRETHETT.

Pages 45-47. 31 July 1793. GEORGE HAIRSTON of Henry County to ALEXANDER HUNTER of the same for the sum of Five hundred pounds sells land by estimate 800 acres located on the south side of Smith River lines agreeable to a deed of THOMAS M. RANDOLPH to EDMUND LYNE..extends to EUSEBUS STONE, round the tract of land known as the Horse Shoe. No wit. Signed: GEORGE HAIRSTON.

Pages 47-48. 4 Dec. 1787. SAMUEL JOHNSON of the county of Henry & ROWLAND TANKERSLEY of the same to EDWARD DELOSURE of said county for the sum of Twenty pounds sells and conveys 400 acres of land on the waters of Leatherwood Creek. Wit: REUB. DANIEL, REUBEN TARRANT, THOMAS DICKERSON, SENR. Signed: SAMUEL JOHNSON, ROWLAND TANKERSLEY. Payment received 4 Dec. 1787.

Page 49. 1 Aug. 1793. CHARLES FARRIS, SENR. of the county of Henry to WALTER KING COLE of the same for the sum of Twenty pounds sells and conveys 25 acres on both sides of Little Marrowbone Creek, joins JOHN PACE and JOHN REA. Signed: CHARLES (X) FARRIS.

Pages 50-51. 24 Nov. 1790. THOMAS MAN RANDOLPH of Goochland County to JOHN MATHEWS of Henry County for the sum of Twenty pounds sells and conveys 22 acres on the south side of the North Mayo River it being part of a larger tract purchased of T. M. RANDOLPH by JOSEPH ROBERTS. Wit: JOHN EARLY, JOSH. RENTFRO, JOSEPH MARTIN. Signed: THOMAS M. RANDOLPH.

Pages 51-52. 24 Nov. 1790. THOMAS MANN RANDOLPH of the county of Goochland to ARCH. HUGHES of Henry County for the sum of Two hundred forty pounds sells 100 acres on the north side of the North Mayo River. Wit: JOSH. RENTFRO, JOHN EARLY, JOSEPH MARTIN. Signed: THOMAS M. RANDOLPH. Proved: 25 July 1791 & 30 Apr. 1793 & 30 July 1793.

Page 53. 27 July 1793. DAVID LANIER and MARY LANIER, his wife, of Henry County to ELIZABETH

DONELSON of the same county for the sum of Fifty pounds sell and convey 97 acres that joins Lomax & Company. Wit: JAMES HENDREN, BENJAMIN LANIER, JOHN LANIER. Signed: DAVID LANIER, MARY (X) LANIER.

Pages 54-55. 21 Sept. 1792. BARNEBA HAILEY and RHODY HAILEY, his wife, of Henry County to THOMAS PHILLIPS of the same, for the sum of Twenty pounds sells 100 acres located on the branches of the South fork of Leatherwood Creek, being part of a tract granted by patent to DANIEL MCBRIDE..joins: JOHN HAILEY, EDMOND TOOMBS, WILLIAM TOOMBS. Wit: EDWARD PHILLIPS, ELIJAH BAYLES, RODAY PHILLIPS. Signed: BARNABA HALEY, RODY (X) HALEY.

Pages 55-57. 9 Nov. 1792. DAVID WATSON of the county of Henry to WILLIAM BRETHETT of the same for the sum of Sixty pounds sells 450 acres of land on the branches of Leatherwood Creek, joins GARROT BURCH...and part of another tract to make out the 450 acres. BETSY JOHNSON wife of SAMUEL JOHNSON formerly proprierty of the above land. Wit: JOHN WATSON, SAMUEL ELLIOTT, HENRY LAWRENCE (X). Signed: DAVID WATSON, BETSY or BETTY JOHNSTON. . . .Possession granted 9 Nov. 1792.

Pages 57-58. 10 Dec. 1790. Inquisition on land located on Beaver Creek sold by THOMAS COOPER and his wife SARAH COOPER to GEORGE HAIRSTON. We, the jury summoned by the Sheriff of Henry County to assess damages to the land of ZACHARIAH PHILPOTT by THOMAS COOPER'S erecting a Water Grist Mill. 1/8 ac. of land condemned and THOMAS COOPER is to pay ZACHARIAH PHILPOTT eight pounds for land and damage. Jury: CHARLES DAVIS, W. PACE, STARK BROWN, ROBERT PEDDECO, JR, JUNOR (X) MEREDITH, ROBERT PEDDECO, SR., JOHN REDD, CHARLES (X) BURNIT, JOHN CAHILL, JOHN BARKSDALE, WILLIAM HEARD, WILLIAM BROWN.

Pages 59-60. 6 Aug. 1793. JOHN ALEXANDER of the county of Henry to DANIEL RAMEY of the same, for the sum of one hundred pounds sells land on the south side of Smith River whereon RAMEY now lives ..182-1/2 acres by survey, it being part of a tract formerly conveyed by MARTIN KEE of Fluvanna County Attorney for JOHN HARMER of the Kingdom of Great Britian to JOHN ALEXANDER in behalf of DANIEL RAMEY and now from JOHN ALEXANDER to DANIEL RAMEY. Signed: JOHN ALEXANDER. Proved: 26 Aug. 1793.

Pages 61-62. 6 Aug. 1793. DANIEL RAMEY of Henry

County to JOHN HEFFLEFINGER late of the same county conveys land on Smith River 182½ acres land bought of JOHN ALEXANDER. This transaction for Four hundred twenty pounds...Payment and possession 26 Aug. 1793. No wit. Signed: DANIEL RAMEY. Proved: 26 Aug. 1793. MARY RAMEY, wife of DANIEL RAMEY, releases right of dower.

Pages 63-64. 21 June 1793. DANIEL RAMEY of Henry County to JOHN CROUCH of the same for Seventy pounds sells 159 acres by survey, dated 19 April 1768, land on the waters of Smith River, joins WILLIAM ALEXANDER. No wit. Signed: DANIEL RAMEY. Proved: 26 June 1793. . . .MARY RAMEY, wife of DANIEL RAMEY, releases dower right.

Pages 64-65. 26 Aug. 1793. GEORGE HAIRSTON of the county of Henry to SANFORD RAMEY of the same, for the sum of Five pounds sells 4 acres joins DR. WALTER KING COLE, NEWSOM PACE and the line of the land that was formerly owned by DR. JOHN BRISCO. Signed: GEORGE HAIRSTON.

Page 65-66. 26 Aug. 1793. GEORGE HAIRSTON of the county of Henry to DR. WALTER KING COLE of the same, for the sum of One hundred pounds sells and conveys 100 acres, by estimate, located on Marrowbone Creek joining SANFORD RAMEY, NEWSOM PACE and JOHN PACE. Signed: GEORGE HAIRSTON.

Pages 66-67. 26 Aug. 1793. GEORGE HAIRSTON of Henry County to PETER PERKINS of Pittsylvania County for the consideration of One hundred pounds sells land at the head of Marrowbone Creek, 300 acres, the same being the plantation that JESSE WILLINGHAM sold GEORGE HAIRSTON. Joins the lines of JOHN RENNO, URIAH HARDMAN, ELEANOR TORBURN, JOHN HARDMAN including land formerly URIAH HARDMAN'S, DANIEL FORD. No wit. Signed: GEORGE HAIRSTON.

Pages 68-69. 9 July 1793. WILLIAM BRETHETT and ELIZABETH BRETHETT his wife of Campbell County, Virginia to CHARLES THOMAS PHILPOTT of Henry County for the sum of Three hundred pounds sells and conveys land on Little Beaver Creek, it being land purchased of ABRAHAM PENN by WILLIAM WHISETT and by the last will and testament of WILLIAM WHISITT bequested unto the said WILLIAM BRETHETT and ELIZABETH BRETHETT his wife total of 300 acres, joins lands of ROBERT STOCKTON. Wit: JOHN REDD, JAMES HOWARD, SAMUEL (X) WATSON. Signed: WILLIAM BRETHETT, ELIZABETH

(X) BRETHETT. Proved: 26 Aug. 1793.

Pages 69-70. 17 Jan. 1793. JOHN COLLIER of the county of Henry to JOHN GRIGGS of the same, for the sum of Fifteen pounds sells land on the branches of Leatherwood Creek consisting of 236 acres, joins JOHN WATSON. Wit: JOSEPH GRAVELY, JOHN WATSON, JOHN GRIGGS, JR. Signed: JOHN COLLIER. Proved: 26 Aug. 1793.

Page 71. 9 Sept. 1792. JAMES OAKES of the county of Pittsylvania to LABREN OAKS of the same for the sum of Three hundred pounds sells land in Henry County located on the south side of Smith River, 100 acres, more or less. Wit: DUTTON LANE, JOSEPH GOODWIN, WILLIAM (X) SHELTON. Signed: JAMES OAKES.

Page 72. 22 Apr. 1793. FRANCIS GILLEY of Henry County to ARCHIBALD MURPHY of Rockingham Co., North Carolina for the sum of Fifty pounds sells 200 acres of land on both sides of Turkey Cock Creek it being part of a grant to FRANCIS GILLEY, deceased in 1781 and this land having been willed to his son FRANCIS GILLEY. Wit: GEORGE GILLEY, RICHARD GILLEY, MOSES WILSON. Signed: FRANCIS GILLEY, MARY (X) GILLEY.

Page 73. 29 Apr. 1793. Power of Attorney. CHARLES COX and ELEANOR COX his wife of Henry County hereunto moving and but more especially for good will, love and affection we bear MARGARET COX we appoint this friend to sell a tract of 50 acres which joins the land of the deceased THOMAS WATTS whereon he lived. The land of ELEANOR COX which she received by the last will and testament of the deceased THOMAS WATTS in the county of Culpepper and parish of St. Marks....in our name to give receipt, etc. Signed: CHARLES COX, ELEANOR (X) COX. Proved: 30 Sept. 1793.

Page 74. No date. Whereas JOHN FONTAINE, deceased did enter into partnership with PATRICK HENRY and GEORGE ELLIOTT for taking up land in North Carolina and did make use of my name among others in friendly confidence as grantee of part. Therefore in consideration whereof I, JOHN MARR appoint MARTHA FONTAINE widow of JOHN FONTAINE, deceased to be my attorney and act for me and dispose of such as she sees fit. Wit: PATRICK HENRY FONTAINE, WALTER SHELTON. Signed: JOHN MARR.

Pages 74-75. 26 Oct. 1793. WILLIAM PALFREY of the county of Henry to WILLIAM STONE of the same for the consideration of the sum of Fifty pounds sells and conveys a parcel of land containing 38 acres located on the north side of Smith River. No wit. Signed: WILLIAM PALFREY.

Pages 75-76. 29 Sept. 1793. I, EDWARD CASON of the county of Henry for the love and affection that I bear unto the children of my beloved wife LUCY CASON and as I am thereunto moving give, grant unto MARY EDWARDS, JUDITH EDWARDS and NANCY JOHNSON one negro woman agreeable to the bond which demands the said negro woman from MRS. SUSANNAH MARR administrator of the estate of JOHN MARR, dec'd. Wit: LANEY (X) COX, ANNEY (X) MORGIN, BETSY NORMAN, JOSEPH GOODWIN, WILLIAM NORMAN. Signed: EDWARD CASON.

Pages 76-77. 16 Oct. 1793. I, ELIZABETH LOCKHEART of the county of Patrick hereunto moving appoint my son THOMAS LOCKHEART of Surry County, North Carolina attorney to recover for me my third of a tract of land in Albermarle County, which was sold by my deceased husband THOMAS LOCKHEART. Wit: JOHN COX, TUNSTALL COX. Signed: ELIZABETH (X) LOCKHEART. Proved: 28 Oct. 1793.

Pages 77-78. 12 Oct. 1793. Bond of EDWARD DANIEL and JOHN DILLARD are hereby bound to the County of Henry..the said EDWARD DANIEL has undertaken to build a bridge across Marrowbone Creek near the road-ford next above HAIRSTON'S Marrowbone Store for the sum of Eighty pounds, 9 shillings, 6 pence. To be built and kept in repair for 7 years. Wit: THOMAS STOVALL, JAMES TAYLOR. Signed: EDWARD DANIEL, JOHN DILLARD.

Pages 78-80. 14 Feb. 1793. EDMUND EDWARDS heir at law of THOMAS EDWARDS, deceased and JAMES EDWARDS and HENRY LANSFORD, executor for the said THOMAS EDWARDS, deceased convey unto JOHN MARR for the sum of Four hundred pounds all the lands of THOMAS EDWARDS, dec'd being in the county of Henry on both sides of Smith River contains by estimate 894 ac. more or less..joins CALEB MAY a line on Home Creek. Wit: RICHARD WORSHAM, GEORGE SWAIN, JOHN PRYOR, CALEB MAY, JAMES (X) MAY. Signed: EDMUND EDWARDS, JAMES EDWARDS, HENRY LANSFORD. . . .State of Georgia, county of Wilks, RICHARD WORSHAM and GEORGE WAIN, Justices of the Peace for Wilks Co., State of Georgia before whom this deed was acknowledged.

Pages 81-83. 25 Nov. 1793. DAVID LANIER and his wife

MARY LANIER and JOHN ALEXANDER and his wife LUCY ALEXANDER of the county of Henry to JOHN HEFFLEFINGER of the same for the consideration of One hundred sixty eight pounds land on the north side of Smith River containing 134½ ac...being part of a larger tract that LANIER purchased of PATRICK HENRY whereon the said LANIER now lives at the mouth of Mulberry Creek. Wit: REUBEN PAYNE, THOMAS BARTON, RICHARD STOCKTON. Signed: DAVID LANIER, JOHN ALEXANDER. Proved: 25 Nov. 1793. . . .Payment and possession 25 Nov. 1793. Dower release of MARY LANIER, same date.

Pages 83-84. 25 Nov. 1793. CHARLES RIGG of Henry County to JOHN DILLARD of the same for the consideration of one certain gray mare conveys land on the north side of the north fork of the Mayo River being 154 acres. No wit. Signed: CHARLES RIGG.

Pages 84-85. 25 Nov. 1793. Bond. JOHN DILLARD appointed Sheriff of the county of Henry, his bondsmen: GEORGE HAIRSTON, HENRY LYNE, JOHN STAPLES and WILLIAM SHELTON. Proved: 25 Nov. 1793.

Pages 85-86. 24 Dec. 1793. THOMAS COOPER of the county of Green and state of Georgia to GEORGE HAIRSTON of Henry County for the sum of ____ sells land on the waters of Reedy Creek and Donalds Creek being 348 acres. Wit: EDWARD ADAMS, ROBERT ANDERSON, WILLIAM MOORE, ARCHD. FARIS. Signed: THOMAS COOPER. Proved: 30 Dec. 1793.

Pages 87-88. 24 Dec. 1793. THOMAS COOPER of the county of Green and state of Georgia to GEORGE HAIRSTON of Henry County for ____ sells and conveys 308 acres on the waters of Reedy Creek, Donalds Creek and Smith River. Wit: EDWARD ADAMS, ROBERT ANDERSON, WILLIAM MOORE, ARCHD. (X) FARIS. Signed: THOMAS COOPER. Proved: 30 Dec. 1793.

Pages 88-89. 3 Dec. 1793. WILLIAM THOMPSON of the county of Henry to GEORGE HAIRSTON of the same for Seventy five pounds sells and conveys land containing by patent 228 acres bearing date 10 Aug. 1759..mentions trees, creeks but not named. Wit: JOHN P. PYRTLE, JOHN COX, WILLIAM WELLS. Signed: WILLIAM THOMPSON. Proved: 30 Dec. 1793.

Page 90. 25 Oct. 1790. JAMES MANKINS of Henry County to WILLIAM GILLIAM of the same for the consideration of One hundred pounds sells 216 acres on the north fork of Russells Creek, the land now in the possession of WILLIAM GILLIAM. Wit: MILLER EASLEY, JOHN MANKIN, JAMES SMITH. Signed: JAMES MANKINS.

Pages 91-92. 31 Dec. 1793. JOHN ACUFF of the county of Henry to JOHN MINTER of the same for Forty pounds sells 100 acres on the branches of the south fork of Leatherwood creek joins lines of CAIN ACUFF and WILLIAM ACUFF. Wit: JOHN CONNAWAY, JOHN HALEY, CAIN ACUFF. Signed: JOHN (X) ACUFF.

Pages 92-93. 24 Oct. 1793. CARTER TARRANT and WILLIAM ACUFF of the county of Henry to JOHN MINTER in consideration of Seventy five pounds sell land on a branch of Leatherwood Creek by estimate 230 acres joins land of REUBEN NANCE and JOHN ACUFF. Wit: LEONARD TURLEY, JOSEPH ANTHONY, JACOB FERRIS, RODAY PHILLIPS, JOHN ANDERSON. Signed: CARTER TARRANT, WILLIAM ACUFF.

Pages 93-94. 1 Oct. 1793. WILLIAM TOOMBS and his wife SUSANAH TOOMBS to JAMES MELVIN for the sum of Eleven pounds sell 50 ac. on the branches of the south fork of Leatherwood Creek, it being part of a tract TOOMBS bought of BENJAMIN WHEAT, joins DANIEL MCBRIDE. No wit. Signed: WILLIAM TOOMBS.

Page 95. 3 Oct. 1793. JOHN COLLIER of the county of Pittsylvania to WILLIAM THOMASSON of Henry County for the consideration of Ten pounds sells 100 acres more or less on the branches of Leatherwood Creek. Wit: FLEMING THOMASSON, BENJAMIN THOMAS, JAMES (X) THOMASSON. Signed: JOHN (X) COLLIER.

Pages 96-97. 18 Jan. 1794. JOHN COLLIER of the county of Pittsylvania to JONATHAN STONE of Henry County for the sum of Twenty pounds sells and conveys land on the waters of Leatherwood Creek, being 100 acres joins JESSE DELOTHER, NICKES AIKEN. Wit: DANIEL CHYSHER (?), BENJAMIN THOMAS, EDWARD JONES. Signed: JOHN (X) COLLIER. Proved: 27 Jan. 1794.

Pages 97-98. JAMES TAYLOR of the county of Henry to JOHN MAY of the same for Fifty pounds sells 37 acres on Marrowbone Creek, now in possession of the said MAY. Wit: E. ADAMS, GEORGE WALLER, JR. Signed: JAMES TAYLOR. Proved: 27 Jan. 1794.

Pages 98-99. 22 Aug. 1793. Request for the Justices of Woodford County, Kentucky to examine MARGARET COOK wife of WILLIAM COOK and secure a release of right of dower needed for deed to PETER SAUNDERS for 350 acres in Henry County (now Franklin County), Virginia...1 Oct. 1793, Woodford Co., Kentucky, release secured.

Page 99.   24 Jan. 1794.   Jurors viewed damages that HENRY CLARK did sustain on his land on both sides of Beaver Creek by the building of a bridge across said creek. Awarded Thirty four shillings, 6 pence. Jurors: JOHN ROWLAND, JOHN PACE, AMBROSE JONES, JAMES MASTEN, ZA. PHILPOTT, CHARLES PHILPOTT, GEORGE WALLER, JOSEPH MARTIN, JOHN STOKES, JOHN REDD, BEN. JONES, BRICE MARTIN.

Pages 100-101. 4 Dec. 1793. JOHN GRAVELY and PEGGEY GRAVELY his wife of the county of Henry to WILLIAM LAURANCE of the same convey for the sum of Sixty pounds 206 acres on Leatherwood Creek beginning at Twitty's corner, crosses Meethouse branch. Wit: JAMES JOHNSTON, JACOB COOLEY, HENRY (X) LAURANCE, ANDREW FORD. Signed: JOHN (X) GRAVELY, PEGGEY (X) GRAVELY. Proved: 4 Dec. 1793.

...I, WILLIAM LAURANCE the present owner of the above land agree that JOHN BURCH, SR. is to have all the land from the fence that now stands as a dividing line between JOHN BURCH and JOHN GRAVELY in the way of a swap by JOHN BURCH SENR. and JOHN BURCH, JR. Dated 4 Dec. 1793. Wit: JAMES JOHNSTON, JACOB COOLEY.

Pages 102-103.   24 Feb. 1784.   Deed of Trust. JOHN HAILEY of Henry County to SAMUEL CALLAND of the county of Pittsylvania, said HAILEY indebted in the amount of Sixty nine pounds fifteen shillings, secures with land on the waters of Leatherwood Creek being the land whereon the said HALEY now lives contains 230 acres, joins lines of WILLIAM BROWN, JOHN NANCE also 2 mares, stock of cattle, household furniture and plantation tools. To be in effect this date, and after 25 Dec. 1795 shall be sold. No wit. Signed: JOHN HAILEY.

Pages 104-105.   24 Feb. 1793. PHILIP ANGLIN of the county of Henry to JOSEPH JINKINS of the same for the consideration of Twenty pounds sells 157 acres on both sides of the north fork of Fall Creek. No wit. Signed: PHILIP ANGLIN. Proved: 24 Feb. 1794.

Pages 105-106.   18 Feb. 1794. HENRY SUMPTER of Henry County to THOMAS BOLLING of the same for Thirty pounds sells 100 acres on Rock Run Creek.. fork paths, one called Bakers and Goings Wagon Road and the other Cox Path to "Bool" (Bull) Mtn. Rd. that is called JOHN COXES Rd. to the other end of the path wich is known as JOHN COX School House path. Includes the house that JESSE LAWLESS now lives in and the School House. No wit. Signed: HENRY SUMPTER.

Pages 107-108. 29 Oct. 1793. JOHN COLLIER of Pittsylvania County to CHARLES DICKERSON of Henry County for the sum of Twenty pounds sells 351 acres, by survey 17 Mar. 1772 on the branches of Leatherwood Creek joins: JAMES BLEVINS, CHRISTOPHER BOLLING. Wit: THOMAS DICKERSON, SENR., WILLIAM THOMAS, BENJAMIN THOMAS. Signed: JOHN (X) COLLIER.

Page 109. 29 Mar. 1794. JACOB CATRON of the county of Henry to WILLIAM WHITTON of the same for the consideration of Twenty pounds sells land on Steward's Creek on the south side of Smith River contains 100 acres. No wit. Signed: JACOB (X) CATRON.

Pages 110-111. 13 Mar. 1794. HARMON COOK of the county of Pittsylvania to THOMAS WILSON, JR. of Henry County for the consideration of Fifty pounds sells land containing by patent dated 20 Oct. 1755, 109 acres more or less on Turkey Cock Creek on a south branch of the Irvin River (Smith). Wit: ROBERT (X) BRASHARES, AARON (X) WILSON, JAMES (X) WILSON. Signed: HARMON (X) COOK, M. (X) COOK. Proved: 31 Mar. 1794.

Pages 111-112. 31 Mar. 1794. HENRY LYNE of the county of Henry to WILLIAM FRENCH of the same for Fifty pounds sells land on both sides of Horsepasture Creek joins Randolph & Company, it being part of a tract, surveyed by DUTTON LAYNE, contains by estimate 400 acres, joins: JAMES EAST and JAMES MAY. No wit. Signed: HENRY LYNE. Proved 31 Mar. 1794.

Page 113. 6 Feb. 1794. RUBEN NANCE and NANCY NANCE his wife of Henry County to JESSE CROUCH for the sum of Fifty pounds sells 200 acres more or less on Rocky Branch of Leatherwood Creek. No wit. Signed: RUBEN NANCE. Proved: 31 Mar. 1794.

Pages 114-115. 31 Mar. 1794. CHARLES BURNETT of the county of Henry to GEORGE HAIRSTON of the same for the sum of Thirty five pounds sells land on the branches of Beaver Creek, by survey 147 acres. No wit. Signed: CHARLES (X) BURNETT. Pr: 31 Mar. 1794.

Pages 115-116. 15 Mar. 1794. JESSE ROBERSON of the county of Pittsylvania to WILLIAM PEARSON of the county of Henry for the sum of Eighty five pounds sells and conveys a tract or parcel of land containing 758 acres, joins land of THOMAS CLAY. Wit: JOSEPH CUNINGHAM, WILLIAM PIERSON, JACOB DAINS. Signed: JESSE ROBERSON.

Pages 116-117. 15 Mar. 1794. JESSE ROBERSON of the county of Pittsylvania to JACOB DAINS of the county of Henry for the consideration of Twenty pounds sells a tract of land containing 242 acres. Wit: JOSEPH CUNINGHAM, WILLIAM PIERSON, WILLIAM PIERSON. Signed: JESSE ROBERSON.

Pages 117-119. 28 Apr. 1794. WILLIAM CRANE of the county of Henry to BENJAMIN MITCHELL of the same for the consideration of Ten pounds sells land on the branches of Sandy River. No wit. Signed: WILLIAM (X) CRANE, REBECKAH (X) CRANE.

Page 119. 20 Mar. 1794. JOHN REDD of Henry County to NATHAN NORRIS of the same for the sum of ____ sell 50 acres on a branch that runs into Reed Creek, joins MARKHAM LOVELL..to where JOHN JAMISON, SR. has his dividing line. No wit. Signed: JOHN REDD.

Pages 120-121. 19 April 1794. JOHN NORRIS of the county of Henry to WILLIAM WARREN of the same for the consideration of Thirty pounds sells and conveys 100 acres more or less on the waters of Reed Creek. No wit. Signed: JOHN NORRIS. Proved: 28 Apr. 1794.

Pages 121-122. 25 April 1794. THOMAS BOLLING (BOULDIN) of the county of Henry to GREEN BOLLING (BOULDIN) for the sum of Forty shillings sells land on Grassy Creek being 310 acres that joins BRICE MARTIN. Wit: GEORGE HAIRSTON, D. LANIER, WILLIAM STOKES. Signed: THOMAS BOULDIN. Proved: 28 Apr. 1794.

Pages 122-123. 28 April 1794. GEORGE HAIRSTON of the county of Henry to WILLIAM JONES of the same for the consideration of Sixty pounds sells and conveys 120 acres on the waters of Beaver Creek and joins the lines of AMBROSE JONES. No wit. Signed: GEORGE HAIRSTON. Proved: 28 Apr. 1794.

Pages 123-124. 29 April 1794. Deed of Release between GEORGE HAIRSTON and SALLY COLE both of

Henry County, said SALLY COLE is the widow and relick of WALTER KING COLE, dec'd. GEORGE HAIRSTON did purchase of said COLE a parcel of land containing between Twelve or Fourteen hundred acres on the south side of Smith River running up Blackberry and Rock Run Creeks, joins the lands of HUNTER, HORD, BAKER and SUMPTER. MRS. COLE still holds her right of dower and by this deed of release, does hereby relinquish her rights of dower. No wit. Signed: SALLY COLE. Proved 29 Apr. 1794.

Page 125. 29 April 1794. Bond of JOHN DILLARD who is Sheriff of Henry County, his bondsmen are: GEORGE HAIRSTON and JOHN WALLER.

Pages 125-126. 19 Feb. 1794. Bill of Sale. JOHN ABINGTON of the county of Patrick for the sum of Forty pounds sells unto WILLIAM FRENCH of the county of Henry 2 negroes, JOIE, a lad of about 17 and BETTY a girl about 10 years old. Wit: HENRY LYNE, BOWLES ABINGTON. Signed: JOHN ABINGTON.

Page 126. 29 April 1794. Bond of GEORGE WALLER, JR. who is appointed Surveyor for the County of Henry. Signed: GEORGE WALLER, JR., GEORGE WALLER, SR., GEORGE HAIRSTON.

Page 127. 29 July 1794. Bond of GEORGE WALLER who is appointed Escheater for the County of Henry. Signed: GEORGE WALLER, JOSEPH MARTIN.

Page 128. 8 Jan. 1794. Deed of Trust. BARNA WELLS endebted to JESSE D. LOZEAR (DELOZAR) both of Henry County, in the amount of Fifty pounds. This Deed of Trust to come due after the 1 day of May 1795, if this sum has not been repaid. Secures with a tract of land being 272 acres and the plantation whereon he now resides. Wit: FLEMING THOMASSON, ELIJAH SMITH. Signed: BARNA WELLS.

Pages 128-129. 25 Aug. 1794. Power of Attorney. THOMAS POSEY who intermarried with ELIZABETH HOBART, daughter of HARRISON HOBART and his wife JEAN and SASARAH (SABERAH) HOBART daughter of said HARRISON HOBART and JEAN his wife all of Henry County, we hereunto moving ordain and appoint our friend JOHN HOBART attorney to demand of the executors of ASA KING, deceased of Charles County, Maryland all legacy left us by the said ASA KING, deceased. Signed: THOMAS POSEY, ELIZABETH (X) POSEY, SABERAH (X) HOBART. Proved: 25 Aug. 1794.

Page 129. 25 Aug. 1794. Power of Attorney. JOSEPH ANTHONY of the county of Henry appoints WILLIAM BARTLETT of the county of Madison and state of Kentucky to be my attorney to transact my business. Signed: JOSEPH ANTHONY. Proved: 25 Aug. 1794.

Page 130. 28 Apr. 1794. THOMAS NUNN, MARY NUNN and JOHN COX of Henry County to JOHN DILLON of the same for the sum of Fifty pounds sells land on the north side of Smith River and on both sides of Rock Run Creek containing 120 acres more or less. Signed: THOMAS NUNN, JOHN COX.

Page 131. No date. Power of Attorney. I, JOHN BURCH of the county of Henry, me hereunto moving appoint my friend WILLIAM STONE of Franklin County, Virginia my attorney to receive a debt due me from JOHN BISWELL SENR., JOHN BISWELL, JR., and JOHN GOVER of Kentucky due from 21 March 1784 with interest. Wit: SAMUEL BIRD, THOMAS DICKERSON. Signed: JOHN BURCH. Proved: 29 Sept. 1794.

Pages 132-133. 14 Apr. 1788. ZADOCK SMITH of the county of Henry to JOHN CLARK of the same for the sum of Fifty pounds sells and conveys land on the waters of the Mayo River, on the south side of a branch of the Nobusiness fork of the Mayo River...line chopped by agreement between JAMES ECTON and JAMES TAYLOR, goes up a branch called Yellow Bank, being 150 acres more or less. Wit: MOSES REYNOLDS, JESSE REYNOLDS, JOHN LILTRELL. Signed: ZADOCK SMITH. ..Payment received and possession granted date above.

Page 136. 14 April 1788. ZADOCK SMITH of Henry County to JOHN CLARK of the same, for One hundred pounds sells 200 acres land on the waters of the Mayo River. Wit: MOSES REYNOLDS, JESSE REYNOLDS, JOHN LILTRELL. Signed: ZADOCK SMITH.

Page 136-137. 28 July 1790. At a Court held for Henry County DAVID ANDERSON, Complainant vs. SAMUEL TARRANT, Defendant, In Chancery... SAMUEL TARRANT gave a Deed of Trust to DAVID ANDERSON for 317 acres on which he now lives. The attorney for DAVID ANDERSON, RICHARD NATHANIEL VEANBLE, is to sell the land at publick auction to the hightest bidder. Paid to the Clerk and to the Sheriff 187# of tobacco, paid to the Surveyors fee and tax 31/6# of tobacco. . . .RICHARD N. VENABLE having given legal notice to the said SAMUEL TARRANT, have sold said land to DAVID ANDERSON and CALEB HART for the sum of

One hundred Fifty pounds. Dated: 23 Oct. 1790. Teste: JOHN COX. . . .Memo: No part of the personal property was sold at this date, it being sold before to satisfy a debt to DAVID ANDERSON & Company. Signed: RICHARD N. VENABLE.

Pages 137-139. 29 Feb. 1794. Deed of Release. MARTHA FONTAINE widow and relict of JOHN FONTAINE deceased, of Henry County to RICHARD BIBB of Prince Edward County. RICHARD BIBB purchased land of JOHN FONTAINE in Charlotte County, ___ acres with a water grist mill that the said FONTAINE had purchased of WALTER ROBERTSON, deceased, the deed was recorded in Charlotte County 7 April 1777, land on the waters of Staunton River. Since the said MARTHA FONTAINE had never given a dower release, she does so at this time. Wit: EDWARD HENRY, PATRICK HENRY FONTAINE, JACOB JENNINGS. Signed: MARTHA FONTAINE. Proved: 25 Aug. 1794 & 29 Sept. 1794.

Pages 139-140. 18 April 1789. JOHN CUNNINGHAM of the county of Henry to JAMES JOHNSON of the same for the sum of One hundred pounds sells and conveys land on both sides of Turkey Cock Creek being 230 acres. Wit: REUBEN TARRANT, JR., SAMUEL JOHNSON, JOHN PREVILLER (?), A. BALLENGER. Signed: JOHN CUNNINGHAM, SARAH CUNNINGHAM. Proved: 27 Apr. 1789 & 31 July 1793.

Pages 141-142. 4 Feb. 1794. LUCY CASON, EDWARD CASON and JOSEPH GOODWIN executors of JAMES EDWARDS, deceased of Henry County to the estate of JOHN MARR, deceased of Henry County. LUCY CASON, EDWARD CASON and JOSEPH GOODWIN for and by virtue of the will of JAMES EDWARDS directing LUCY CASON to make a deed to the said estate of JOHN MARR, deceased for the sum of Two hundred pounds conveys land on the south side of Smith River by estimate 299 acres joins WILLIAM EDWARDS. Wit: JOHN PRYOR, CHARLES COX, ROBERT (X) SMITH. Signed: LUCY (X) CASON, EDWARD CASON, JOSEPH GOODWIN.

Pages 142-143. 4 Feb. 1794. LUCY CASON, EDWARD CASON, and JOSEPH GOODWIN executors of JAMES EDWARDS, deceased...by virtue of the will of the said JAMES EDWARDS directing LUCY CASON to make a deed to the estate of JOHN MARR, deceased, land on the south side of Smith River, joins line of THOMAS EDWARDS as it meanders to a box wood corner at the Indian Grave Ridge being 91 acres. Wit: JOHN PRYOR, CHARLES COX, ROBERT (X) SMITH. Signed: LUCY (X) CASON, EDWARD

CASON, JOSEPH GOODWIN.

Page 144. 25 June 1794. GRIFFITH DICKINSON of the county of Pittsylvania to the Estate of JOHN MARR, deceased for the sum of Fifteen pounds sells 93 acres in Henry County on the north side of Smith River...to a white oak line called for by Chizzells Patent but can not be found. Wit: JOHN PRYOR, THOMAS B. MC ROBERTS, JOHN CALL. Signed: GRIFFITH DICKINSON.

Pages 145-146. 31 Dec. 1792. JOHN WYATT of the county of Halifax to THOMAS CHAPMAN of Henry County for the sum of Seventy five pounds sells land in Henry County on the branches of the south fork of Leatherwood Creek and Rock Spring branch. Wit: REUBEN NANCE, BENJAMIN THOMAS, JOHN CONNAWAY. Signed: JOHN WYATT.

Page 146. 31 Oct. 1786. JOHN SIMMONS and his wife NANCY SIMMONS of Henry County to JOHN WEAVER of the same for the consideration of One hundred fifty pounds sells land on Marrowbone Creek, joins the lines of GEORGE HAIRSTON, SAMUEL LANIER and RICHARDSON. Wit: JOSEPH ANTHONY, JACOB FERRIS, JOSIAH FERRIS. Signed: JOHN (X) SIMMONS, NANCY (X) SIMMONS.

Page 147. No date. JAMES PARBERRY of the county of Franklin sell to THOMAS GRAVES of Henry County two negroes for the sum of One hundred pounds, one wench named Lucy and one boy Peter. Wit: JOSEPH MARTIN, REUBEN PAYNE, JOHN ROWLAND. Signed: JAMES PARBERRY.

Page 148. 24 Oct. 1794. HUGH WOODS and his wife SARA ANN WOODS of Franklin County sell unto ROBERT STOCKTON of Henry County a parcel of land on the north side of Smith River, crosses Fall Creek and Middle Creek for Forty five pounds. Wit: ROBERT STOCKTON, JR., THOMAS FITZPATRICK, J. WOODS. Signed: HUGH WOODS, SARAH ANN (X) WOODS.

Page 149. No date. Upon the principal of love, justice, mercy and truth and in obedience to the Command of the Creator of all things who commands us to do unto all men as we would, the eye should do unto us and to break every yoke and let the oppressed go free and agreeable to the Bill of Rights which opposed the Power of Brittain. I do hereby these presents renounce all claim to any power over man against their be him white or black and I do upon the

Housetop confess my sins and hope that God for Christs sake will pardon me for what is past and yet I now freely and immediately liberate and quit claim to a negro man named JOHN but commonly called JACK and a negro woman named LUCY his wife, a negro man named BRUMLY, a girl named SUSANAH now 10 years old to go free at the expiration of 8 years from this date and also a negro RACHEL 8 years old to go free at the expiration of 10 years from this date. In witness whereof I hereunto affix my hand and seal this 29th day of Sept. 1794. Signed: JOHN WATSON. Proved: 29 Oct.1794. ...The within instrument of emancipation was acknowledged to be the act of JOHN WATSON this 29th Oct.1794.

Page 150. 27 Apr. 1795. JOHN NANCE and MARY NANCE his wife of Henry County to BIRD NANCE of the same county for the consideration of Fifty pounds sells and conveys 100 acres more or less on the branches of the south fork of Leatherwood Creek, joins CHARLES BURNETT'S spring Branch, BENJAMIN RENS, ROBERT STOCKTON and GEORGE HAIRSTON. No wit. Signed: JOHN NANCE. Proved: 27 Apr. 1795.

Pages 151-154. 5 Feb. 1795. Deed of Trust. JOHN WELLS and JAMES MORTON of Henry County to ABRAHAM PENN administrator for JOHN MARR, deceased, JOHN DILLARD of Henry County and ARCHELUS HUGHES of Patrick County..having formerly given Bond Security for the credit of BARNABY WELLS, deputy Sheriff to JAMES LYON, Sheriff for tobacco paid by DAVID LANIER. WELLS and MORTON put up two tracts the first 362 acres the second 138 acres and one negro boy called Dennis also 500 acres, and MORTON the 200 acres tract whereon he now lives. Wit: BARNA WELLS, FRANCIS COX, THOMAS DICKENSON, JR. Signed: JOHN WELLS, JAMES MORTON. Proved 30 Mar. 1795 & 28 Apr. 1795. . . .Memo: I exceed to the above deed for the aforesaid purpose. 5 Feb. 1795. Signed: DAVID LANIER. Teste: ARMSTEAD JONES, JOHN M. ALEXANDER.

Page 153. 29 Apr. 1795. MARTHA FONTAINE widow and relict of JOHN FONTAINE of Henry County to CALEB BAKER of Prince Edward County. JOHN FONTAINE died intestate and having sold CALEB BAKER land in Prince Edward County for One hundred twenty pounds the said MARTHA FONTAINE had never relinquished her right of dower..she does do so by this deed. Wit: N. W. DANDRIDGE, P. H. FONTAINE, JOHN RAMEY. Signed: MARTHA FONTAINE. Proved: 29 Apr. 1795.

Page 154. 28 Apr. 1795. Bond of JOHN DILLARD being

appointed Sheriff for the County of Henry, his Bondsman, GEORGE HAIRSTON.

Page 154.   28 Apr. 1895.   Power of Attorney. JAMES LYON of the County of Patrick appoints his friend WILLIAM LINDSAY to transact business for him relative to his former Sheriff's business. Signed: JAMES LYON.

Pages 155-156.   17 Nov. 1788.   MOSES HODGE of the County of Pittsylvania to JACOB DEEN of Henry County for the consideration of Sixty pounds sells land in Henry County 200 acres more or less, part of a 400 acres formerly surveyed for WILLIAM RICKEL, located on both sides of the south branch of the south fork of Sandy River and bounded by deed of conveyance from JOSEPH MABRY to NICHOLAS PERKINS and recorded in Pittsylvania County. Wit: DAVID HARRIS, HENRY SANFORD, THOMAS MARSHALL, GEORGE G. HARRIS. Signed: MOSES HODGE.

Pages 156-157.   8 Apr. 1795.   JAMES MURPHY, SENR. and ELIZABETH MURPHY his wife of the County of Henry to JOSEPH TOWNLIN of the same for the sum of Twenty pounds conveys and sells 104 acres by estimate at the head of Daniel Creek. No wit. Signed: JAMES MURPHY, SENR.

Pages 157-158.   27 Apr. 1795.   JOSEPH GRAVELY of Henry County to ELIJAH RICHARDSON of the same for the sum of Thirty pounds sells 100 acres more or less on the branches of the middle fork of Leatherwood Creek beginning at the line of Gravely and Oldham line to Davis line, crossing Grassy fork of Leatherwood Creek, formerly surveyed by JOHN SHORT. Signed: JOSEPH (X) GRAVELY.

Pages 158-159.   22 Dec. 1794.   ANTHONY BITTING of Stokes County, North Carolina to SHADRACK DENT of Henry County for the sum of Fifty pounds sells 150 acres more or less joins the lines of RICHARD DONALD, to the top of the mountain that divides Daniel Creek and Beaver Creeks. Wit: ANN CLARK, HENRY CLARK, GEORGE WALLER, JR. Signed: ANTHONY BITTING.

Pages 159-160.   27 Apr. 1795.   THOMAS NUNN of Henry County to EUSEBUS STONE, SENR. of the same for the sum of Twelve pounds sells and conveys 190 acres of land on the waters of Smith River joins the lines of JOHN PALFREY, NEWSOM PACE and Little Rock Creek. Signed: THOMAS NUNN.

Pages 160-161. 27 Apr. 1795. WILLIAM PEARSON, SENR. of the county of Henry to GEORGE HAIRSTON of the same for the consideration of Eight pounds sells 758 acres by platt, which land is part of THOMAS CLOYS Order of Council, sold to PEARSON by JESSE ROBERTSON. No wit. Signed: WILLIAM PEARSON. Proved: 27 Apr. 1795.

Pages 161-162. 29 Jan. 1795. DAVID QUARLES and his wife JUDITH QUARLES of Henry County to JOHN QUARLES of the same for the sum of Fifty pounds sells 80 acres of land beginning at the mouth of Ray's Creek, joins GEORGE HAIRSTON and the Big Marrowbone Creek. No wit. Signed: DAVID (X) QUARLES. Proved: Henry Court Jan. 1795.

Page 163. 11 Aug. 1794. I, THOMAS FARRIS bought a sorel horse of MARTHA FONTAINE for which I gave my note for 1,000# of inspected tobacco payable the 25th Dec. 1794. In consideration I have this day sold and delivered unto MARTHA FONTAINE a sorel mare which I had of a certain THOMPSON. Teste: JACOB JENNINGS. Signed: THOMAS (X) FARRIS. Proved: 21 Jan. 1795. . . .I assign the within Bill of Sale to JOSEPH RYAN. Signed: MARTHA FONTAINE, 21 Jan.1795.

Pages 163-164. 8 Nov. 1794. JESSE SMITH of Henry County to CHARLES FARRIS of the same for the sum of Fifteen pounds sells and conveys 90 acres of land on the branches of Marrowbone Creek, joins WASHINGTON LANIER, SAMUEL LANIER, Dec'd, BLIZZARD MAGRUDER. It being where JESSE STITH now lives and being part of the tract patented to JOHN RICHARDSON. This land is now in the possession of said CHARLES FARRIS. Wit: WASHINGTON LANIER, JAMES TAYLOR, ARCHIBALD (X) FARRIS. Signed: JESSE (X) STITH.

Pages 164-165. 17 Nov. 1794. JESSE STITH and AMEY STITH his wife of Henry County to THOMAS WILLIAMS for the sum of Fifteen pounds sells a parcel of land on the waters of Marrowbone Creek containing 100 acres. Wit: JOHN COX, WASHINGTON LANIER, OZBURN WILLIAMS. Signed: JESSE STITH (X).

Pages 165-166. 14 Feb. 1795. DANIEL HANKINS of the county of Pittsylvania to JOHN JONES of Henry County for the sum of Forty nine pounds sells and conveys 141 acres on Leatherwood Creek, crosses the fork at Suckegg. Wit: JOSEPH JONES, STEPHEN WATKINS, JOSEPH CLIFFT. Signed: DANIEL HANKINS. Proved: 23 Feb. 1795.

Page 167.   23 Feb. 1795.   HENRY JONES and his wife SUSANNAH JONES of the county of Henry to JOSEPH JONES, the son of the said HENRY JONES for the sum of Five shillings sells and conveys a tract of land containing 400 acres on the waters of Sandy River. No wit. Signed: HENRY (X) JONES. Proved: 23 Feb. 1795. . . .Deed examined and delivered date above.

Pages 168-169.   26 Aug. 1794.   THOMAS CHANDLER of the county of Henry to SAMUEL ELLIOTT of the same for the consideration of Sixty pounds sells and conveys 720 acres more or less on the waters of Leaterwood Creek joins GEORGE RUNNOLDS and WILLIAM BURNETT. Wit: EDMUND COVINGTON, NANCY (X) COVINGTON, FRANCIS COX, JEREMIAH (X) PEARSON. Signed: THOMAS CHANDLER, CHARITY (X) CHANDLER. Proved: 26 Aug. 1794 & 23 Feb. 1795. . . .Payment received 26 Aug. 1794.

Pages 169-170.   21 Oct. 1794.   JOSEPH CARR and his wife ANNA CARR of the county of Henry to JOHN COX of the same for the sum of Fifty five pounds sells land on both sides of Rock Run where CARR now lives it being 100 acres more or less, joins GEORGE HAIRSTON, HENRY SUMPTER. Wit: HENRY LYNE, JOHN SALMON, BENJAMIN DILLEN, JAMES BAKER, AUGUSTINE LAWLESS. Signed: JOSEPH KARR. Proved: 29 Dec.1794.

Pages 170-171.   20 Oct. 1794.   ABSALOM ADAMS of Henry County to BARTLETT WASHINGTON of the same for the sum of Sixty pounds sells 100 acres on Rock Run Creek joins HENRY SUMPTER, DAVIS BRANCH, JAMES BAKER and ISHAM CRADOCK. Wit: JAMES BAKER, JOHN WITT, JOHN COX, HENRY LYNE, JOHN SALMON. Signed: ABSALOM ADAMS. Proved: 23 Feb. 1795.

Page 172.   29 Dec. 1794.   JOHN DILLION and his wife SARAH DILLION of the county of Henry to JOSEPH PHIFER of the same for the sum of Twenty pounds sells land on the south side of Rock Run Creek of the Smith River containing 100 acres more or less, part of a larger tract granted said JOHN DILLION by patent 20 Feb. 1794, joins JOHN BARKSDALE, crosses the Iron Works Road to Rowlands line. No wit. Signed: JOHN DILLION. Proved: 29 Dec. 1794.

Page 173.   27 Oct. 1794.   JOHN DILLION of Henry County to JOSEPH PHIFER of the same for the consideration of Seventy pounds sells land on the north side of Smith River and on both sides of Rock Run Creek, being 120 acres. No wit. Signed: JOHN DILLION. Proved: 29 Dec. 1794. . . .Deed examined and delivered

29 Dec. 1794.

Page 174. 5 Dec. 1794. WILLIAM WARREN of the county of Henry to HENRY HARRIS of the same for the sum of Ten pounds sells and conveys a parcel of land containing 16 acres on the south side of Reed Creek. Signed: WILLIAM WARREN.

Page 175. 24 Nov. 1794. JOHN NORRIS of the county of Henry to HENRY HARRIS of the same for the sum of Twenty pounds sells land on the waters of Reed Creeks being 235 acres. Signed: JOHN NORRIS.

Pages 176-177. 29 Dec. 1794. DAVID QUARLES and WILLIAM QUARLES, JR. of Henry County to GEORGE HAIRSTON of the same for the sum of Three hundred and Fifty pounds 240 acres on the south side of Smith River joins JOHN REA, Marrowbone Creek, Rea's Creek and in sight of JOHN QUARLES fence, NEWSOM PACE. Signed: DAVID QUARLES, JUDITH QUARLES, WILLIAM QUARLES, JR., MARY QUARLES. Proved: 29 Dec. 1794. . . Proved, examined and delivered 29 Dec. 1794.

Page 177. 29 Nov. 1794. Dower release of SARAH ANN WOOD wife of HUGH WOOD who sold land to ROBERT STOCKTON.

Page 178. 29 Dec. 1794. Bond. Whereas, JOSEPH PEDEGO produced credentials of ordenation from the Baptist Society and is licensed to celebrate the rights of matrimony. Bondsmen: ROBERT STOCKTON and HENRY CLARK.

Page 179. 5 Nov. 1794. To the Worshipfull the Court of Henry County. Gentlemen: I consider the right of administrating the estate of my son EDWARD HENRY deceased as belonging to me. But I do waive that right and do hereby desire and request that the administration of the estate of my son EDWARD HENRY be granted to my daughter MARTHA FONTAINE. Wit: N.W. DANDRIDGE, PATRICK HENRY FONTAINE. Signed: PATRICK HENRY.

Pages 179-180. 20 Aug. 1794. THOMAS CHANDLER of the county of Henry to SAMUEL ELLIOTT of same for the sum of Sixty pounds sells land on the waters of Leatherwood Creek by survey being 200 acres more or less joins GEORGE RUNNOLDS, WILLIAM BURNETT. Wit: EDMUND COVINGTON, NANCY (X) COVINGTON, FRANCIS COX, JEREMIAH (X) PERSON. Signed: THOMAS CHANDLER, CHARITY (X) CHANDLER. Proved: 23 Feb. 1795.

Pages 181-183. 22 Feb. 1780. MARTIN KEY of Fluvanna County attorney in and for WALTER KING of Great Britian to JOHN ALEXANDER of Henry County. About the year 1770 MARTIN KEY did sell 456 acres of land belonging to WALTER KING for the sum of Two hundred twenty eight pounds. This is where the said JOHN ALEXANDER now lives. Wit: NICHOLAS SPEARS, THOMAS BUSH, DANIEL RAMEY. Signed: MARTIN KEY. Proved: 23 Mar. 1780 & 30 Mar. 1795.

Pages 183-184. 30 Mar. 1795. THOMAS NUNN of Henry County to EUSEBUS STONE, JR. of the same for Ten pounds sells land on the north side of Smith River, begins at Stone's corner on Smith River, 50 acres more or less. No wit. Signed: THOMAS NUNN. Proved: 30 Mar. 1795.

Pages 184-185. 13 Dec. 1794. BALLENGER WADE of the county of Henry to JESSE ATKISSON of the same for the sum of Fifteen pounds sells 15 acres that joins the land where JESSE ATKISSON lives. No wit. Signed: BALLENGER WADE. Proved: 30 Mar. 1795.

Pages 185-186. 15 Dec. 1794. JESSE ATKISSON of Henry County to BALLENGER WADE of the same for the sum of Fifteen pounds sells land containing 15 acres and joins the land where the said WADE lives. Wit: GEORGE TAYLOR, JESSE ATKISSON, JR., MARY ATKISSON. Signed: JESSE ATKISSON. Proved: 30 Mar. 1795.

Pages 186-187. 24 Nov. 1794. ARCHELAUS REYNOLDS of the county of Henry to GEORGE HAIRSTON of the same for the consideration of Thirty pounds sells 80 acres on Leatherwood Creek above Hailes Mill joins Yallow Bank Creek. Wit: THOMAS NUNN, EDWARD ADAMS, JOSEPH STOVALL. Signed: ARCHELAUS REYNOLDS. Proved: 30 Mar. 1795.

Pages 188-189. 24 Nov. 1794. JOSHUA DILLINGHAM of the county of Henry to GEORGE HAIRSTON of the same for the sum of One hundred pounds sells 2 tracts on both sides of Reedy Creek, one is 188 acres purchased of JOHN HEARD the seconds 100 acres purchased of JAMES MCWILLIAMS. Wit: THOMAS NUNN, JOSEPH STOVALL, EDWARD ADAMS. Signed: JOSHUA DILLINGHAM. Proved: 30 Mar. 1795.

Pages 191-192. 18 Mar. 1795. WILLIAM WATSON of the county of Henry to GEORGE HAIRSTON of the same for the consideration of Sixty pounds sells and conveys land on the branches of Stuarts Creek of

Smith River contains 356 acres more or less and joins lines of WILLIAM CAYTON. No wit. Signed: WILLIAM WATSON. Proved: 25 May 1795.

Pages 192-193. 5 June 1795. Deed of Gift. BLIZZARD MAGRUDER of the county of Henry for the love, goodwill and affection that he bears his sister CHRISTIAN MAGRUDER of Henry County he gives her a tract of land containing 2,984 acres more or less on the waters of Beaver Creek, Leatherwood Creek and Snow Creek. Wit: GEORGE WALLER, WILL. WALLER, EDMUND WALLER. Signed: BLIZZARD MAGRUDER. Proved: 29 June 1795.

Pages 193-194. 29 June 1795. JOHN DILLION and SALLY DILLION his wife of the county of Patrick to WILLIAM DRAPER of the county of Henry for ____ pounds sells land on both sides of Rock Run of Smith River, the land whereon WILLIAM DRAPER now lives, by estimate 112 acres, it being part of a larger tract that was granted JOHN DILLION in Richmond 20 Nov. 1794. No wit. Signed: JOHN DILLION. Proved: 29 June 1795.

Pages 194-195. 24 June 1795. DAVID WEATHERFORD of Henry County to JAMES WILSON of the same for the sum of Twenty pounds sells 75 acres on Leatherwood Creek joins Randolph & Company. Wit: WILLIAM (X) STEVENS, MOSES (X) WILSON, GEORGE (X) GILLEY. Signed: DAVID WEATHERFORD, MARY WEATHERFORD. Proved: 29 June 1795.

Pages 196-197. 25 July 1795. WATERS DUNN administrator of the estate of THOMAS NELSON deceased of Wilks County, Georgia to WILLIAM NORMAN of Henry County for the sum of Twenty five pounds sells and conveys 174 acres that was granted THOMAS NELSON 1 Feb. 1769, located on the draughts of the Smith River joins lines of MARTIN WEBB. Wit: TUNSTALL COX, JOHN COX, JR., MARKHAM LOVELL. Signed: WATERS DUNN. Proved: 28 July 1795.

Pages 197-198. 28 July 1795. ABRAHAM PENN of the county of Patrick to GEORGE HAIRSTON of Henry County for the sum of Forty pounds sells land in Henry County on the waters of Beaver Crees, 351 acres joins STEPHEN CARTER and is the plantation where WILLIAM KETCHAM now lives. No wit. Signed: ABRAHAM PENN. Proved: 28 July 1795.

Pages 1980199. 29 July 1795. ANTHONY BITTING of

Stokes County, North Carolina to JOHN STOKES of Henry County, Virginia for the sum of One hundred fifty pounds sells land on Beaver Creek being 408 acres more or less joins JACOB FARIS, BREATHET'S line and is on the mountain that divides the waters of Beaver and Daniel Creek. No wit. Signed: ANTHONY BITTING. Proved: 29 July 1795.

Pages 199-200. 29 July 1795. WILLIAM COLLINS REA of the county of Henry to GEORGE HAIRSTON of the same for the consideration of One hundred twenty pounds sells 249 ac. on both sides of Little Marrowbone Creek, lines: COOPER and Bolings Creek. No wit. Signed: WILLIAM COLLINS REA. Proved: 29 July 1795. . . .Memo: The within WILLIAM C. REA is intitled to the grounds where his father and mother is buried.

Page 201. 1 Apr. 1795. Dower Release. Amherst County, Virginia. MILLEY BALLINGER wife of ARCHELLUS BALLENGER hereby releases her right of downer to a tract of land, 425 ac. in Henry County, Virginia that was sold to WILLIAM BAYLES SENR. and his children. Justices of the Peace of Amherst: DANIEL WHITE and WILLIAM WARWICK. Proved: 31 Aug. 1795.

Pages 202-203. 31 Aug. 1795. RICHARD STOCKTON of the county of Franklin to JAMES HOWARD of Henry County for One hundred fifty pounds sells land in Henry County on the waters of Beaver Creek joining Copland 315 acres. No wit. Signed: RICHARD STOCKTON, ELIZABETH STOCKTON. Proved: 31 Aug. 1795.

Pages 203-204. 30 Aug. 1795. FRANCIS JINKINS and NANCY JINKINS his wife of Henry County to EDWARD WATKINS of the same for the sum of Three pounds sells 285 acres by survey on the waters of Fall Creek and Marrowbone, joins THOMAS JAMISON, W. HARBOUR, and DAVID WITT, the said land and tenaments now in the possession of EDWARD WATKINS. No wit. Signed: FRANCIS (X) JINKINS. Proved: 31 Aug. 1795. . . . NANCY JINKINS releases her right of dower.

Page 205. 2 April 1794. Power of Attorney. JOSEPH FUQUA does appoint his friends DAVID LANIER and GEORGE HAIRSTON his attorneys to transact all his business in the state of Virginia, receive and pay all debts due or owed. Wit: NANCY LANIER, DANIEL REAMY, ELIZABETH LANIER, RICHARD REYNOLDS, JOHN CARTER. Signed: JOSEPH FUQUA. Proved: 28 Sept. 1795.

Pages 205-207. 4 Nov. 1789. JOHN DUNKIN (DUNCAN) and MILLY DUNKIN his wife of Henry County to JOHN NUNNS of the same for the consideration of One hundred thirty pounds sells 180 acres on the Little Dan River. Wit: ROBERT HEDSPETH, ROBERT HOOKER, SAMUEL HOOKER, THOMAS PARKER. Signed: JOHN (X) DUNCIN, MILLY (X) DUNCIN. Proved: 26 Apr. 1790 & 26 Oct.1795.

Pages 207-208. 20 July 1795. LABON OAKES of the county of Henry to SAMUEL LANE of Dinwiddie County for the sum of One hundred twenty pounds sells land on the shole banks of the River. Wit: ARCHIBALD MURPHY, MASON KELLEY, DUTTON LANE. Signed: LABON OAKES. Proved: 26 Oct. 1795.

Pages 208-209. 25 Apr. 1795. THOMAS CHOWNING of the county of Henry to PHILIP BROSHEARS of the same for Twenty pounds sells 100 acres more or less on the north side of Turkey Cock Creek joins the land of FRANCIS GILLEY, deceased. Wit: JOHN PACE, W. PACE, ARCHIBALD MURPHY. Signed: THOMAS CHOWNING. Proved: 26 Oct. 1795.

Pages 209-210. 26 Oct. 1795. THOMAS WILSON of the county of Henry to ROBERT BORSHEARS of the same for Thirty pounds sells 54 acres on Little Turkey Cock Creek. Wit: WILLIAM MITCHELL, JAMES BRASHER, PHILLIP BRASHER. Signed: THOMAS WILSON. Proved: 26 Oct. 1795.

Pages 210-211. 25 Aug. 1795. Bond of THOMAS COOPER, SENR. of Hancock County, Georgia and JOSEPH STOVALL of Patrick County, Virginia are bound unto GEORGE HAIRSTON of Henry County, Virginia. ELIZABETH STOVALL administrator of THOMAS STOVALL, deceased is about to remove to Georgia taking with her the estate of THOMAS STOVALL deceased. Wit: JOHN WALLER, JOHN WEEKS. Signed: THOMAS COOPER, JOSEPH STOVALL. Proved: 26 Oct. 1795.

Pages 212-213. 28 Sept. 1795. Bond of JOHN CAHILL. JOHN CAHILL shall truly do and finish painting of the Courthouse of Henry County on or before 28 Dec. 1796. The roof painted red, the body and gable ends painted white. The inside to be sky blue, the lawyers bar, justices seat and sheriff box painted in the same manner, doors and windows to answer the outside painting, the chair board white. Wit: H. SALMON, JR. Signed: JOHN CAHILL, GEORGE HAIRSTON. Proved: 26 Oct. 1795.

Pages 213-216. 30 Nov. 1795. Bond of JOHN SAMON as Sheriff of Henry County with his bondsmen: GEORGE HAIRSTON, HENRY LYNE, FRANCIS COX, BALLENGER WADE and JOHN PACE. Proved: 30 Nov. 1795. . . . Bond also to Collect taxes for the Treasury of the Commonwealth, with same witnesses.

Pages 217-218. 30 Nov. 1795. JOHN HARRIS of the county of Henry to JOHN GROGAN of the same for the sum of Fifty pounds sells 50 ac. joining CLAYBROCK'S. Wit: WILLIAM CARTSON, CHARLES COX, JAMES HAMPTON. Signed: JOHN HARRIS. Proved: 30 Nov. 1795.

Pages 219-220. __ Apr. 1795. GEORGE SUMPTER of the county of Henry to GEORGE HAIRSTON of the same for Thirty pounds sells land on the headwaters of Horsepasture Creek, joins JOHN WATSON and the Wagon Road. Contains 227 acres. Wit: JOHN COX, JAMES STUART, MARY COX. Signed: JOSEPH DILLION. JOSEPH DILLION also gives release. Proved: 30 Dec. 1795.

Pages 220-221. 3 Sept. 1788. THOMAS FLOWERS of the county of Henry to HENRY GUFFEE of the same for Twenty five pounds sells 200 acres on the waters of Smith River on Buffalow Creek, head of Old Still Branch lines of JOHN LACKEY, THOMAS HOFF, JOHN KINDRICK, SAMUEL ALLEN. Wit: ADAM LACKEY, JOHN LACKEY, RICHARD PILSON. Signed: THOMAS FLOWERS. Proved: 20 Feb. 1789 & 30 Dec. 1795.

Pages 222-223. 6 Nov. 1795. ISHAM BROWDER TATUM and RACHEL BROWDER TATUM of Henry County to JOHN JONES of the same for One hundred seventeen pounds ten shillings sells 204 acres on both sides of the south fork of Sandy River, the land was granted to NICHOLAS DORNELL 1 Mar. 1781. Wit: JOSEPH JONES, WILLIAM (X) CRAIN, JEREMIAH DUNSON. Signed: ISHAM BROWDER TATUM. Proved: 28 Dec. 1795.

Pages 224-225. 3 Oct. 1795. BARTLETT WASHINGTON of the county of Henry to JOHN GOING of the same sells 100 acres on Rock Run Creek, joins HENRY SUMPTER, DAVIS BRANCH, JAMES BAKER, ISHAM CRADOCK. Wit: JAMES BAKER, WILLIAM BARKSDALE, JOHN WITT, SUSANAH (X) DILLION, HENRY SUMPTER, JR. (X). Signed: BARTLETT WASHINGTON. Proved: 28 Dec. 1795.

Pages 226-227. 19 Aug. 1795. JAMES CLAYBROOK of the county of Henry to JOHN GROGAN of the same for the sum of Fifty pounds sells 50 acres...

beginning at the River, to a creek. Wit: TUNSTALL COX, S. HORD, WILLIAM NORMAN, HENRY LYNE, JESSE CLAYBROOK. Signed: JAMES CLAYBROOK. Proved: 30 Nov. 1795.

Pages 227-228. 25 Jan. 1790. Power of Attorney. BENJAMIN SMITH appoints BENNETT SCEARCEY and ROBERT SCEARCEY of the Southwestern Territory (Merodest--t) to convey to WILLIAM HORD a right in fee simple to a tract in the said District of MISO. being 428 acres, which land I obtained for military service in the late War with Britton by virtue of land warrant #663. No wit. Signed: BENJAMIN SMITH. Proved: 25 Jan. 1796.

Page 228-230. 25 Dec. 1795. MARTHA FONTAINE, Administratrix of EDWARD HENRY, deceased of the county of Henry to JAMES MASTIN of the same for the sum of Thirty pounds sells 250 acres on a branch of Mulberry Creek, being part of a survey by PATRICK HENRY. Wit: AXTON WHITECOTTON, JAMES STUART, NATHL. W. DANDRIDGE. Signed: MARTHA FONTAINE. Proved: 28 Dec. 1796.

Pages 230-231. 25 Jan. 1796. CHARLES COX, THOMAS KELLY and CATY KELLEY of Henry County appoint their friend MASON KELLEY attorney to receive from WILLIAM BENNETT of King George County all their part of the estate of CASSON BENNETT, deceased, he has their authority to receive and obtain all that is due them. Wit: DUTTON LANE, JR., TIMAN CLARK, WILLIAM NORMAN. Signed: CHARLES COX, THOMAS KELLY, CATY (X) KELLY. Proved: 25 Jan. 1796.

Page 232. 9 Jan. 1796. Whereas sometime in the year 1776, I, JOHN REDD, stipulated with Gen. GEORGE R. CLARK for a tract of land lying in the state of Kentucky at or near Drennon's Lick which contract he has failed to comply with. Know ye, JOHN REDD has appointed WILLIAM HORD my attorney to settle and determine regarding my claim. Wit: J. W. WATSON, JOHN WATSON. Signed: JOHN REDD. Proved: 25 Jan. 1796.

Pages 233-234. 28 Sept. 1795. Whereas I, JOHN WATSON for the natural love and goodwill I bear unto my daughter SALLY BET HEATH, I give to her and her husband WILLIAM HEATH a part of three tracts of land on the waters of Horsepasture Creek and Smith River, joins land of JAMES EAST, DUTTON LANE 267 acres, joins JOHN WATSON 190 acres and 125 acres (not clear whether this is the total of the 3 tracts or amount he is conveying). Wit: DANIEL DEJARNATT, SAMUEL CRUTHCHER, JOHN COX, CHARLES CRUTHCHER. Signed: JOHN WATSON. Proved: 29 Feb. 1796.

Pages 235-236. 24 Dec. 1794. JOHN SMITH of the county of Patrick to GEORGE HAIRSTON of Henry County for the consideration of Fifty pounds sells land in Henry and Patrick Counties, the largest quantity in Henry on the branches of the Mayo River 140 acres being part of a tract SMITH had of JOHN STAPLES joins ANTHONY SMITH and JOHN STAPLES. Wit: JOSEPH STOVALL, DRURY SOLOMON, JACOB ADAMS. Signed: JOHN SMITH. Proved: 29 Feb. 1796.

Pages 237-238. 9 Oct. 1795. SAMUEL HUGHES of the county of Henry to SAMUEL CALLAND of Pittsylvania County for the sum of One hundred thirty three pounds conveys land in Henry County on the waters of Turkey Cock Creek 275 acres joins JOHN CUNNINGHAM and EDWARD SMITH. Wit: ANDREW FORD, JABEZ GRAVELY, JACOB COOLLEY, JOHN TOMPKIN. Signed: SAMUEL (X) HUGHES. Proved: 30 Nov. 1795 & 29 Feb. 1796.

Page 239. 12 Aug. 1795. ELIZABETH MORTON of the county of Henry sells all her personal estate to her brother JAMES MORTON, estate consists of: one negro AGGA, all beds and household furniture and stock of all kinds for the sum of Five hundred pounds. Wit: JAMES JOHNSTON, MARTIN DALTON, JOSEPH MORTON. Signed: ELIZABETH (X) MORTON. Proved: 29 Feb. 1796.

Page 240. 10 Nov. 1795. JOHN REA of the county of Henry to WILLIAM FRANCIS of the same for Six pounds sells 46 acres on the Smith River joins DAVID QUARLES and WILLIAM DILLON. Wit: WILLIAM J. PACE, LANGSTON PACE, JAMES REA. Signed: JOHN REA, MARY REA. Proved: 5 Mar. 1796.

Pages 241-242. 25 Jan. 1796. THOMAS CHOWNING of the county of Henry to THOMAS WILSON of the same for Twenty pounds sells 50 acres...begins at the ridge path in Broshears and Sams old line. Wit: WILLIAM HEWLETT, JOHN DAVIS, WILLIAM MITCHELL. Signed: THOMAS CHOWNING. Proved: 25 Apr. 1796.

Page 242-243. 23 Jan. 1796. THOMAS CHOWNING of the county of Henry to JOHN DAVIS of the same for the sum of Twenty pounds sells 50 acres... lines: JAMES BOLING, the mouth of the long branch on Little Turkey Cock Creek. Wit: WILLIAM HEWLETT,

THOMAS WILSON, WILLIAM MITCHELL. Signed: THOMAS CHOWNING. Proved: 25 Apr. 1796.

Pages 244-245. 6 Nov. 1795. PETER PERKINS of the county of Pittsylvania to THOMAS BOULDIN of Henry County for the sum of Ninety pounds sells land by estimate 300 acres, joins lines of JOHN WEAVER, URIAH HARDMAN, Marrowbone Creek, ELLENDOR TARBORN'S old line and JOHN HARDMAN. The land formerly belonged to GEORGE HAIRSTON. Wit: GREEN BOULDIN, WILLIAM BOULDIN, JESSE ATKISSON. Signed: PETER PERKINS. Proved: 25 Apr. 1796.

Pages 246-247. 9 Nov. 1795. DAVID WEATHERFORD of the county of Henry to JOHN HAMMOND of the same for the sum of Fifty pounds sells 60 acres on Leatherwood Creek joins COL. HENRY'S. Wit: GEORGE (X) GILLEY, JAMES (X) SHORT, PHILIP CONNOR. Signed: DAVID WEATHERFORD, MARY WEATHERFORD. Proved: 25 Apr. 1796.

Pages 248-249. 25 Apr. 1896. JAMES REA and MOLLY REA his wife of Henry County to ABNER REA their son for One hundred forty pounds sells land on the waters of Smith River and Little Marrowbone Creek, part of two tracts that the said JAMES REA purchased of ANDREW REA and a MR. ROBERTSON. No wit. Signed: JAMES REA. Proved 25 Apr. 1796.

Pages 250-251. 8 Feb. 1796. DAVID BUNCH of the county of Henry to THOMAS WILKINS of the same for the sum of Thirty pounds sells 89 acres on the branches of Leatherwood Creek. Wit: JOHN MINTER, JOHN GRIGS, MICAL GRIGS. Signed: DAVID BUNCH, MARTHY BUNCH. Proved: 25 Apr. 1796.

Page 252. 28 Feb. 1796. MARTIN BUNCH of the county of Henry to JOHN GRIGGS,SENR. of the same for Thirty pounds sells 68 acres on the branches of Leatherwood Creek and Beaver Creek. Wit: JOHN MINTER, MICAL GRIGS, THOMAS WILKINS. Signed: MARTIN BUNCH, ANNA BUNCH. Proved: 25 Apr. 1796.

Pages 253-254. 23 Jan. 1796. BENJAMIN BUNCH of the county of Henry to FRANCIS BUNCH for a valuable sum sells 100 acres more or less on the branches of the Mayo River. Wit: JAMES EVENS, WILLIAM MOTLEY, WILLIAM HAYES. Signed: BENJAMIN (X) BUNCH. Proved: 25 Apr. 1796.

Page 255. 25 Apr. 1796. WILLIAM ROBERSON of the

county of Henry to WILLIAM S. COX of the same for
Fifty pounds sells 25 acres on the waters of Smith
River, joins MRS. FONTAINE and QUARLES. No wit.
Signed: WILLIAM ROBERTSON. Proved: 25 Apr. 1796. . .
EASTER ROBERTSON, wife of WILLIAM ROBERTSON releases
her right of dower.

Pages 256-257. 29 Mar. 1796. THOMAS BOLLING of Henry
County to JOHN COX, JR. of the same
for Thirty pounds sells 100 acres more or less on the
branches of Rock Run, Goings Wagon Rd., Cox's Path to
Bull Mountain Rd. that is called JOHN COX'S road, JOHN
COX School path, the house that JESSE LAWLESS lives
in and the School House. No wit. Signed: THOMAS (X)
BOLLING. Proved: 26 Apr. 1796.

Pages 258-259. 29 Mar. 1796. DAVID LANIER Trustee
for JAMES MORTON, ABRAHAM PENN Administrator of JOHN MARR, deceased and JOHN DILLARD to
WILLIAM LINDSAY of Patrick County for the sum of ___
sells 101 acres located in Henry County a total of 200
acres more or less, it is the plantation whereon JAMES
MORTON now lives. Wit: WILLIAM WALLER. Signed: DAVID
LANIER. Proved: April 1796.

Pages 259-260. 12 Mar. 1796. PETER LEAK and HANNAH
LEAK, his wife of the county of Henry
to WILLIAM SHELTON of the same for Sixty pounds sells
by estimate 50 acres on Horsepasture Creek joins
ALEXANDER HUNTER and JOHN DILLARD. Wit: THOMAS DICK-
ENSON, JOHN STAPLES, GREENE BOULDIN. Signed: PETER
LEAK, HANNAH LEAK. Proved: 30 Mar. 1796.

Pages 261-262. 11 Apr. 1796. ANTHONY SMITH and
AGNES SMITH his wife of Patrick County
to JOHN STAPLES of Henry County for the sum of Sixty
pounds sells 150 acres on Horsepasture Creek that
joins said STAPLES. Wit: WILLIAM SHELTON, SAMUEL
MORRIS, JR., JOHN SPENCER, JOHN DILLARD. Signed:
ANTHONY SMITH, AGNES (X) SMITH. Proved: 30 May 1796.

Pages 262-264. 28 May 1796. WILLIAM LINDSAY of
Patrick County to JOHN WALLER of Henry
County for the sum of One hundred Fifty pounds sells
200 acres in Henry County on the waters of Sandy
River, the land whereon JAMES MORTON now lives. Wit:
JOHN SALMON, GEORGE WALLER, GEORGE WALLER, JR. Sign-
ed: WILLIAM LINDSAY. Proved: 30 May 1796.

Pages 264-265. 4 Mar. 1796. Deed of Trust. HEZEKIAH
SALMON of Henry County is indebted

unto KATHERINE ELIZABETH BURGESS in amount of Twenty five pounds due 5th of April coming, secures with one negro wench Betty said property of HEZEKIAH SALMON. Wit: JOHN SALMON, ABIGAIL SALMON, SAMUEL STEPHENS. Signed: HEZEKIAH SALMON. Proved: 30 May 1796.

Pages 265-266. 28 Apr. 1796. Bond of HENRY LYNE is is the Coroner of Henry County. Bondsmen: JOHN ALEXANDER, JOHN COX, THOMAS NUNN. Proved: 30 May 1796.

Pages 267-268. 25 July 1796. JOHN MAY and CHARITY MAY his wife of Henry County to JONADABB WADE of the same for the consideration of One hundred fifty pounds sells 156 acres on the waters of Marrowbone Creek joins JAMES TAYLOR. No wit. Signed: JOHN MAY, CHARITY MAY. Proved: 25 July 1796.

Pages 268-269. 29 Aug. 1796. GEORGE FULLER HARRIS of the county of Pittsylvania to WILLIAM ROBERTSON, JR. of Henry County for the sum of Fifty pounds sells 78 acres on Cascade Creek joins land of JAMES ROBERTS. No wit. Signed: GEORGE F. HARRIS. Proved: 29 Aug. 1796.

Page 270. 29 Aug. 1796. JOHN FLETCHER of the county of Patrick appoints JOSEPH ANTHONY his attorney to transact business in Kentucky that the said JOHN FLETCHER is entitled to. No wit. Signed: JOHN FLETCHER. Proved: 29 Aug. 1796.

Pages 271-272. 29 Aug. 1796. JACOB COOLEY of Henry County to JOHN GRIGGS of the same for the consideration of Twenty five pounds sells 50 acres on Rattle Snake Branch of Leatherwood Creek joins JOHN DOWDIE. Wit: JOHN CONNAWAY, ABNER STULS, NICHOLAS AKIN. Signed: JACOB COOLEY. Proved: 29 Aug. 1796. ...NANCY COOLEY the wife of JACOB COOLEY release her right of dower to the above.

Pages 273-274. 24 Mar. 1796. BENJAMIN HARRISON and his wife SALLY HARRISON Administratrix of WALTER KING COLE, deceased to HENRY LYNE, JOHN ALEXANDER, DAVID LANIER and THOMAS JETT, securities for SALLY HARRISON...whereas SALLY HARRISON doth grant and sell one tract of land near Richmond, Henrico County on Bacon Quarter Tract contains 200 acres more or less, joins WILLIAM DUVALL and ROBERT MITCHELL. This land was given SALLY HARRISON, wife of BENJAMIN HARRISON, by her father SAMUEL MITCHELL. Wit: JOHN ROWLAND, WILLIAM C. REA, SANFORD REAMEY. Signed:

BENJAMIN HARRISON, SALLY HARRISON. Proved: 29 Aug. 1796.

Page 275. No date. I do hereby certify that I never said that JAMES ANDERSON was forsworn in the testimony he given a warrant brought by PHILIP RYAN against one tried before MAJOR LANIER: or if I did so, it is a false accusation for I believe the said ANDERSON to be a man of truth and integrity. Wit: JOHN DAVIS, REUBEN NANCE, SAMUEL TURLEY, MOSES (X) SMITH. Signed: JAMES (X) PHILLIPS. Proved: 29 Aug. 1796.

Pages 275-277. 22 Dec. 1795. WILLIAM WELLS of the county of Henry to JOHN WATSON of the same for One hundred pounds sells 150 acres on both sides of Little Reed Creek, joins COPLAND'S order line and above Burchett's Mill. Wit: JOHN NORRIS, NATHAN NORRIS, JOHN MAMESON. Signed: WILLIAM WELLS, REBAKEH WELLS. Proved: 25 Apr. 1796 & 29 Aug. 1796.

Pages 277-278. 22 Sept. 1796. SALLY REA, wife of ANDREW REA releases her right of dower to land sale of 125 acres to PHILLIP ANGLIN. Proved: 26 Sept. 1796.

Pages 278-279. 1 Sept. 1796. THOMAS GRAVES of Henry County to GEORGE HAIRSTON of the same for the sum of Sixty pounds sells 50 acres, it being part of a tract GRAVES purchased of DILLIAN BLEVINS and said BLEVINS sold part to WILLIAM BLEVINS, SENR. before said GRAVES made his purchase, the land was formerly owned by PHILIP THOMAS, it is plantation where DANIEL NEWMAN formerly lived on Smith River. Wit: JACOB LINDSAY. Signed: THOMAS GRAVES. Proved: 27 Sept. 1796.

Pages 280-281. MARY LANIER wife of DAVID LANIER releases her right of dower to land transaction of 622 acres to JOHN OSBORNE for the benefit of CAMPBELL & WHEELER of Dinwiddie County, it was for two tracts. Proved: 31 Oct. 1796.

Pages 281-282. 5 Mar. 1796. WILLIAM JOHNSON and his wife MARY JOHNSON of Patrick County to JOHN DEMPSEY of Patrick County for the sum of Twenty pounds sells land in Henry County on Mill Creek 50 acres more or less one line begins on a high ridge by the side of a path called Ridge Path. Wit: RICHARD TUCKER MAINER, JEARRY MANOER, SAMUEL PERRY. Signed: WILLIAM (X) JOHNSON. Proved: 3 Oct. 1796.

Pages 283-284. _____, 1796. JOSEPH LYELL of the county of Brunswick and ANN LYELL his wife to MOSES QUARLES, JR. of Henry County for the sum of One hundred seventy five pounds sells 175 acres on both sides of Roberts Creek of the Sandy River. Wit: JAMES FISHER, JOHN MOODE, JONATHAN FISHER, STERLING QUARLES, JAMES QUARLES, SAMUEL QUARLES. Signed: JOSEPH LYELL, ANN LYELL. Proved: 31 Oct. 1796.

Pages 284-285. 4 Oct. 1796. WILLIAM QUARLES of the county of Henry to DAVIS BURGESS of the same for Forty pounds sells 39 acres by pattern on the north side of Smith River. Wit: JOHN PACE, WILLIAM DILLEN, THOMAS STUART. Signed: WILLIAM (X) QUARLES. Proved: 1 Nov. 1796.

Pages 286-287. _____, 1796. HENRY SUMPTER of Henry County to GEORGE HAIRSTON of the same for One hundred pounds sells by estimate 1,000 acres on Rock Run Creek waters and branches of Smith River which was granted HENRY SUMPTER by patent 1 Mar. 1781 patent for 1,404 acres, 3 tracts sold heretofore to ABSALEM ADAMS, THOMAS BOLING and JOSEPH CARR. Signed: HENRY SUMPTER. Proved: 1 Nov. 1796. . . .AGNES SUMPTER, wife of HENRY SUMPTER releases dower right.

Pages 288-289. 22 June 1795. CHARLES FARRIS, SENR. of Henry County to CHARLES FARRIS, JR. of the same for Twenty pounds sells 93 acres on Marrowbone Creek, joins JOHN HARDMAN. Wit: WASHINGTON LANIER, JOHN WEAVER. Signed: CHARLES (X) FARRIS. Proved: 1 Nov. 1796.

Pages 289-290. 1 Nov. 1796. CHARLES FARRIS, JR. of Henry County to THOMAS EAST of the same for Twenty pounds sells 93 acres on a branch of Marrowbone Creek. Wit: ABNER REY, WILLIAM HEARD, RICHARD STOCKTON. Signed: CHARLES (X) FARRIS. Proved: 1 Nov. 1796.

Page 291. 20 Nov. 1796. THOMAS GRAVES of Henry County to JOSEPH MARTIN of the same for the consideration of Three hundred pounds sells a tract of 296 acres on the south side of Smith River, begins at a walnut near Graves' fish trap, joins GEORGE HAIRSTON. No wit. Signed: THOMAS GRAVES. Proved: 28 Nov. 1796.

Pages 292-293. 28 Nov. 1796. GEORGE GILLEY of Henry County to WILLIAM HEWLITT of the same for One hundred pounds sells by estimate 254 acres on the south side of Smith River, land purchased of FIELD

& CALL. Wit: THOMAS FITZPATRICK, JOHN BURGESS, WILLIAM M. MITCHELL. Signed: GEORGE (X) GILLEY. Proved: 28 Nov. 1796.

Pages 293-294. 28 Nov. 1796. JOHN WILSON of Pittsylvania County to GEORGE HAIRSTON of Henry County for the sum of Fifteen pounds sells 139 acres by estimate as per patent on Marrowbone Creek. Wit: N. W. DANDRIGE, THOMAS FITZPATRICK, JAMES STEWART. Signed: JOHN WILSON. Proved: 28 Nov. 1796.

Page 295. 1 July 1796. Bill of Sale. BENJAMIN HARRISON, JR. (of Henry County) Administrator in right of SALLY his wife the administrator of W. K. COLE, deceased, for the sum of Fifteen pounds ten shillings sells unto WALLERS NUNN one negro boy named Peter. Wit: N. W. DANDRIDGE. Signed: BENJAMIN HARRISON, JR. Proved: 26 Dec. 1796.

Pages 296-297. 19 Nov. 1796. WILLIAM CALL of the county of Prince George, surviving partner of FIELD & CALL, to GEORGE GILLEY of Henry County for the sum of Seventy pounds...paid as ---- made with him by COL. JOHN WILSON, late factor and agent for the said FIELD & CALL, tract on the side of Smith River, 254 acres being land that FIELD & CALL purchased of CHARLES BURNS in payment of a debt. Signed: WILLIAM CALL. Proved: 26 Dec. 1796. . . . Town of Petersburg...WILLIAM CALL appeared before ELIAS PARKER, Mayor of the said town and acknowledged it to be his act and deed.

Pages 298-299. 12 Sept. 1796. BIRD NANCE and MARY his wife of the county of Henry to JOHN NIXON of Charlotte County for the sum of Sixty five pounds sells 100 acres on the branches of the south fork of Leatherwood Creek, joins CHARLES BURNETT'S spring branch and ROBERT STOCKTON. Wit: JOHN CONNAWAY, REUBEN NANCE, ELIJAH MOORE, THOMAS RICHARDSON. Signed: BIRD NANCE, MARY NANCE. Proved: 30 Jan. 1797.

Pages 299-300. 14 Sept. 1796. JACOB CATON of the county of Henry to WILLIAM JOSEPH of the same for Thirty pounds sells 200 acres on the south side of Smith River joins JOHN GROGAN, and Kendricks branch. Wit: JOHN DAVIS, CORNELIUS CAYTON, TILMAN CLARK. Signed: JACOB CATON. Proved: 30 Jan. 1797.

Pages 301-302. 30 Jan. 1797. JACOB CATON of the

county of Henry to CORNELIUS CATON of the same for the sum of Fifty pounds sells and conveys 200 acres more or less on the south side of Smith River joins MORGAN'S Road, KELLY and GROGINS. No wit. Signed: JACOB (X) CATON. Proved: 30 Jan. 1797.

Pages 302-303. 23 July 1796. WILLIAM BAYLES of Henry County to JOHN WELLS of the same for Twenty five pounds sells and conveys land on the east side of Turkey Cock Creek joins HUNT, HARDAWAY, HANKINS and JOHNSON, the same track ARCHILLIS BALLENGER sold to WILLIAM BAYLES, it being 50 acres, part of the tract that HUNT now lives on. Wit: JAMES JOHNSTON, HENRY (X) LAWRENCE, SELLMAN EDWARDS. Signed: WILLIAM BAYLES. Proved: 30 Jan. 1797.

Pages 304-305. 25 Oct. 1796. BLIZARD MCGRUDER of Henry County to THOMAS BOULDIN of the same for the sum of Thirty seven pounds ten shillings sells 750 acres more or less on the waters of Grassy Creek, joins the lines of WILLINGHAM (now BOULDIN) MCKINNEY, JOHN SALMON, BOULDIN (formerly JOHN SIMMONS). Wit: MARY TALMON, WILLIAM BOULDIN, THOMAS BOULDIN, JR. Signed: BLIZARD MCGRUDER. Proved: 30 Oct. 1797.

Pages 305-306. 6 Jan. 1797. THOMAS BOULDIN of Henry County to GREEN BOULDIN of the same for the sum of Fifty seven pounds fifteen shillings sells a parcel of land on Grassy Creek being 270 acres. Wit: JOHN REDD, JOHN SPENCER, B. MARTIN. Signed: THOMAS BOULDIN. Proved: 30 Jan. 1797.

Pages 307-308. 25 Dec. 1792. JOHN HICKS of the county of Brunswick to JOHN KING and GEORGE KING of the county of Henry, for the sum of Four Hundred Fifty pounds sells and conveys a tract of land being 1,147½ acres...lines: BURNETT'S fence, Beaver Creek Mtn., Beaver Creek and Burnlies path. Wit: WILLIAM BROWN, RUFFIN BROWN, JOHN KING. Signed: JAMES HICKS, JUDITH HICKS. Proved: 28 Jan. 1793 & 30 Jan. 1797.

Page 308. 25 July 1796. Deed of Gift. FRANCIS COX of the county of Henry to my daughter ELLENDER GRAVELY, a gift of a negro gal Tildy, the daughter of Judith. Wit: JOHN MINTER, JABEZ GRAVELY. Signed: FRANCIS COX. Proved: 30 Jan. 1797.

Page 309. 24 Nov. 1795. Bond of JOHN SALMON appointing him Sheriff of Henry County with his securities GEORGE HAIRSTON, BALLENGER WADE, HENRY

LYNE and JOHN REDD.   Proved: 30 Jan. 1797.

Page 310.   30 Jan. 1797.   JOHN HALEY of Henry County to PETER GARLAND of Rockingham County, North Carolina for the sum of Five pounds sells land on the branches of Leatherwood Creek, being the land that was intended for my son BARNY HALEY, joins JOHN KING, WILLIAM BROWN and JOHN NANCE, contains 100 acres. No wit. Signed: JOHN HALEY. Proved: 30 Jan. 1797.

Page 311.   28 Jan. 1797.   ZACKERIAH PHILPOTT of Henry County to CHARLES T. PHILPOTT of the same for the sum of One hundred fifty pounds sells land on Beaver Creek tract contains 500 acres more or less begins at Beaver Creek at the mouth of Long Branch. Wit: JOHN PHIPOTT, SAMUEL PHILPOTT. Signed: ZACKERIAH PHILPOTT. Proved: 30 Jan. 1797.

Page 312.   27 July 1792.   WILLIAM RICKLE of Henry County to THOMAS ARTHUR of the same for the sum of Twenty pounds sells land in Pittsylvania and Henry County, on both sides of Young's Creek joins the lines of SAMUEL SHEWMATE and WILLIAM NANCE it being 59 acres. Wit: JACOB DAINS, WILLIAM ROBERSON, WILLIAM CUNNINGHAM. Signed: WILLIAM (X) RICKLE. Proved: 26 Nov. 1792 & 27 Feb. 1797.

Pages 313-314.   10 Feb. 1797.   JOHN STEVENS of Henry County to WILLIAM STEVENS of the same for the sum of Three pounds sells 20 acres on the waters of Home Creek adjoining the land of WILLIAM STEVENS. Wit: MOSES WILSON, LABON (X) HAMPTON, WILLIAM STEPHENS, JR. Signed: JOHN (X) STEPHENS, MILLY (X) STEPHENS. Proved: 27 Feb. 1797.

Pages 314-315.   1 Feb. 1797.   JOHN INGRAM and wife ELIZABETH INGRAM of Patrick County to JOHN PHILPOTT of Henry County for the sum of Fifty pounds sells land in Henry County on Smith River being 110 acres joins THOMAS FINE, the north side of Smith River and Butteringham Town Creek. Wit: JOEL CHITWOOD, HUMPHREY (X) POSEY, MARY ANN PHILPOTT, FRANKEY (X) CUNNINGHAM. Signed: JOHN (X) INGRAM. Proved: 27 Feb. 1797.

Pages 316-317.   24 Dec. 1796.   THOMAS WILLIAMS of Henry County to ARCHIBALD FARRIS of the same for Thirty pounds sells by estimate 100 acres more or less where the said WILLIAM lives on Marrowbone Creek joins WASHINGTON LANIER. Wit: JAMES TAYLER, HUGHES TAYLER, FANNY BUNCH. Signed: THOMAS WILLIAMS.

Proved: 27 Feb. 1797. . . .Memo: 24 Dec. 1796...possession of land and premises taken.

Pages 318-319. 26 Oct. 1796. WILLIAM MILLS of Henry County to ELIJAH SAMS of the same for the sum of One hundred pounds sells more or less 300 acres on both sides of Matrimony Creek. Wit: JESSE (X) MURPHY, PETER (X) RUGG, JOHN (X) PRICE. Signed: WILLIAM MILLS. Proved: 27 Feb. 1797.

Pages 320-321. 9 Mar. 1797. Deed of Trust. JOSEPH PHIFER of Henry County to JAMES BAKER in the amount of Eighteen pounds. The said PHIFER indebted to BAKER, secures with 220 acres land whereon the said PHIFER now resides bounded by JOHN BARKSDALE, NEWSUM PACE, THOMAS NUNN, WILLIAM DRAPER and the land formerly of JOHN ROWLAND. After the 1st of October next will sell for best price, balance to JOSEPH PHIFER. Wit: JOHN COX, JEREMIAH STONE, LEWIS (X) FRANKLIN. Signed: JOSEPH PHIFER. Proved: 27 Mar.1797.

Pages 321-322. April Court 1796. GEORGE HAIRSTON and THOMAS EAST attorney for WILLIAM WRIT acting executor of GEORGE GILMORE, deceased, came into Court and agreed that BRICE MARTIN, THOMAS BOULDEN, SENR. and GEORGE WALLER, JR. divide and take off one fourth part of 890 acres of land lying on the Poison'd fields of Grassy Creek, formerly property of RANDOLPH, HARMER & KING. Signed: JOHN COX. Proved: 27 Mar. 1797. . . .In obedience with a Court Order we layed off 222½ acres. Signed: BRICE MARTIN, THOMAS BOULDIN, GEORGE WALLER, JR.

Page 322-323. 27 Mar. 1797. GEORGE HAIRSTON of Henry County to BURREL BASSETT of the same for the sum of One hundred fifty pounds sells and conveys by survey 222½ acres more or less on Strands Creek, a branch of the Smith River, known by the name of Poison Fields which land was conveyed by W. K. COLE to PETER FRANCISCO and by FRANCISCO to me, being part of an undivided tract which reference to other deeds will more fully describe. Signed: GEORGE HAIRSTON. Proved: 27 Mar. 1797. . . .ELIZABETH, the wife of GEORGE HAIRSTON releases her right of dower.

Page 324. 28 Jan. 1797. GEORGE TAYLOR of the county of Henry to his son JAMES TAYLOR gives and grants 50 acres on the south side of the Mayo River. . . .N.B. This tract or parcel of land is all my son JAMES TAYLOR is to have of my estate. Signed: GEORGE TAYLOR. Proved: 27 Mar. 1797.

Pages 325-326. 27 Mar. 1797. JESSE ATKISSON and RUTH his wife of Henry County to STEPHEN ATKISSON of the same for the sum of Ten Pounds sells land on the south side of the North Mayo River joins JESSE ATKISSON, BALLENGER WADE, JESSE ATKISSON, JR., the land in the possession of said STEPHEN ATKISSON being 76 acres more or less. Wit: JESSE ATKISSON, JR., SIR JAMES BOULDIN, WILLIAM BOULDIN. Signed: JESSE ATKISSON, RUTH ATKISSON. Proved: 27 Mar. 1797.

Pages 326-327. 27 Mar. 1797. JESSE ATKISSON and RUTH his wife of the county of Henry to JESSE ATKISSON, JR. for the sum of Ten pounds sells and conveys land on the south side of the North Mayo River adjoining the land of JESSE ATKISSON, STEPHEN ATKISSON, BALLENGER WADE being 90 acres more or less this land now in the possession of JESSE ATKISSON, JR. Wit: STEPHEN ATKISSON, SIR JAMES BOULDIN, WILLIAM BOULDING. Signed: JESSE ATKISSON, RUTH ATKISSON. Proved: 27 Mar. 1797.

Pages 328-329. 4 Mar. 1797. DANIEL WILSON of the county of Henry to NATHANIEL WILSON of the same for the sum of One hundred pounds sells and conveys land on the waters of Home Creek joins the lines of COX, WATKINS and contains 200 acres more or less. Wit: MOSES WILSON, BANAR (X) CUMTON, LABAN (X) HAMPTON. Signed: DANIEL WILSON. Proved: 24 Apr. 1797.

Page 329-330. 24 Apr. 1797. JOSEPH MARTIN of Henry County to CARR WALLER of the same, for and in consideration of a sum in fee simple sells, grants and conveys 160 acres of land...this said land was conveyed by THOMAS MATHES (MATHEWS??) to JOHN BOTTOM the father of JOEL BOTTOM and ROWLAND BOTTOM who conveyed it to JOSEPH MARTIN. No wit. Signed: JOSEPH MARTIN. Proved: 24 Apr. 1797.

Pages 330-331. 17 April 1797. THOMAS STEWART of the county of Henry to JOHN HAMMONDS of the same, for the sum of Twenty seven pounds sells 80 acres more or less on Leatherwood Creek, joins lines of MERRY WEBB. No wit. Signed: THOMAS STEWART, USLEY STEWART. Proved: 24 Apr. 1797.

Pages 332-333. 24 Apr. 1797. JOHN DILLARD and SARAH DILLARD, his wife of Henry County to PETER PERKINS and THOMAS BOULDIN of the same, for the sum of Seventy five pounds sell land on the north side of the north fork of the Mayo River, 154 acres, the land now in possession of the said PERKINS and

BOULDIN. Wit: SIR JAMES BOULDIN, WILLIAM BOULDIN, THOMAS BOULDIN. Signed: JOHN DILLARD. Proved: 24 Apr. 1797. . . .SARAH DILLARD, the wife of JOHN DILLARD releases her right of dower to the said land above described.

Pages 334-335. 27 Apr. 1797. JOHN KELLY of the county of Henry to JOSEPH GOODWIN of the same for the sum of Six pounds sells and conveys 20 acres more or less that joins JOSEPH GODWIN on Rock Key Branch. No wit. Signed: JOHN KELLY. Proved: 27 Apr. 1797.

Pages 335-336. 17 Apr. 1797. WILLIAM ROBISON (ROBERTSON, ROBERSON) of Henry County to PHILIP CONNOR of the same for and in consideration of Forty pounds sells 96 acres by survey, on the south side of Smith River, joins FRANCIS GILLEY, JR. & Graveyard Branch. Wit: JOHN HAMMOND, MOSES (X) WILSON, HENRY (X) SMITH. Signed: WILLIAM ROBERSON, ESTHER (X) ROBERSON. Proved: 24 Apr. 1797.

Pages 337-338. 17 Apr. 1797. JONADAB WADE and SAMUEL C. MORRIS of Henry County to PETER LEAK of the same for the consideration of One hundred twenty five pounds sells 154 acres by estimate, in Henry County on the waters of Little Horsepasture Creek joins PETER LEAK, GILMORE OFFICER, ALEXANDER HUNTER and JAMES OFFICER. This land now in possession of said LEAK. No wit. Signed: JONADAB WADE, MARY ANN WADE, wife of JONADAB WADE, SAMUEL C. MORRIS. Proved: 27 Apr. 1797. . . .MARY ANN WADE, wife of JONADAB WADE, releases her right of dower to the above mentioned land.

Pages 339-340. 24 Apr. 1797. MARTHA FONTAINE of the county of Henry to JOSEPH MARTIN of the same for the sum of Ten pounds sells and conveys 100 acres on the waters of Tabbots Creek and joins the lines of MARTIN and FONTAINE. Wit: DAVID PANNILE, P. H. FONTAINE, NATH. W. DANDRIDGE, JR. Signed: MARTHA FONTAINE. Proved: 24 Apr. 1797.

Pages 340-341. 14 Nov. 1796. JAMES EDWARDS of Rockingham County, North Carolina and JOHN GROGAN of Henry County, Virginia, ISHAM EDWARDS of Franklin County, Virginia and HENRY GROGAN of Rockingham County, North Carolina to JOHN PRICE of Henry County for the sum of Two hundred pounds sells and conveys 483 acres on the waters of Matrimony Creek. Wit: ARCHIBALD MURPHY, ELIJAH SAMMS, JACOB DILLENDER.

Signed: JAMES EDWARDS, JOHN GROGAN, ISHAM EDWARDS, HENRY GROGAN. Proved: 27 Apr. 1797.

Pages 342-343. 19 Apr. 1797. JOHN NORRIS, JOHN JAMERSON and MARKHAM LOVELL of Henry County to CLEMENT MURPHY of the same for the sum of One hundred pounds sells three tracts or parcels of land all adjoining each other on the waters of Redd Creek, it being 90 acres, joins also NATHAN NORRIS. No wit. Signed: JOHN NORRIS, JOHN JAMERSON, MARKHAM LOVELL. Proved: 24 Apr. 1797.

Pages 343-344. 24 April 1797. JAMES MEREDITH of the county of Henry to ABNER STULTS of the same sells and conveys 75 acres more or less on the head branch of the South fork of Leatherwood Creek joins MAGRUDER, GIRGGS' old ridge path, THOMAS WILKINS, WILLIAM BROWN, for the consideration of Forty six pounds. No wit. Signed: JAMES (X) MEREDITH. Proved 25 Apr. 1797.

Page 345. 5 Apr. 1797. Power of Attorney. I, JOSEPH MARTIN of Henry County, me hereunto moving appoint my son BRICE MARTIN my true and lawful attorney to convey any of my lands in the state of Virginia or Kentucky. No wit. Signed: JOSEPH MARTIN. Proved: 25 Apr. 1797.

Page 346. No date. Power of Attorney. I, WILLIAM HILL of the county of Henry do appoint THOMAS JETT of the same, my lawfull attorney for the express and particular purpose of conveying by special warrants to WILLIAM HENRY or his heirs all my right and title to certain lands containing 812½ acres, this being the one half of 1600 acres in Kentucky which land is located by survey by the said WILLIAM HENRY and the balance of the said property THOMAS JETT is to dispose of as he thinks proper. No wit. Signed: WILLIAM HILL. Proved: 25 Apr. 1797.

Pages 347-348. October 1796. DAVID LANIER and MARY LANIER his wife, JOHN HEFFLEFINGER and MARY HEFFLEFINGER his wife to GEORGE HAIRSTON all of Henry County, for the sum of Four hundred fifty pounds sell and convey 350 acres of land on Irvins now called Smith River on the north side beginning where DAVID LANIER land from PATRICK HENRY begins...see this deed for a better description, joins FONTAINE, BOLING and MARTIN. Wit: JOHN H. LANIER, DAVID LANIER, ELIZABETH LANIER, JOHN ALEXANDER, JOHN SMITH, JOHN ROWLAND, JR. Signed: DAVID LANIER, MARY (X) LANIER,

JOHN HEFFLEFINGER, MARY (X) HEFFLEFINGER. Proved: 29 May 1797.

Pages 348-350. 3 May 1797. HUMPHREY POSEY and his wife ELIZABETH POSEY of the county of Patrick to EDWARD PHILPOTT of Henry County for the sum of Two hundred pounds sell land in Patrick and Henry Counties on both sides of Smith River, joins GRAY'S line and contains 245 acres more or less. Wit: JESSE CARTER, JOHN PHILPOTT, HUGH MARTIN, SAMUEL CRUTCHFIELD, WILSON VAUGHN, JEREMIAH ROBERTS, ABRAM MAYES. Signed: HUMPHREY (X) POSEY, ELIZABETH (X) POSEY. Proved: 29 May 1797.

Pages 350-352. 6 Sept. 1796. Indenture of Assignment, JOHN OSBORNE of Petersburg, Merchant, CAMPBELL & WHEELER Merchants of the same and DAVID LANIER to GEORGE HAIRSTON. DAVID LANIER by deed dated 1 June 1789 conveyed to the said OSBORNE two tracts of land (where the said DAVID LANIER lives) on Smith River and the other on the south side of Smith River adjacent to Marrowbone. By the said deed OSBORNE might after the 1 Jan. 1791 sell the said lands to satisfy LANIER'S debts. The debt now is Three hundred and thirty three pounds and GEORGE HAIRSTON to take a Deed of Trust to the said lands. Wit: JOHN ROWLAND, JOHN STAPLES, BENJAMIN LANIER. Signed: JOHN OSBORNE, CAMPBELL & WHEELER, DAVID LANIER, GEORGE HAIRSTON. Proved: Oct. 1796 & 29 May 1797.

Pages 353-354. 16 June 1797. WILLIAM HEATH and SALLY BET HEATH his wife of Henry County to JOHN TRAVIS of the same for the sum of Five hundred eleven dollards sells 29 acres in Patrick County and the balance in Henry County on the waters of Horsepasture Creek and Smith River...it being the whole of a tract as per deed WATSON to HEATH in Patrick Office and part of two other tracts per deed WATSON to HEATH and LAWLESS to HEATH in Henry County Office...joins lines of HENRY DILLION, WOODSON and WATSON it being a total of 311 acres more or less. Wit: SAMUEL STEPHENS, TUNSTALL COX, HEZEKIAH SALMON. Signed: WILLIAM HEATH, SALLY BET HEATH. Proved: 26 June 1797.

Page 355. 20 Aug. 1797. ANTHONY BITTING of Stokes County, North Carolina to HENRY CLARK of Henry County, Virginia for the sum of Seven pounds ten shillings sells and conveys 53 acres by estimate in Henry County joins WILLIAM STOKES, DANIEL and DENT. No wit. Signed: ANTHONY BITTING. Proved: 31 July 1797.

Pages 356-357. 31 July 1797. THOMAS EAST of Henry County to ARCHIBALD FARRIS of the same for the sum of Twenty pounds sells 118 acres of land on the branches of Marrowbone Creek joins his own land and BLIZARD MAGRUDER. No wit. Signed: THOMAS EAST. Proved: 31 July 1797.

Page 358. 28 Aug. 1797. CAIN ACUFF of Henry County to GEORGE HAIRSTON of the same for the sum of Fifty pounds sells land, by estimate 100 acres it being part of a tract granted JOHN ACUFF by patent, joins JOHN NANCE. No wit. Signed: CAIN ACUFF. Proved: 28 Aug. 1797. . . .ESTHER ACUFF, wife of CAIN ACUFF releases her right of dower.

Pages 359-360. 28 Aug. 1797. RUSSEL COX of Henry County to GEORGE HAIRSTON of the same for the sum of Fifteen pounds sells and conveys 200 acres more or less on both sides of the Bold branch of Leatherwood Creek and Meadow Branch, joins GEORGE REYNOLDS. No wit. Signed: RUSSEL COX. Proved: 28 Aug. 1797.

Pages 360-361. 28 Aug. 1797. DAVID MAYSE of Henry County to GEORGE HAIRSTON of the same for the sum of Five shillings sells 50 acres of land on the Long Branch, begins at the old line of HENRY MAYSE, deceased. No wit. Signed: DAVID (X) MAYSE. Proved: 28 Aug. 1797.

Page 362. 28 Aug. 1797. JACOB CAYTON of Henry County to GEORGE HAIRSTON of the same for the consideration of Fifty three pounds sells 200 acres of land that joins MORGAN'S Road, the lines of MARR and KELLY. No wit. Signed: JACOB (X) KEATON. Proved: 28 Aug. 1797.

Pages 362-364. 16 April 1796. ANTHONY SMITH and AGNES SMITH his wife of Henry County to JOHN SPENCER, WILLIAM SPENCER, JAMES SPENCER and GEORGE WASHINGTON SPENCER sons and heirs of JAMES SPENCER, deceased for the sum of Fifty pounds sell land on the waters of Horsepasture Creek...said land joins the land of the heirs, JOHN STAPLES and WILLIAM MILLS said tract contains 75 acres and this land is now in the possession of the said heirs of JAMES SPENCER, deceased. Wit: STEPHEN LEE, NATHANIEL SHELTON, HEZEKIAH SALMON, NATHANIEL BASSETT, WILLIAM BREWER. Signed: ANTHONY SMITH, AGNES (X) SMITH. Proved: 30 May 1796 & 28 Aug. 1797.

Pages 365-366. 8 July 1796. MARTHA FONTAINE of the county of Henry to WILLIAM S. COX of the same for the sum of Ten pounds fifteen shillings sells and conveys 75 acres of land joining his own and WILLIAM ROBERTSON. Wit: P. H. FONTAINE, NATHANIEL W. DANDRIDGE, THOMAS COX. Signed: MARTHA FONTAINE. Proved: 30 Jan. 1797.

Pages 366-367. 28 Aug. 1797. THOMAS WHITE RUBLE (no county or state mentioned) to JOHN REDD for the sum of Three hundred pounds sells one mority of a tract of land containing 100 acres in Henry County on both sides of Town Creek joins DANIEL SMITH, refer to lines in SHADRACK TURNER'S will, see the patent dated 12 Oct. 1779 at Williamsburg for other descriptions. No wit. Signed: THOMAS W. RUBLE. Proved: 28 Aug. 1797.

Pages 367-368. 22 May 1789. DAVID HARBOUR of the county of Montgomery, State of Virginia to JAMES POTEET, SENR. fo the County of Henry for the consideration of Two hundred pounds sells and conveys a certain parcel or tract of land contains by estimate 313 acres and is located on the south fork of Goblingtown Creek. Wit: JESSE SPURLOCK, DRURY SPURLOCK. Signed: DAVID HARBOUR. Proved: 25 May 1789. . . .MARY HARBOUR, the wife of DAVID HARBOUR, releases her right of dower to the above transaction.

END OF DEED BOOK 5

DEED BOOK 6

Pages 1-2. 25 Nov. 1796. WASHINGTON LANIER of the county of Henry to ARCHIBALD FARRIS of the same for the sum of Seventy five pounds sells and conveys a tract or parcel of land containing 117 acres on a creek, trees given as corners. Wit: JOHN STAPLES, PETER LEAKE, CHARLES FARDING. Signed: WASHINGTON LANIER, ELIZABETH (X) LANIER. Proved: 31 July 1797 Court.

Pages 2-3. 24 Sept. 1797. JOHN MINTER of the county of Henry to GEORGE HAIRSTON of the same for the sum of One hundred fifty pounds sells a tract of land by estimate to be 330 acres more or less on the branches of the south fork of Leatherwood Creek, joins the lines of REUBEN NANCE, CAIN ACUFF and MC-CULLOCK. This includes the tenements JOHN MINTER purchased of CARTER TARREN, WILLIAM ACUFF and EDWARD HALEY. Wit: THOMAS GRAVES, NAT'L. W. DANDRIDGE, JR., GEORGE WALLER, JR. Signed: JOHN MINTER. Proved: 25 Sept. 1797.

Pages 4-5. 25 Sept. 1797. JACOB DILLENDER and RHODY DILLENDER, his wife of Henry County to GEORGE HAIRSTON of the same for the sum of Twenty six pounds sells 181 acres by survey, located on Turkey Cock Creek of Smith River and joins HAIRSTON'S land. No wit. Signed: JACOB (X) DILLENDER, RHOCY (X) EILLENDER. . . .RHODY DILLENDER, wife of JACOB DILLENDER releases her right of dower.

Pages 5-6. 19 Feb. 1780. An agreement between MORDECAI HORD and PATRICK HENRY both of Henry County. MORDECAI HORD sells to PATRICK HENRY 350 acres on the Smith River where GARDNER lives and passes all his right without warranty but agrees that as soon as he obtains a right from MARTIN KEY he will execute a deed for the said land to PATRICK HENRY in fee simple. PATRICK HENRY gives for the said land all his right to a plot and certificate for 2,000 acres of land on the Ohio River near the Great Bone, surveyed by JAMES DOUGLASS and warrant from the Land Office also One thousand pounds more in current money and is to pay HORD One thousand pounds more for damages if HORD fails to obtain a right to the land from MARTIN KEY but said One thousand pounds forfiet to be discharged by payment of gold or silver at rates of 1 for 20 pounds in paper. Viz: Fifty pounds hard money for the said One thousand pounds. PATRICK HENRY is to have immediate use of the land. 400 acres of land out of the 2,000 acres to go to COL. WILLIAM CHRISTIAN. Wit: HENRY LYNE, MARVEL NASH. Signed: MORDECAI HORD, P. HENRY. Proved 25 Sept. 1979 Court.

Pages 6-7. 24 Apr. 1797. Bill of Sale. DAVID LANIER of Henry County sells unto SANFORD RAMEY of the same, one negro girl named Judy who is 19 years of age, is of healthy and sound mind and body for the sum of Fifty two pounds. Wit: THOMAS EAST, NAT. W. DANDRIDGE, JR. Signed: DAVID LANIER. Proved: 25 Sept. 1797.

Pages 7-8. 19 May 1797. Bill of Sale. SUSANAH MARR, Administrator of the estate of JOHN MARR, deceased sells to DANIEL WILSON, THOMAS CHOWNING and ISHAM LANSFORD the following negroes, horses and household furniture, viz: Henry, Aggy, Jerey, Nelson, Hanah, Squire, Eady, Elley, Morning, Clementina, Honor, Aron, Jinney, Sharper, Allet and Phann, 2 gray horses about 12 years old, one dark gray mare 3 yrs., 1 bald horse, 3 bays, 7 beds and furniture, 2 desks, 1 bookcase, 1 chey press, folding table, 9 pots, 3 dutch ovens also one negro man Ned and one woman named Lucy, 1 negro girl Franky this being the property of JOHN MARR deceased and also my own private property. Wit: WILLIAM MITCHELL, WILLIAM NORMAN, RUS. HUGHES. Signed: SUSANAH MARR.

Pages 8-9. No date. DANIEL WILSON, THOMAS CHOWNING and ISHAM LANSFORD obtained this day of Bill of Sale from SUSANAH MARR for the above property. Now it is understood that the above DANIEL WILSON, etc. should not be called on nor be obliged to pay money on account of a Bond entered into this day with SUSANAH MARR and MARK HARDEN for to enable them to obtain a writ Surp--- Court? from District Court a New London then and in that case we release the said property and return to S. MARR. Proved: 30 Oct. 1797.

Pages 9-10. 14 July 1797. WILLIAM LINDSAY of Patrick County to THOMAS JAMISON of Henry County. WILLIAM LINDSAY is indebted to JAMES OAKLEY in the amount of Forty pounds and in order to secure and pay him he gives this Deed of Trust to THOMAS JAMISON, of two negros a girl slave Sarah 14 years of age and a boy 10 years old. These to be sold if the debt is not paid 25 December next year. Wit: ELENOR TARBOURN, THOMAS GRAVES, JACOB MICHAUX. Signed: WILLIAM LINDSAY, THOMAS JAMISON. Proved: 30 Oct.1797.

Pages 11-12. 5 April 1796. MARTHA FONTAINE of the

county of Henry to SAMUEL HESTER of Mecklenburg County for the sum of Two hundred pounds sells land on the waters of Leatherwood Creek joins THOMAS BARTON, and MRS. HENRY, contains 206 acres. Wit: BANISTER ROYSTER, JOSEPH RYAN, N. W. DANDRIDGE, JR., JOHN RAMEY. Signed: MARTHA FONTAINE. Proved: 26 Sept. 1796 & 1 Nov. 1797.

Pages 12-13. 1 Nov. 1797. THOMAS COOPER and ELIZABETH COOPER his wife of the county of Henry to GEORGE HAIRSTON of the same for the sum of Seventy five pounds sells land on Marrowbone Creek by estimate 95 acres more or less joins JAMES REA'S old line and HAIRSTON. Wit: GEORGE WALLER, JR., T. ALEXANDER. Signed: THOMAS (X) COOPER, ELIZABETH (X) COOPER. Proved: 1 Nov. 1797. . . .ELIZABETH COOPER, wife of THOMAS COOPER released her right of dower.

Pages 14-16. 3 Nov. 1797. Deed of Trust. JACOB DAINES and NANCY DAINES his wife to GEORGE HAIRSTON, DAINES owes HAIRSTON..conveys for the sum of Fifty pounds land on the waters of Sandy River by estimate 442 acres joins HENRY JONES, JOSEPH JONES, SAMUEL SHOEMAKE, it being land DAINES formerly lived on. Lines agreeable to a deed to DAINES from HODGES and others. Wit: WILLIAM HEARD, THOMAS EAST. Signed: JACOB DAINES, NANCY DAINES. . . .Memo: JACOB DAINES debt to GEORGE HAIRSTON is 26 pounds 19 shillings and 10-½ pence, if not paid prior to 1 March next (with interest) to be sold at the above price. . . .NANCY DAINES, wife of JACOB DAINES, releases right of dower.

Page 17. 27 Nov. 1797. THOMAS CHOWNING of Henry County to WILLIAM MITCHELL of the same for the sum of Thirty pounds sells 70 acres on the north side of Smith River east side of Middle Creek, it being part of 200 acres assigned THOMAS CHOWNING by JOHN KELLY. No wit. Signed: THOMAS CHEWNING. Proved: 27 Nov. 1797.

Pages 18-19. 30 Oct. 1797. GEORGE BRITTAIN of Henry County to PERINAS WILLIAMS of Pittsylvania County for the sum of One hundred pounds sells land in Henry and Pittsylvania County 144 acres in Pittsylvania by patent 1 Sept. 1791 another part in Henry County purchased of Captain JAMES ROBERTS and WILLIAM STEPHENS as per deed in Henry County. GEORGE BRITTAIN now lives land that joins WILLIAM STEPHENS, DANIEL WILSON, CAPT. HENRY LANSFORD on Home Creek, both tracts contain 350 acres more or less. Wit: T. MARSHALL, WILLIAM (X) SPANS, LEWIS JONES, JOSEPH CLARK.

Signed: GEORGE BRITTAIN, JUDITH (X) BRITTAIN. Proved: 27 Nov. 1797.

Pages 19-20. 6 Oct. 1797. WILLIAM ROBERTSON of Henry County to WILLIAM BAYS of the same sells land on the waters of Cascade it being 178 acres to Gepsons Branch, joins G. F. HARRIS and JOSEPH AMBROSE. The consideration is for Ninety pounds. Wit: WILLIAM STEPHENS, JR., MOSES (X) WILSON, PHILIP CONNOR. Signed: WILLIAM ROBERTSON. Proved: 27 Nov. 1797.

Pages 21-22. 27 Nov. 1797. ZACKARIAH PHILPOTT of Henry County to GEORGE HAIRSTON of the same for the consideration of Twenty five pounds sells land on the waters of Beaver Creek by estimate 20 or 30 acres joins the land now claimed by CHARLES PHILPOTT which he purchased of WILLIAM BRETHEAT, and the said BRETHEAT of WILLIAM LOVELL to THOMAS COOPER'S old line (Now HAIRSTONS) opposite HAIRSTON'S Mills. No wit. Signed: ZACKARIAH PHILPOTT. Proved: 27 Nov. 1797.

Pages 22-23. 27 Nov. 1797. FRANCIS NORTHCUTT, JOSEPH JONES and JOHN PACE of the county of Henry to THOMAS EGGLETON. At a session of Court 1 Nov. 1796 it was ordered in a Case in Chancery then depending between BARNA WELLS Plantif and JESSE DELOZER, Defendant that NORTHCUTT, JONES and PACE sell at publick auction 220 acres where the Defedant formerly lived and out of the proceeds pay the Plantif the sum of Forty pounds with interest. THOMAS EGGLETON paid Fifty three pounds 1 shilling for the 220 acres, payment hereby received. No wit. Signed: FRANCIS NORTHCUTT, JOSEPH JONES, JOHN PACE. Proved: 27 Nov. 1797.

Pages 24-25. 27 Nov. 1796. Bond of DAVID LANIER who is appointed Sheriff of Henry County. Bondsmen: GEORGE HAIRSTON, WILLIAM MOORE, BENJAMIN HARRISON, JR., BENJAMIN LANIER. Bond acknowledged Nov. 27, 1797 Court.

Pages 25-26. 27 Nov. 1796. Same bondsmen appointing DAVID LANIER to Collect taxes for the county of Henry.

Pages 27-28. 22 Dec. 1797. ROBERT PEDIGOY, SENR. of Henry County & ROBERT PEDIGOY, JR., of the same to JOHN WATSON of the county of Pittsylvania for the sum of Thirty one pounds five shillings conveys 100 acres on Lick Branch of Leatherwood Creek joins MCBRIDE and GRIFFIN GRIFFITH. No wit. Signed:

ROBERT PEDIGOY, SENR., ROBERT PEDIGOY, JR. Proved: 25 Dec. 1797.

Pages 29-30. 25 Dec. 1797. GEORGE HAIRSTON of Henry County to ROBERT PEDIGO for the sum of Twenty pounds sells 139 acres on Mulberry Creek contains by survey the 139 acres, it being land deeded HAIRSTON from JOHN WILSON of Pittsylvania County. No wit. Signed: GEORGE HAIRSTON. Proved: 25 Dec. 1797.

Pages 30-31. 25 Dec. 1797. ROBERT PEDIGO and his wife of Henry County to GEORGE HAIRSTON for Fifty pounds sells by survey 248 acres joins JO. MASTERS and SMITH. No wit. Signed: R. (R.) PEDIGO. Proved: 25 Dec. 1797.

Pages 32-33. 26 Feb. 1797. PATRICK HENRY and DORATHEA HENRY his wife of Charlotte County to WILLIAM LINDSAY of Patrick County for the sum of Five shillings, land in Henry County on the waters of Leatherwood Creek containing by survey 150 acres which lands PHIL. RYAN now lives and said RYAN purchased said tract of JOHN FONTAINE in his lifetime. Begins at THOMAS JETT'S line, to EDWARD HENRY'S to said creek. Wit: GEORGE HAIRSTON, JOHN NORTON, WILLIAM OLLIVER, JR. Signed: PATRICK HENRY, DORATHEA HENRY. Proved: 29 May 1797.

Page 33. 26 Feb. 1797. PATRICK HENRY and DORATHEA HENRY, his wife, of Charlotte County to THOMAS JETT of Henry County for the sum of Five shilling land on the south side of Leatherwood Creek on Ralph's Branch, 150 acres begins at JETT'S line...he sold to HOBSON to JOSEPH BOULDIN to EDWARD HENRY, WILLIAM FONTAINE sold to HOBSON...being lands sold by JOHN FONTAINE to JAMES JOHNSON. Wit: GEORGE HAIRSTON, JOHN NORTON, WILLIAM OLLIVER, JR. Signed: PATRICK HENRY, DORATHEA HENRY. Proved: 27 Mar. 1797.

Pages 34-35. 25 July 1797. WILLIAM LINDSAY of Patrick County to GEORGE HAIRSTON of Henry County for the consideration of Two hundred pounds sells and conveys lands in Henry County on Leatherwood Creek joins THOMAS JETT, JOSEPH HOBSON, JAMES JOHNSON, EDWARD HENRY. This 150 acres conveyed by JOHN FONTAINE, deceased to PHIL. RYAN and RYAN to WILLIAM LINDSAY and the deed of conveyance from PATRICK FENRY to WILLIAM LINDSAY. Wit: BENJAMIN HARRISON, JR., SIR JAMES BOULDIN, HARRISON BOYD. Signed: WILLIAM LINDSAY. Proved: 27 Nov. 1797.

Pages 36-37. 22 Dec. 1797. ROBERT PEDIGO of Henry County to GRIFFIN GRIFFITH of the same for the sum of Forty pounds sells 100 acres of land on the waters of Leatherwood Creek joins LOMAX & Company. No wit. Signed: ROBERT PEDIGO. Proved: 25 Dec. 1791.

Page 38. 26 Feb. 1798. JOSEPH GRAVELY of Henry County to HENRY SHAKLEFORD of the same for the sum of Forty five pounds sells 160 acres more or less on Grass fork of Leatherwood Creek joins LOMAX & Company and to a line agreed upon by JOSEPH GRAVELY and NICKLES AKIN. No wit. Signed: JOSEPH GRAVELY. Proved: 26 Feb. 1798.

Pages 39-40. 20 Dec. 1797. ELIZABETH DONELSON and WILLIAM TUNSTALL of Pittsylvania County to JOSEPH MARTIN of Henry County for the sum of One hundred dollars sell and convey a parcel or tract of land by estimate 97 acres joins LOMAX & Company's Order Line, it is the same land conveyed to ELIZABETH DONELSON by DAVID LANIER 7 July 1793 recorded in Henry County as that deed will more full show. Wit: DANIEL LOVELL, ARCHD. B. DANDRIDGE, JOHN (X) RIDDLE, NATHL. W. DANDRIDGE, RICHARD TUNSTALL. Signed: ELIZABETH DONELSON. Proved: 26 Feb. 1798.

Pages 41-43. 25 Dec. 1797. JOHN MURCHIE of Chesterfield County, only surviving executor and trustee of the last will and testament of ROBERT DONALD, deceased of the said county to JOHN REDD of Henry County conveys 637 acres as per survey (original in Pittsylvania County) and commonly known as ROWLANDS Old Tract as per deed from the late THOMAS M. RANDOLPH to the said ROBERT DONALD 26 Feb. 1780. ROBERT DONALD by his last will and testament 23 June 1791 in Chesterfield County that the said land was to be sold by the executors. The consideration is Six hundred thirty seven pounds, for the two tracts 411 acres and 291 acres bounded by HENRY BARSDALE CUNNINGHAM and by Smith River. Wit: GEORGE PENN, JESSE CORN, SALLY PENN, WILLIAM CARTER, J. WOODS. Signed: JOHN MURCHIE, executor of ROBERT DONALD, dec'd. Proved: 26 Feb. 1798.

Pages 44-45. 1 Jan. 1798. DAVID M. RANDOLPH and MARY RANDOLPH his wife to GEORGE HAIRSTON for the sum of Four hundred fifty pounds sells 1,660 acres on the waters of Leatherwood Creek lately surveyed by COL. JOHN FONTAINE and to the said MARY RANDOLPH wife of DAVID M. RANDOLPH by T. M. RANDOLPH conveyed by deed 23 Mar. 1792. Wit: BENJAMIN HARRISON,

JR., BEN. RANDOLPH, T. BRAXTON, WILLIAM FITZHUGH
BRAXTON, JOHN REDD, JESSE CORN, WILLIAM CARTER, JOHN
HALE, J. WOODS. Signed: DAVID M. RANDOLPH. Proved:
26 Feb. 1798.

Pages 45-48.   21 Dec. 1797. Deed of Trust. NATHANIEL
               WILKERSON, RICHARD ADAMS, WILLIAM HAY,
JOHN HAROU (?), WILLIAM DUVAL and GEORGE NICKELIEN
Trustee of the interest which the Commonwealth hath in
certain land where PATRICK COUTTS, deceased died seized to JOHN PHILPOTT whereas the General Assembly by
an act for vesting in Trustee the interest which the
Commonwealth land whereof PATRICK COUTTS deceased pass-
ed 16 Dec. 1790 authorized Trustees which has been
sold by WILLIAM COUTTS who was Administrator or by
BENJAMIN LEWIS, ALEXANDER W. ROBERT and JOHN MCKEAND
Administrators of said PATRICK COUTTS deceased admin-
istrated by WILLIAM COUTTS deceased for the sum of
Thirty pounds sell to JOHN PHILPOTT the residue of the
land in the county of Lunenburg but now in Henry
County 218 acres part was sold by the Sheriff to pay
tax and was granted to ROBERT BARRET, Clerk by patent
25 July 1768...lines Butterham Town Creek, THOMAS
FENNIS' line, north side of Smith River, crosses the
Mill Creek. Wit: JOHN REDD, JESSE CORN, JOSEPH MARTIN.
Signed: RICHARD ADAMS, JOHN HAROU, WILLIAM DUVALL.
Proved: 29 Jan. 1798.

Page 48. 15 Aug. 1797. Power of Attorney. WILLIAM
          LINDSAY of Patrick County with the purpose
of negoceating my business with the executors of my
grandfather JAMES LINDSAY'S estate appoint JACOB
MICHAUX to transact business and receive monies due
me as an heir of JACOB LINDSAY. No wit. Signed:
WILLIAM LINDSAY. Proved: 25 Feb. 1798.

Pages 49-50.   6 Feb. 1798. WILLIAM CRANE and REBECCA
               CRANE his wife to WILLIAM CRUM of the
county of Bedford for the sum of Thirty pounds sell
and convey 249 acres on the branches of Sandy River
being part granted unto JOHN MITCHELL by letter patt-
ent by date 12 Nov. 1779, see this for further details.
Wit: JOHN CARTER, TITUS (X) HUNTER, JOSEPH JONES.
Signed: WILLIAM CRANE. . . .REBECCA CRANE wife of
WILLIAM CRANE release dower rights.

Pages 50-52. 11 Mar. <u>1779</u>. PETER WORKMAN of the
              county of Rowan, State of North Carolina
to ANTHONY TITTLE of Henry County for the sum of Forty
pounds sells and conveys a parcel of land contains 115
acres by estimate on the north fork of Goblintown

Creek formerly the land where GEORGE WORKMAN lived. Wit: THOMAS HARBOUR, JOHN TITTLE, HENRY RETHEL. Signed: PETER (X) WORKMAN. Proved: 14 May 1779 & 26 Feb. 1798.

Pages 52-53. 20 Jan. 1798. FREDERICK HUTCHENS of Henry County to AMBROSE WHITE of the same sells 72 acres more or less on the south side of the South Mayo River it bein land granted HUTCHENS by JOHN SIMS 2 Mar. 1784 joins HENRY FRANCE. Wit: BALLENGER WADE, WILLIAM HAYS, SENR., WILLIAM HAYS,JR. Signed: FRED. (X) HUGENS. Proved: 26 Feb. 1798.

Page 54. 10 Jan. 1798. Bill of Sale. AUGUSTINE WOODLIFF of Henry Co. to WILLIAM MOORE for the sum of Eighteen pounds sells one red cow 7 yrs. old, 1 cow 5 yrs. old, 2 cows 2 yrs. old, 1 heifer 3 yrs., 1 horse 5 yrs., 2 feather beds with furniture. Wit: JOSEPH MARTIN, BANISTER ROYSTER, PETER ROYSTER. Signed: AUGUSTINE WOODLIFF. Proved: 27 Feb. 1798.

Pages 55-56. 31 Aug. 1797. SAMUEL STAPLES of Patrick County to ARCHIBALD HATCHER of Henry County for the sum of Fifty pounds sells 130 acres in Henry County joins JAMES SHELTON, deceased, WILLIAM SHELTON, JOHN DILLARD and is on the north side of Horsepasture Creek and JOHN STAPLES, STAPLES line was formerly JOSIAH SMITH'S. Wit: SAMUEL DUVAL, AUGUSTINE THOMAS, BALLENGER WADE. Signed: SAMUEL STAPLES. Proved: 25 Sept. 1797 & 27 Feb. 1798.

Pages 56-57. 30 Dec. 1797. WILLIAM COLLINS REA and WINNEFRED REA his wife of Henry County to GEORGE HAIRSTON of the same for the sum of Five pounds sells by survey 33 acres on Marrowbone Creek joins WILLIAM DILLEN. Wit: THOMAS GRAVES, PETER LEAKE. Signed: WILLIAM COLLINS REA, WINNEFRED (X) REA. Proved: 27 Feb. 1798.

Page 58. No date. Release. GEORGE HAIRSTON had a deed of conveyance from JACOB DAINES for two tracts of land one of which is where said DAINES now lives, DAIN sold one tract to JOHN ROWLAND and JACOB DAINES has paid the money due G. HAIRSTON. GEORGE HAIRSTON hereby releases all right or claim to the said land. Signed: GEORGE HAIRSTON.

Pages 58-60. 28 Feb. 1798. JACOB DAINES and NANCY DAINES his wife of Henry County to JOHN ROWLAND for the sum of Ninety pounds sell a parcel of land by estimate 200 acres being part of a 400 acre tract formerly surveyed for WILLIAM RICKLE on both sides of the south side of the south branch of the South Fork of Sandy River and is bounded in and by a deed of conveyance from JOSEPH MABRY to NICHOLAS PERKINS, also to SAMUEL SHOUMATE, HENRY JONES. No wit. Signed: JACOB DAINS. Proved: 28 Feb. 1798.

Pages 60-62. 2 Sept. 1797. JAMES TAYLOR of Henry County to DAVID MULLINS of Goodgeland County (Goochland??) for the sum of Two hundred fifty pounds sells a parcel of land contains 370 acres more or less it being the tract whereon TAYLOR now lives on Marrowbone Creek, joins JONADAB WADE, ARCHIBALD FARRIS, BLIZARD MCGRUDER and JAMES LARIMORE. Wit: THOMAS R. G. ADAMS, JOHN WENIRSE(?), GEORGE TAYLOR, WILLIAM MOORE. Signed: JAMES TAYLOR. Proved: 26 Mar. 1798. . .Memo: 2 Sept. 1797 possession granted and payment received.

Page 63. 30 Dec. 1797. ROBERT JOYCE of the county of Rockingham and state of North Carolina for the purpose of negociating my business with the executors of JAMES LINDSAY, deceased Estate appoint JACOB MICHAUX my attorney to act in my behalf. Wit: JOHN PATTERSON, RICHARDSON HERNDON. Signed: ROBERT JOYCE. Proved: 25 Mar. 1798.

Pages 63-64. 17 Jan. 1798. JARRETT PATTERSON of the county of Rockingham and state of North Carolina do appoint as my lawful attorney JACOB MICHAUX to transact my business with the Executors of the estate of JAMES LINDSAY, deceased. Wit: ROBERT JOYCE, RICHARDSON HERNDON. No signature for signing. Proved: 26 Mar. 1798.

Pages 64-65. 23 Mar. 1798. JOSEPH PEDIGO of the county of Henry to JOHN NORRIS of the same for the sum of Twenty five pounds sells and conveys land on the waters of Beaver Creek by estimate 100 acres joins JORDON and WALKER. No wit. Signed: JOSEPH PEDIGO. Proved: 26 Mar. 1798.

Pages 66-67. 21 Mar. 1798. JOSEPH PEDIGO of the county of Henry to ZEBULON NORRIS of the same for the sum of Twenty five pounds sells 100 acres by estimate, joins COPLAND and crosses a branch. No wit. Signed: JOSEPH PEDIGO. Proved: 26 Mar. 1798.

Pages 67-68. 23 Mar. 1798. JOHN REDD of Henry County to BENJAMIN JONES of the same for the consideration of One hundred fifty pounds does sell and convey a parcel of land on Little Beaver Creek by estimate 300 acres more or less joins the lines of HOLMES and GEORGE HAIRSTON. No wit. Signed: JOHN REDD. Proved: 26 Mar. 1798.

Pages 68-69. 9 Mar. 1798. JOHN REDD of Henry County to THOMAS W. RUBLE for the sum of Two hundred pounds sells 100 acres on both sides of Butterrum Town Creek, it being the land the said RUBLE conveyed to the said REDD whereon the Iron Works now stands, joins DANIEL SMITH, thence the dividing line as reference to the Will of SHADRACK TURNER. No wit. Signed: JOHN REDD. Proved: 26 Mar. 1798.

Pages 69-71. 10 May 1796. CHARLES DICKERSON of South Carolina, formerly of Henry County, Virginia to GEORGE HAIRSTON for the consideration of Fifty pounds sells by estimate of the Patent 351 acres on the branches of Leatherwood Creek, joins the lands of JAMES BLEVINS and CHRISTOPHER BOLING. Wit: JACOB COOLLEY, H. SALMON, JR., EDW. DELOZEAR, ROBERT DICKERSON. Signed: CHARLES DICKERSON. Proved: 26 Mar. 1798. ....At a Court 1 Mar. 1796 this indenture proved and ordered to be certified and afterwards at a Court 26 March 1798 recorded.

Pages 71-72. 19 Jan. 1798. EDWARD COCKRAM and MARY COCKRAM his wife of Franklin County to JOHN GROGAN of Henry County for the sum of One hundred pounds sells land that is part of the same tract that CHARLES COX now lives on, contains 135 acres. Wit: ISHEM EDWARDS, LETTICE (X) GROGEN, HENRY PEDEGO. Signed: EDWARD (X) COCKRAM, MARY (X) COCKRAM. Proved: 26 Mar. 1798.

Pages 73-74. 23 Mar. 1798. Deed of Gift. KINNEY MCKINSEY of the county of Henry for love and affection to his beloved wife PHEBY MCKINSEY gives all of his estate both real and personal consisting of lands, negros, to wit: Mary and Alse, stock of cattle, horses, hogs, household furniture during her natural life. If said wife shall bear a child it is to possess all the estate that may remain after PHEBY MCKINSEY'S decease. My daughter MARY BAUGHAN is to be remembered out of the estate in the amount of One shilling. Also the love and good will I bare to JANE HENSLEY, daughter of my present wife I give her a negro girl Betty when she arrives at lawful age. Should PHEBY MCKINSEY have no child she is to dispose of my estate as she thinks proper. KINNEY MCKINSEY appoints JOHN WALLER, THADDEUS SALMON, JOHN SALMON,

SENR. to act in a manner as they think proper. Wit: LEWIS HENSLEY, WILLIAM WALLER, JOHN SALMON. Signed: KINNEY MCKINSEY. Proved: 26 Mar. 1798.

Pages 74-76. 29 Sept. 1797. PATRICK HENRY and DORETHEA HENRY his wife of Charlotte County to JOSEPH HOPSON of Halifax County. Whereas, JOHN FONTAINE, deceased in his lifetime purchased of the said PATRICK HENRY 2,000 acres of land on Leatherwood Creek and Smith River and did pay him, but departed this life without a conveyance for the said land. JOHN FONTAINE did enter into a contract to sell to THOMAS JETT 432 acres on Leatherwood Creek, part of the 2,000 acres, whereon the said THOMAS JETT now resides and now the said THOMAS JETT has sold the land to JOSEPH HOPSON. PATRICK HENRY is fulfulling the true intent of the contract made by JOHN FONTAINE gives deed to JOSEPH HOPSON for the same. Wit: P. H. FONTAINE, NATH. W. DANDRIDGE, JR., A. B. DANDRIDGE, OBEDIENCE RYAN, PHIL. RYAN. Signed: PATRICK HENRY, DORATHEA HENRY. Proved: 26 Mar. 1798.

Pages 76-78. 23 Oct. 1797. GEORGE HAIRSTON of Henry County & THOMAS BEDFORD of Mecklenburg County to JOHN COX of Henry County for the sum of Seventy five pounds sells and convey a parcel of land on the waters of Smith River, contains by estimate 584 acres, it being the land whereon the said JOHN COX now lives and was granted GEORGE HAIRSTON, THOMAS BEDFORD and JOHN MARR by patent at Richmond 1 Feb. 1781 joins the land of HORD (formerly RANDOLPH & Company). Wit: HENRY LYNE, SAMUEL H. JENNINGS, TUNSTALL COX. Signed: GEORGE HAIRSTON, THOMAS BEDFORD. Proved: 26 Mar. 1798.

Pages 78-79. 6 Mar. 1798. JOHN HORD and RUTH HORD, his wife, of the county of Henry to GEORGE HAIRSTON of the same for the consideration of Two hundred forty pounds sells a tract of land on the waters of Horsepasture Creek containing 400 acres more or less joins GREGORY DURHAM, JESSE WITT and JOSEPH MORRIS. No wit. Signed: JOHN HORD, RUTH HORD. Proved: 26 Mar. 1798.

Page 80. 26 Mar. 1798. JOHN HORD and RUTH HORD, his wife of the county of Henry to ALEXANDER HUNTER of the same for the sum of Five hundred pounds sell a tract of land on Smith River contains 450 acres more or less, it being the place where JOHN HORD now lives. This is the land his father MORDECAI HORD left JOHN HORD and also land that he purchased of his brother WILLIAM HORD. No wit. Signed: JOHN HORD. Proved: 26 Mar. 1798.

Page 81. 26 Mar. 1798. ALEXANDER HUNTER of the Parish of Patrick and County of Henry, Planter, for the love and affection that he bears unto his daughter RUTH HORD the land on Smith River 450 acres whereon JOHN HORD now lives, it being land that MORD. HORD left his son JOHN HORD and also land he bought of his brother WILLIAM HORD. This is including all improvements. No wit. Signed: ALEXANDER HUNTER. Proved: 26 Mar. 1798.

Pages 82-83. 19 Jan. 1798. JAMES MEREDITH of Henry County to JOHN GRIGGS of the same for Twelve pounds sells 60 acres on Beaver Creek, joins THOMAS WILKINS, ABNER STULS, MC GROODER. Wit: WILLIAM BROWN, SENR., WILLIAM BROWN, JR. Signed: JAMES (X) MEREDITH. Proved: 30 Apr. 1798.

Pages 83-84. 28 Nov. 1797. JOSEPH LYSEL and ANN LYSEL his wife of the county of Brunswick to HENRY MORRIS of the same county for the sum of Five hundred pounds purchases a parcel of land on the branches of Leatherwood Creek and Roberts Creek contains 100 acres joins land of JOSEPH MORTON. Wit: THOMAS DANCE, DRURY QUARLES, JOHN LYELL. Signed: JOSEPH LYSEL, ANN LYSEL. Proved: 30 Apr. 1798.

Page 85. 9 Apr. 1798. JOHN WATSON of Pittsylvania County to ROBERT PEDIGO of Henry County for the sum of Twenty four pounds sells 100 acres on the branches of Leatherwood Creek, beginning at SAMUEL WATSON'S line and LOMAX & Company. Wit: JOSEPH PEDIGO, NATHAN NORRIS, ZEBULAN NORRIS. Signed: JOHN (X) WATSON. Proved: 23 Apr. 1798.

Pages 86-87. 13 Apr. 1798. WILLIAM PACE and SUSANNA PACE his wife of Henry County to DANIEL REAMY of the same for the consideration of One hundred pounds sells land on Smith River on the south side joins RANDOLPH, by survey 162 acres and another tract of 152 acres joins NEWSOM PACE and SANFORD REAMY. No wit. Signed: WILLIAM PACE, SUSANNA (X) PACE. Proved: 30 Apr. 1792.

Page 88. 29 Oct. 1793. WILLIAM HOLT of Henry County

to JOSEPH ANTHONY of the same. JOSEPH ANTHONY is paying for 50 acres of a Treasury Warrant and is to pay one-half of the expense of laying off and surveying the said tract, and WILLIAM HOLT makes lawful title to 50 acres that joins the said JOSEPH ANTHONY. Wit: HENRY CLARK, HENRY MORRIS, SNR. Signed: WILLIAM (X) HOLT. Proved: 30 Apr. 1798.

Page 89. 6 Apr. 1798. KINNEY MCKINSEY of Henry County to WILLIAM HOLT of the same for the sum of One hundred thirteen pounds ten shillings sells 100 acres more or less beginning at a hickory near the Sholes by Reuben's fish trap up the River to JOHN WALLER'S line to the top of the ridge. Wit: JOSEPH ANTHONY, HENRY MORRIS, SR. Signed: KINNEY (X) MC-KINSEY. . . .PHEBE MCKINSEY, wife of KINNEY MCKINSEY, releases her right of dower.

Pages 90-91. 31 Aug. 1797. BENJAMIN BUNCH and MARY BUNCH his wife of Henry County to JAMES LARRIMORE of the same in consideration of a valuable sum conveys land that the said BUNCH purchased of WILLIAM KELLUM, it being 211 acres on the branches of Mayo River and joins FAR.... BUNCH. Wit: ALEXANDER MOORE, SPENCER CALLIM, GARROT WILLIAMS. Signed: BENJAMIN (X) BUNCH, MARY (X) BUNCH. Proved: 30 Apr. 1798.

Page 92. 9 Dec. 1797. ELIZABETH STONE wife of WILLIAM STONE, deceased of Henry County for the natural love and affection she bears unto her son THOMAS STONE and to her daughter SUSANAH STONE give, grant and convey all my claim and right and title that I may have to a negro girl Tiller. Wit: JOSEPH NUNN, EUSEBUIS STONE, DOSHE STONE. Signed: ELIZABETH (X) STONE. Proved: 30 Apr. 1798.

Pages 93-94. 30 Apr. 1798. JOHN WALLER of the county of Henry to JOSEPH STOVALL of the same for the consideration of Two hundred pounds sells and conveys a parcel of land on the waters of Sandy River, by estimate 200 acres, it being the land whereon JAMES MORTON formerly lived and conveyed to JOHN WALLER from WILLIAM LINDSAY, a description more fully appears there. No wit. Signed: JOHN WALLER. Proved: 30 Apr. 1798.

Pages 94-95. 2 Jan. 1798. JOHN STOKES of the county of Henry to WILLIAM STOKES of the same for the consideration of Fifty pounds, but more especially for the love and affection that JOHN STOKES bears. JOHN STOKES hereunto moving hath given, granted and conveyed to WILLIAM STOKES land on the waters of Beaver Creek joins Bitings Spring Branch and joins the land lately purchased by HENRY CLARK of Anthony Bitting, joins JACOB FARRIS, JOSEPH ANTHONY, CARR WALLER..being the land he had of Gen. MARTIN. Wit: SAMUEL DUVAL, IGNATIOUS SIMMS, JAMES VERELL. Signed: JOHN STOKES. Proved: 1 May 1798.

Pages 96-97. 2 Jan. 1798. JOHN STOKES of the county of Henry and ELIZABETH STOKES, his wife to POLLY STOKES for the sum of Fifty pounds, but more especially for love and affection give all the land I now possess exclusive of the part deeded my son WILLIAM STOKES, on Beaver Creek joins GEORGE HAIRSTON, SHADRACK DENT, HENRY CLARK that he purchased of ANTHONY BITTING. To have and hold, nevertheless reserving unto JOHN and ELIZABETH STOKES during their lives the old tract whereon the said JOHN STOKES now resides. Wit: SAMUEL DUVAL, IGNATIOUS SIMMS, JAMES VERELL. Signed: JOHN STOKES. Proved: 1 May 1798.

Pages 97-98. 20 Jan. 1798. JOHN MANNING and SUCKEY MANNING his wife and RICHARD MITCHELL and ELIZABETH MITCHELL his wife of Franklin County to GEORGE HAIRSTON of Henry County for the sum of Ninety pounds sells 277 acres on Beaver Creek, on the Bold Branch, joins ROBERT STOCKTON, THOMAS COOPER and Simms Creek. No wit. Signed: JOHN MANNING, RICHARD MITCHELL. Proved: 29 Jan. 1798.

Pages 99-100. 24 May 1798. ROBERT PEDIGO, SENR., and ROBERT PEDIGO, JR., attorney for JOHN DAVIS and ELIZABETH DAVIS, his wife of Henry County to CHARLES JONES for the sum of Seventy pounds sells a parcel of land on the waters of Leatherwood Creek, 315 acres bound by DANIEL MCBRIDE'S new line, GRIFFIN'S corner & LOMAX & Company. Wit: JOHN KING, THOMAS KING, WILLIAM DESHAZO. Signed: ROBERT PEDIGO, SR., ROBERT (X) PEDIGO, JR. Proved: 28 May 1798.

Pages 100-101. 28 May 1798. ALEXANDER HUNTER of Henry County to RUTH HORD wife of JOHN HORD, for natural love and affection to his daughter who is moving give a parcel of land lying on Smith River being 450 acres, being the tract whereon JOHN HORD now lives and the land which was left him by his father MORDECIA HORD and likewise all that tract which JOHN HORD purchased of his brother WILLIAM HORD. To RUTH HORD for her lifetime then to her heirs. No wit. Signed: ALEXANDER HUNTER. Proved: 28 May 1798. (This is the same deed as DB 6 page 81.)

Pages 101-102. 28 May 1798. JOHN SALMON and ELIZABETH SALMON his wife to THOMAS BOULDIN, SENR. all of Henry County for the sum of Fifty pounds paid by GREEN BOULDIN a tract of 100 acres more or less joins ARCHIBALD ROBINSON and JOHN SIMMONS. Wit: GREEN BOULDIN. Signed: JOHN SALMON, ELIZABETH (X) SALMON. Proved: 28 May 1798.

Pages 103-104. 20 April 1798. JOSEPH TOWNLEN of the county of Franklin to SHADRACK DENT of Henry County for the sum of One hundred pounds sells a tract of land in Henry County on the branches of Daniels Creek by estimate 104 acres. No wit. Signed: JOSEPH (X) TOWLING. Proved: 28 May 1798. . . .PURLLA TOWNLEN releases her right of dower.

Pages 104-105. 2 Dec. 1797. Deed of Gift. MARY REAMY for the love and affection she bears unto PAMELA JONES gives unto her a negro boy named Jack. Wit: CHARLES T. PHILPOTT, THOMAS JONES. Signed: MARY REAMY. Proved: 28 May 1798.

Pages 105-106. 13 Apr. 1798. JOHN P. PYRTLE of Henry County to BARTLETT WADE for One hundred pounds sells by estimate 250 acres on the waters of Reedy Creek joins JUNOR MEREDITH, near the old Meeting House. Signed: JOHN P. PYRTLE. Proved: 28 May 1798. . . .MARY PYRTLE, wife of JOHN P. PYRTLE, releases her right of dower to the above transaction.

Pages 107-108. 7 Nov. 1797. JOSEPH LYELL and ANN LYELL his wife of Brunswick County to RICHARD LYELL and JONATHAN LYELL of the same county for the sum of Four hundred pounds sells and conveys a tract of land containing 1,000 acres on the branches of Leatherwood Creek and Roberts Creek joins the lines of JOSEPH MORTON (now GEORGE HAIRSTON). No wit. Signed: JOSEPH LYELL, ANN LYELL. Proved: 25 June 1798.

Pages 109-110. 21 June 1798. JOSEPH PEDEGOY of Henry County to ROBERT PEDEGOY of the same for the sum of Forty pounds sells and conveys a tract of land contains 300 acres more or less, it being the same tract of land JOSEPH PEDEGOY had of the above ROBERT PEDEGOY on the waters of Beaver Creek. No wit. Signed: JOSEPH PEDEGOY. Proved: 25 June 1798.

Pages 110-111. 30 Apr. 1798. THOMAS STEWART and USELAH STEWART his wife, of the county of Henry to WILLIAM DUNN of the same for the sum of Fifty pounds sells land on Leatherwood Creek joins ROBERTSON, HENRY, HAMMONS, contains 84 acres. Wit: JOHN PACE, THOMAS PACE, WILLIAM ROBINSON. Signed: THOMAS STEWART, USELAH (X) STEWART. Proved: 25 June 1798.

Page 111. 24 June 1798. Receipt. Received of ROBERT PEDIGOE in behalf of JOSEPH PEDEGOE full satisfaction for a wagon and geers and one horse that was due to me from JOSEPH PEDEGOE in consideration of a wagon and geers and 1 horse which I paid JOSEPH PEDEGOE for land which I have since given up to JOSEPH PEDEGOE. Wit: WILLIAM HEARD. Signed: JOHN KING. Proved: 25 June 1798.

Pages 112-113. 25 June 1798. GEORGE HAIRSTON and ELIZABETH HAIRSTON his wife of the county of Henry to THOMAS BOULDIN of the same for the sum of One hundred pounds sells 200 acres more or less on Smith River joins DANIEL REAMY and SANFORD REAMY. No wit. Signed: NEWSOM PACE. Proved: 25 June 1798.

Pages 114-115. 25 June 1798. WILLIAM PACE of Henry County to LANGSTON PACE of the same for the sum of One hundred pounds sells 100 acres more or less being part of the tract I now live on, joins COL. HAIRSTON, DANIEL REAMY and SANFORD REAMY. No wit. Signed: W. PACE. Proved: 25 June 1798.

Pages 115-117. 14 July 1798. JOHN TRAVIS of Henry County to WILLIAM HEATH, SAMUEL K. JENNINGS, TUNSTALL COX, CARR WALLER and JAMES OFFICER, Trustees in trust for the uses and purposes hereinafter mentioned: For the sum of Five shillings conveys a lot in Henry County joining HENRY DILLEN, contain one acre, for the Trustees shall erect and build a place of worship for the use of members of The Methodist Episcopal Church in the USA and shall at all time forever hereafter permit preachers to expounds Gods Holy Word. At one Trustee's death, another is to be appointed. Wit: J. W. WATSON, THOMAS H. WATSON, ROBERT COX. Signed: JOHN (X) TRAVIS. Proved: 30 July 1798.

Pages 117-118. 21 July 1798. WILLIAM SMITH and CAROLINE SMITH, his wife of Henry County to WILLIAM ROBERTSON for the sum of Thirty four pounds sells 75 acres on Fall Creek joins SHERWOOD MAYSE. Wit: THOMAS JAMESON, LIGIN MAYSE, DAVID MAYSE. Signed: WILLIAM (X) SMITH. Proved: 30 July 1798.

Pages 119-120. No date. Marriage Contract. A Marriage is intended between HEZEKIAH SALMON and RACHEL COOPER both of Henry County. The use and right of RACHEL COOPER'S property consisting of one gray mare and her colt, four head of neat cattle, 1 bull, 14 head of hogs, 1 feather bed and furniture, 1 dutch oven, 1 pot, frying pan, 1 chest, 1 table, 2 large jugs, 1 bedstead, 20 geese, bee stand and other household and kitchen furniture now in her possession shall be regulated in form following, viz: They are in case to be liable for the payment of any debt whatsoever contracted by HEZEKIAH SALMON but to be used by the parties during their couriture and if they live together in matrimony till the decease of either of parties then the surviour then to have the use during their natural lifetime. The property shall vest in the RACHEL COOPER and her heirs as if they had not been united. If RACHEL COOPER should die first, she has the right to regulate in her last will and testament as to disposition. COL. JOHN DILLARD and CAPT. WILLIAM SHELTON are trustees. Should RACHEL COOPER die first and HEZEKIAH SALMON waste or destroy any part of the property it is to be put in the hands of RACHEL COOPER'S heirs. Should HEZEKIAH SALMON die first, RACHEL COOPER shall inherit all of his estate. Wit: SAMUEL K. JENNINGS, WILLIAM C. REA, SIR JAMES BOULDIN. Signed: HEZEKIAH SALMON, RACHEL (X) COOPER. Proved: 30 July 1798.

Pages 120-121. 30 Apr. 1798. THOMAS PHILLIPS of Pittsylvania County to WILLIAM SIMPSON of Henry County for the sum of Thirty pounds does sell and convey a parcel of land contains 100 acres more or less on the south fork of Leatherwood Creek, joins HAILEY'S Mill pond, COL. GEORGE HAIRSTON, old Ridge Road, near the old plantation formerly of DANIEL MCBRIDE. No wit. Signed: THOMAS (X) PHILLIPS. Proved: 30 July 1798.

Pages 122-123. 27 Aug. 1798. GEORGE HAIRSTON and ELIZABETH HAIRSTON his wife of Henry County to JOHN WALLER of the same for the sum of Three hundred pounds sells land on the waters of Horsepasture Creek 400 acres more or less joins GREGORY DURHAM, JESSE WITT, JOSEPH MORRIS, PETER LEAK. No wit. Signed: GEORGE HAIRSTON, ELIZABETH HAIRSTON. Proved: 27 Aug. 1798.

Pages 123-125. 26 Sept. 1798. WILLIAM HUNTER, executor of JOHN GOODE, deceased, of Franklin County to JUNOR MEREDITH of Henry County for the sum of One hundred twenty pounds sells 160 acres on Little Ready Creek joins land of WILLIAM HEARD. No wit. Signed: WILLIAM HUNTER. Proved: 24 Sept. 1798.

Pages 125-126. 28 Apr. 1798. Bill of Sale. SUSANNA MARR sells for the sum of Sixty pounds two shillings to WILLIAM OAKES of Pittsylvania County a negro woman named Dinah and a girl child Mary. Wit: M. HARDIN, JONAS MEADERS HOLLAND. Signed: SUSANNA MARR. Proved: 27 Oct. 1798. . . .Note: If the said negros should die between this day and 25 December next that shall be my loss and I will replace them. Signed: SUSANNA MARR.

Pages 126-127. No date. Power of Attorney. JOHN BEEK and NATHANIEL SCALES executors of JOSEPH SCALES, late of Henry County, deceased do appoint THOMAS JACKSON of Hawkins County, Tennessee lawful attorney to obtain for the heirs of JOSEPH SCALES a distribution or share of all the land taken up in co-partners with NICHOLES PERKINS, CONSTANT PERKINS, JOHN MARR and others, the land that is in Tennessee. Wit: THOMAS HARDMAN, W. M. MARR, O. BURNETT. Signed: JOHN BEEK, NATHANIEL SCALES. Proved: 30 Oct. 1798.

Pages 127-128. 25 Apr. 1798. JAMES MCCRAW of Antrim Parish, County of Halifax to JOHN STONE of Patrick County, for the consideration of One hundred twenty pounds sells land in Henry County on both sides of Fall Creek a branch of Horsepasture Creek by survey 258 acres, being land granted MCCRAW at Richmond 8 Oct. 1783. Wit: JESSE OWEN, JOHN C. MC CRAW, JOHN CURSEY, NATHL. BASSETT, JOHN (X) PHILLIPS, JOHN SPENCER, WILLIAM SPENCER, WILLIAM (X) SOLOMON, TUNSTALL COX, HENRY KOGER. Signed: JAMES MCCRAW. Proved: 24 Sept. 1798.

Pages 129-130. 26 Nov. 1798. GEORGE HAIRSTON of Henry County to WILLIAM ROBERTS of the same for the consideration of Forty five pounds sells and conveys a parcel of land containing 80 acres more or less on the waters of Leatherwood Creek joins HAILEY old Mill. No wit. Signed: GEORGE HAIRSTON. Proved: 26 Nov. 1798.

Pages 130-131. 26 Nov. 1798. JOHN GOING of Henry County to JOHN STONE of the same, for the sum of Sixty pounds sells 100 acres on the Rock Run Creek joins HENRY SUMPTER, now GEORGE HAIRSTON, DAVIS' Branch, JAMES BAKER and ISHAM CRADDOCK. No wit.

Signed: JOHN GOING. Proved: 26 Nov. 1798.

Pages 131-132. 26 Nov. 1798. WILLIAM RICE of Henry County to JAMES OAKES of the same for the sum of Three hundred pounds sells a tract of land on Smith River on the north side contains 226 acres. No wit. Signed: WILLIAM RICE. Proved: 26 Nov. 1798. . . . .ANN RICE, wife of WILLIAM RICE, releases her right of dower.

Pages 133-134. 24 Oct. 1797. WILLIAM MILLS and ELIZABETH MILLS his wife of Henry County to GEORGE HAIRSTON of the same for the sum of One hundred pounds sells land on the waters of Matrimony Creek by estimate to be 60 acres more or less. Wit: THOMAS GRAVES, ROBERT ANDERSON, BENJAMIN LANIER. Signed: WILLIAM MILLS, ELIZABETH MILLS. Proved: 27 Nov. 1797.

Pages 134-135. 26 Nov. 1798. Bond of DAVID LANIER with GEORGE HAIRSTON, BENJAMIN HARRISON, WILLIAM MOORE, BENJAMIN LANIER and THOMAS JETT as his securities is appointed to be Sheriff and to collect Taxes for the county of Henry by a Commission from the Governor dated 24 Aug. 1797. Proved: 26 Nov. 1798.

Pages 135-137. 13 Dec. 1797. SAMUEL WOODSON of Henry County to WILLIAM MILLS of the same for the sum of One hundred pounds sells land on the north fork of Matrimony Creek, crosses Marrowbone Creek, contains 440 acres. Wit: JOS. MARTIN, JOHN REDD, JESSE CORN. Signed: SAMUEL WOODSON. Proved: 29 June 1978.

Pages 137-138. No date. DANIEL WILSON, THOMAS CHOWNING and ISHAM LANSFORD to SUSANNAH MARR, Administratrix of JOHN MARR, deceased. SUSANNAH MARR did on the 19 May 1797 convey by a Bill of Sale. DANIEL WILSON, THOMAS CHOWNING and ISHAM LANSFORD and other heirs the following: negros: Harry, Aggy, Jerey, Nelson, Hannah, Squire, Eady, Elly, Mourning, Clementa, Honor, Aaron, Jinney, Sharpes, Allet, Pheen; 7 horses, furniture, one negro man Ned and a woman Lucy a girl Franky. The above mentioned men were security in a bond to obtain writ of supercedeas at Court in New London on a judgement obtained against SUSANNAH MARR by JOHN W. REA. The judgement has been satisfied and the above property is now released. Wit: M. HARDEN, WILLIAM MITCHELL, JOHN PACE. Signed: DANIEL WILSON, THOMAS CHOWNING, ISHAM LANSFORD.

Proved: 26 Nov. 1798.

Pages 138-140. 17 Apr. 1798. Deed of Trust. JOSEPH FIFER to JOHN SMITH. Said FIFER indebted Thirty pounds secures with a tract of land on both sides of Rock Run of the Smith River by estimate 220 acres more or less where the said JOSEPH FIFER lives, joins JOHN BARKSDALE, NEWSOM PACE, THOMAS NUNN, WILLIAM DRAPER and the land formerly of JOHN ROWLAND. After the 25 Dec. next shall be sold to satisfy debt. Wit: JOHN COX, NANCEY WILLIAMSON, JOSEPH COX, MARY JENNINGS, ROBERT COX. Signed: JOSEPH (X) FIFER. Proved: 29 Nov. 1798. . . .Insert: 1 Oct. 1799 - by one Black Mare 60 Dollars Ł18.0.0.

Pages 140-142. 31 Dec. 1798. GEORGE HAIRSTON of Henry County to JOSEPH HOBSON of the same for the sum of Two hundred twelve pounds sells land on Leatherwood Creek joins lines of THOMAS JETT (now HOPSON), JAMES JOHNSON (now JETT) 150 acres which land was sold by JOHN FONTAINE deceased to PHILIP RYAN by RYAN to WILLIAM LINDSAY and a deed of conveyance from PATRICK HENRY to WILLIAM LINDSAY. No wit. Signed: GEORGE HAIRSTON. Proved: 31 Dec. 1798.

Pages 142-143. 22 Oct. 1798. Commonwealth of Virginia to THOMAS HENDERSON, PETER HARRIS and CUTHBURTH SHELTON or any two of them Justices of the Peace of Grainger County, Tennessee, whereas JAMES TAYLOR conveyed unto DAVID MULLINS of Henry County, Virginia 370 acres of land and ANN TAYLOR, wife of JAMES TAYLOR can not travel to Henry County, Virginia Court house, please examine ANN TAYLOR for dower release. Signed: JOHN COX. Proved: 15 Nov. 1798 & 31 Dec. 1798. . . .State of Tennessee, Grainger County: ANN TAYLOR, wife of JAMES TAYLOR, does hereby release her right of dower to the above mentioned 370 acres of land. Dated 15 Nov. 1798. Signed: PETER HARRIS, CUTHBERT SHELTON.

Pages 144-145. 21 June 1798. Dower release. MARY DAINES, wife of JACOB DAINES gives her right of dower release in a transaction between JACOB DAINES and JOHN ROWLAND. Recorded: 31 Dec. 1798.

Page 145. No date. Power of Attorney. WILLIAM GARDNER of Patrick County hereunto moving appoints HENRY LYNE of Henry County to recover from ROBERT PEDEGO money that would be judged reasonable in consideration of a tract of land he sold me then lying in Henry County now Patrick County on the waters of

Smith River which land has since been claimed by CHARLES TALBOT who had prior right. Empower my attorney to recover from ROBERT PEDIGOE as he thinks proper. Signed: THOMAS STARLING, JOHN COX. Signed: WILLIAM GARDNER. Proved: 28 Jan. 1799.

Pages 146-147. 3 Jan. 1799. SARAH BETH HEATH (SALLY BET HEATH) wife of WILLIAM HEATH hereby gives and releases her right of dower to land that WILLIAM HEATH sold unto JOHN FARRIS, 311 acres. Proved: 28 Jan. 1799.

Pages 147-148. 25 Jan. 1799. CHARLES COX, SENR. of the county of Henry to CHARLES COX, JR. of the same for the sum of Fifty pounds sells a parcel of land approximately 80 acres on Turkey Pen Branch, being the tract and plantation whereon the said CHARLES COX, SENR. now resides. Wit: WILLIAM NORMAN, THOMAS COX, HENRY GROGAN. Signed: CHARLES COX, ELLENDER (X) COX. Proved: 28 Jan. 1799.

Pages 148-149. 24 Jan. 1799. WILLIAM HEATH and SALLY B. HEATH, his wife of the county of Henry to JOHN French for the sum of One thousand dollars sells 100 acres of land on the waters of Horsepasture Creek joins lines of HENRY DILLEN, deceased, DUTTON LAND, EAST'S old patent, the Old Road and the use of the spring used by me. Wit: JOHN COX, JOHN COX, JR., TUNSTALL COX. Signed: WILLIAM HEATH, SALLY B. HEATH. Proved: 28 Jan. 1799.

Page 150. 1 Jan. 1799. CHARLES COX, SENR. to THOMAS COX of the county of Henry for the sum of Fifty pounds sells part of the same tract CHARLES COX now lives on, by estimate to be 80 acres. Wit: WILLIAM NORMAN, CHARLES COX, HENRY GROGEN. Signed: CHARLES COX, SENR., ELLENDER (X) COX. Proved: 28 Jan. 1799.

Page 151. 10 Dec. 1798. BRICE GARNER of the county of Washington state of Tennessee to JAMES HOWARD of Henry County, Virginia in consideration of Two hundred Spanish milled dollars on Little Beaver Creek. Wit: WILL. PORTER, WILLIAM STOKES, SAMUEL (X) WATSON, ANN STOCKTON. Signed: BRICE GARNER. Proved: 28 Jan. 1799.

Pages 152-153. 25 Feb. 1796. WILLIAM BAILES, JR., ELIJAH BAILES, JESSE BAILES, BAILEY BAILES, NANCY BAILES, ANDREW MOOR and PEGGY his wife, BENNETT HARRIS and FRANKY his wife, *BARNA WILL and SARAH his wife to GEORGE HAIRSTON all of Henry County for the sum of Seventy pounds sell all that plantation on both sides of Turkey Cock Creek by estimate 375 acres joins lines of WILLIAM BAILES, SENR. and SMITH. *Most likely to be BARNA WELLS. Wit: WILLIAM LARRANCE, JOHN BURCH, HENRY LARRANCE, JACOB LINDSAY, CONSTT. HARDEMAN, CONSTT. PERKINS. Signed: WILLIAM BAYLES, ELIJAH BAYLES, NANCY BAYLES, ANDREW MOORE, BAILEY BAYLES. Proved: 26 Sept. 1796.

Pages 154-156. 25 Mar. 1799. JOSEPH MARTIN of Henry County to PATRICK H. FONTAINE of the same...said MARTIN and FONTAINE entered into a contract to purchase military lands in Tennessee and JOSEPH MARTIN gave Power of Attorney to PATRICK H. FONTAINE who in turn purchased land of STOCKLEY DONESON. JOSEPH MARTIN cancelled the contract. FONTAINE purchased three tracts (1) 640 acres in Sumner County, Tennessee on the waters of Stone's Creek or River surveyed 2 December 1792, patented 20 July 1796. (2) 640 acres Sumner Co., Tenn. on Stone River and Pond Lick Creek (3) 640 acres Sumner Co., Tenn., on Stone River 3 miles above Buffalo Road. JOSEPH MARTIN conveys all or any of his right or title to PATRICK HENRY FONTAINE. Signed: JOSEPH MARTIN. Proved: 25 Mar. 1799. . . .Memorandum: JOSEPH MARTIN or his heirs has no claim or right to the above in any manner.

Pages 156-157. No date. WILLIAM MITCHELL of the county of Henry to WILLIAM BERKELEY Treasurer for the Commonwealth of Virginia, this mortgage in the amount of $2,500.00, land on both sides of Smith River 320 acres, at mouth of Turkey Cock Creek (excludes the tract conveyed by THOMAS CHOWNING to WILLIAM MITCHELL). The condition is that WILLIAM MITCHELL or his heirs shall and will pay the balance of taxes due in the county of Washington for the years 1782, 1783, 1784 agreeable to an Act of the Assembly passes 24 Jan. 1799 intitled an Act concerning EDWARD TATUM, DANIEL CARLIN and WILLIAM MITCHELL. No wit. Signed: WILLIAM MITCHELL. Proved: 25 Mar. 1799.

Pages 157-158. Jan. Court 1799. WILLIAM FRENCH desires leave to build a water grist mill on both sides of Horsepasture Creek, the Sheriff to summon 12 fit persons Tuesday, 12 February to judge if this is a proper place...12 Feb. 1799, Jury judges damages will be nothing: P. GARLAND, BENJAMIN HARRISON, DAVID MULLINS, ARCHIBALD HATCHER, JAMES LARRIMORE, WILLIAM SHELTON, PETER LEAKE, JESSE WITT, DAVID MAYSE, EDWARD DANIEL, JOHN SMITH, ARCHIBALD FARRIS.

Proved: 25 Mar. 1799.

Page 159.   25 Mar. 1799.   WILLIAM GARDNER of the county of Patrick assigns all right and title to 200 acres of land on Flat Creek of Smith River which was conveyed by deed duly recorded in Henry County from THOMAS FLOWERS which lands CHARLES MILLS, TALBOT and others by law of this State ejected WILLIAM GARDNER from holding title. CHARLES MILLS received in his suit costs and damages against WILLIAM GARDNER, and I hereby assign ROBERT PEDIGO free from mollestation and claim of my heirs. Wit: HENRY LYNE, JOHN KING, JOHN SALMON. Signed: WILLIAM GARDNER. Proved: 25 March 1799.

Pages 160-161.   5 Nov. 1794.   ACHILLES BALLENGER of the county of Amherst to WILLIAM BAYLES, JR., ELIJAH BAYLES, JESSE BAYLES, BAILEY BAYLES, SALLEY BAYLES, NANCY BAYLES, PEGGY MOORE and FRANKY HARRIS of Henry County for the sum of One hundred twenty pounds land and plantation on the waters of Turkey Cock Creek being 275 acres by estimate. Wit: BARNA WELLS, WILLIAM MITCHELL, WILLIAM BAYLES, SENR., JOHN (X) MITCHELL. Signed: ACHILLES BALLENGER. Proved: 25 May 1795 & 29 Apr. 1799.

Page 162.   25 Mar. 1799.   ALEXANDER MOORE has undertaken to rebuild the upper bridge over Marrowbone Creek and to keep it in good repair for the period of 7 years. Wit: JESSE ATKISSON, THOMAS BOULDING. Signed: ALEXANDER MOORE, JOHN DILLARD. Proved: 29 Apr. 1799.

Page 163.   29 Apr. 1799.   KINNEY MCKINSEY and PHEREBY MCKINSEY of Henry County to DANIEL SMITH of the same for the sum of One hundred pounds sells and conveys a parcel of land on the Smith River, begins at a branch that runs thru MCKINSEY'S apple orchard and joins WILLIAM HOLT, 100 acres more or less. No wit. Signed: KINNEY (X) MCKINSEY, PHEBEY (X) MCKINSEY. Proved: 29 Apr. 1799.

Pages 164-165.   21 May 1799.   WILLIAM BROWN of the county of Henry to SAMUEL MARSHALL of Mecklenburg County for the sum of One hundred pounds sell land on the waters of Leatherwood Creek, whereon the said WILLIAM BROWN now lives, 260 acres in all. Wit: ELISHA ARNOLD. Signed: WILLIAM BROWN. . . . PEGGY BROWN, wife of WILLIAM BROWN, release her right to dower.

Pages 165-167. 26 Apr. 1799. SAMUEL JOHNSTON of the county of Warren, state of Georgia to JOSHUA PROCTOR of Henry County, Virginia for the sum of Thirty five pounds sell land patented to me on Grasy fork of Fishing fork of Leatherwood Creek dated 1781, except the part sold to MATHEW WELLS conveyed by me to JAMES HALEY at the request of MATHEW WELLS. Wit: WILLIAM LOVELL, MARY LOVELL. Signed: SAMUEL JOHNSTON. Proved: 27 Apr. 1799.

Warren County, Georgia. . . .WILLIAM LOVELL acting Justice of the Peace for Warren County, Georgia and due faith ought to be given his signature. Signed: T. PERSONS. . . .I certify T. PERSONS is Clerk of Warren County, Georgia and credit should be given to his signature. Signed: SAMUEL ALEXANDER. 27 Apr. 1799.

Page 167. 27 May 1799. WILLIAM HEWLETT of Henry County hereunto moving appoints his son JOHN WATKINS HEWLETT attorney to recover and dispose of a tract of land unjustly held by CLAPTON PERSON of Harrison County, Kentucky, tract of 300 acres. Signed: WILLIAM HEWLETT. Proved: 27 May 1799.

Pages 168-169. 26 May 1799. WILLIAM BROWN executor of JOHN WILLIAMS, deceased to GEORGE HAIRSTON all of Henry County, for the sum of Forty five pounds sells and conveys a parcel of land on the waters of Leatherwood Creek joins FRANCIS NORTHCUTT and WILLIAM BROWN, it being 100 acres. No wit. Signed: WILLIAM BROWN. Proved: 27 May 1799.

Pages 169-170. 25 Mar. 1799. THOMAS WILKINS of Henry County to WILLIAM TOOMBS of the same for the sum of One hundred pounds sells 89 acres that joins STULTS, BROWN, KING and GRIGGS. No wit. Signed: THOMAS WILKINS. Proved: 24 June 1799.

Pages 170-173. 19 Jan. 1799. CHRISTINE MAGRUDER of the county of Washington and state of Maryland to CHARLES CARROLL, THOMAS SPRIGGS, NATHANIEL ROCHESTER and IGNATIOUS TAYLOR for the sum of One thousand pounds sells land in the county of Henry and state of Virginia on the branches of Leatherwood and Beaver Creek joins lands of GRAVELY, COLLIER, COPLAND and BLIZARD MAGRUDER contains 2,984 acres. Wit: RICHARD POTTS, WILLIAM FITZHUGH, GEORGE SCOTT. Signed: CHRISTINE (X) MAGRUDER. Proved: 24 June 1799. . . . 19 Jan. 1799 Payment received. Signed: CHRISTINE MAGRUDER. . . .State of Maryland, County of Washington. 19 Jan. 1799. CHRISTINE MAGRUDER appeared in Court and agreed that this transaction is her act and deed.

Page 174. 13 June 1799. BLIZARD MAGRUDER to RICHARDSON HERNDON for the sum of Fifty four dollars sells 54 acres on the waters of the Mayo River joins ARCHABALD FARRIS. Wit: WILLIAM F. MILLS, ARCHIBALD HATCHER, ... KLEMAN. Signed: BLIZARD MAGRUDER. Proved: 24 June 1799.

Pages 175-176. 24 June 1799. WILLIAM DILLEN of Henry County to JOHN QUALLS of the same for the sum of Sixty dollars sells and conveys a parcel of land on the waters of Marrowbone Creek being 200 acres more or less begins at a line between DILLEN & QUALLS, on a path that leads from HARRISON'S field called Staples to GEORGE HAIRSTON'S to where BAILEY now lives. No wit. Signed: WILLIAM (X) DILLIAN. Proved: 24 June 1799.

Pages 176-177. 14 June 1799. JOHN SPENCER and RUTH SPENCER his wife of Henry County to JOHN SMITH for the sum of One hundred eighty nine pounds sell land on the south side of Horsepasture Creek being part of the land JAMES SPENCER, deceased estated contains by estimate 126 acres at the dividing line between JOHN and WILLIAM SPENCER. Wit: THOMAS TUGGLE, GEORGE WALLER, NATHAN SHELTON. Signed: JOHN SPENCER, RUTH SPENCER. Proved: 24 June 1799.

Pages 178-179. 25 May 1799. JOHN SPENCER of Henry County to JOHN STAPLES of the same for One hundred fifty dollars sells land on the waters of Horsepasture Creek and a part of the tract where the said JOHN SPENCER now lives and joins JOHN STAPLES contains 50 acres more or less begins on a branch above the JOHN SPENCER plantation...dividing line between SPENCER and JAMES SHELTON, deceased. Wit: GEORGE J. STAPLES, WILLIAM SPENCER, WILLIAM BOULDIN. Signed: JOHN SPENCER. Proved: 24 June 1799. . . .RUTH SPENCER wife of JOHN SPENCER, releases her right of dower.

Pages 179-180. 1 Apr. 1799. DAVID LANIER, JOHN WELLS and JUDITH WELLS his wife to HENRY MORRIS, SENR. of the county of Brunswick for the sum of Four hundred pounds sell a parcell of land on the waters of Leatherwood Creek contains 362 acres joins the lines of LOMAX & Company and the County Road. Wit: JOHN H. LANIER, DAVID LANIER, JR., DAVID LANIER. Signed: DAVID LANIER, JOHN WELLS. Proved: 24 June 1799.

Pages 181-182. 1 Apr. 1799. DAVID LANIER, JOHN WELLS and JUDITH WELLS his wife of Henry County and MATHEW WELLS and TABITHIA WELLS his wife of Pittsylvania County to HENRY MORRIS, SENR. of Brunswick County for the sum of Four hundred pounds sell and convey a tract of land, 738 acres on the waters of Leatherwood Creeks joins WELL'S old line, Scud Branch. Wit: JOHN H. LANIER, DAVID LANIER, JAMES LANIER. Signed: DAVID LANIER, JOHN WELLS, MATHEW WELLS. Proved: 24 June 1799 & 25 Feb. 1800. . .
Memo: It is to be understood that MATHEW WELLS and TABITHIA WELLS his wife made parties to the written indenture are responsible only for 132 acres being part of a tract MATHEW WELLS purchased of SAMUEL JOHNSTON. Signed: HENRY MORRIS, SENR.

Page 183. 30 July 1799. JARROTT PATTERSON of Rockingham County, North Carolina appoint JACOB MICHAUX of Patrick County, Virginia to collect of REUBEN LINDSAY and DANIEL LINDSAY executors of JAMES LINDSAY, deceased the proportinoable part of the legacy which my wife JUDITH PATTERSON is intitled as one of the legatees of JAMES LINDSAY, deceased. Wit: BIRD DEATHERIDGE, JOHN HARRIS. Signed: JARROTT PATTERSON. Proved: 28 Sept. 1799.

Page 184. No date. We, ROBERT JOYCE and ELIZABETH JOYCE, his wife, and daughter of JAMES LINDSAY, deceased of Rockingham County, North Carolina hereunto moving appoint JACOB MICHAUX of Patrick County, Virginia attorney to collect of REUBEN LINDSAY and DANIEL LINDSAY executors of JAMES LINDSAY, deceased the part which ELIZABETH LINDSAY alias JOYCE is intitled as a legatee of JACOB LINDSAY. Wit: JOHN HARRIS, BIRD DEATHERAGE. Signed: ROBERT JOYCE, ELIZAETH JOYCE. Proved: 28 Sept. 1799.

Pages 185-186. 27 May 1799. WILLIAM STOKES of Henry County to GEORGE HAIRSTON of the same for the sum of Fifty pounds sells land on the waters of Rugg Creek or Smith River 197 acres joins said HAIRSTON and Turkey Pen Branch. Wit: DAVID LANIER, ROBERT HAIRSTON, JOHN MINTER. Signed: WILLIAM STOKES. Proved: 26 Aug. 1799.

Pages 186-188. 16 Aug. 1799. WILLIAM BRETHEART of Campbell County to JOHN DOWDIE of Bedford County for the sum of One hundred pounds sells and conveys by estimate 450 acres in Henry County on the branches of Leatherwood Creek joins lines of JARROT BURCH, DELOZORS, LOMAX & Company, also part of another tract to make up the 450 acres joins SHORTS, HOOKER'S old line...being the land conveyed to WILLIAM BRETHEART by DAVID WATSON. Wit: JOHN COX, SHD. DENT, ZACKARIAH PHILPOTT. Signed: WILLIAM BRETHEART. Proved: 26 Aug. 1799.

Pages 188-189. 16 Sept. 1799. Campbell County, State of Virginia. ELIZABETH BRETHEART wife of WILLIAM BRETHEART, releases her right of dower to a deed to CHARLES THOMAS PHILPOTT by estimate 300 acres. Proved: 30 Sept. 1799.

Pages 189-190. 27 June 1799. JOHN GRAVES of Fayette County, Kentucky appoints JAMES PARBERY of Franklin County, Virginia his attorney to recover the sum of Forty pounds from the estate of WILLIAM GRAVES, my deceased father. Wit: JAMES STEVENS, THOMAS GRAVES. Signed: JOHN GRAVES. Proved: 30 Sept. 1799. . . .Fayette County, Kentucky. THOMAS GRAVES appeared before PETER MASON and A. MONTGOMERY 27 June 1799 and acknowledged the Power of Attorney in Henry County, Virginia.

Pages 191-192. 18 Oct. 1788. JARARD BURCH of the county of Greene and state of Georgia to JOHN WELLS of Henry County for the sum of Sixty pounds sells land on the waters of Leatherwood Creek, it being 362 acres joins LOMAX & Company. Wit: JAMES CUNINGHAM, FLEMING THOMASSON, THOMAS DICKERSON, JR. Signed: JARARD BURCH. Proved: 16 Apr. 1789 & 30 Sept. 1799. . . .Possession granted 18 Oct. 1788.

Page 193. 25 Nov. 1799. Bond of JOHN WELLS that appointed him Sherif by the Governor of Virginia the 21st of Oct. 1799. Signed: JOHN WELLS, GEORGE HAIRSTON, JOHN ROWLAND. Proved: 25 Nov. 1799.

Page 194. 28 Oct. 1799. WILLIAM BROWN of Henry County appoints JOSEPH ANTHONY to collect all debts due me as my lawfull attorney. Wit: TUNSTALL COX. Signed: WILLIAM BROWN. Proved: 28 Oct. 1799.

Pages 194-195. 25 Nov. 1799. JOHN WELLS is appointed to collect all taxes and taxes for the county of Henry. Proved: 25 Nov. 1799.

Pages 196-197. 17 Aug. 1799. WILLIAM DUNN of Henry County to JOHN HAMMONDS of the same for the sum of Fifty pounds sells and conveys land now occupied by said WILLIAM DUNN and formerly the property of THOMAS STEWART, contains 84 acres on Leatherwood Creek. Wit: PHILIP CONNOR, HENRY (X) SMITH, MILLEY (X) BIRD. Signed: WILLIAM (X) DUNN, MARY (X) DUNN. Proved: 25 Nov. 1799.

Pages 198-199. 26 Oct. 1799. THOMAS BOULDIN, SENR. of Henry County to GREEN BOULDIN of the same for the sum of Fifty pounds sells and conveys by estimate 134 acres of land on the waters of Grassey Creek. Wit: HENRY CLARK, SHD. DENT, JOHN WEAVER. Signed: THOMAS BOULDIN. Proved: 25 Nov. 1799. . . . MARTHA BOULDIN the wife of THOMAS BOULDIN, releases her right of dower.

Pages 199-200. 19 Nov. 1799. JOHN DEMPSEY of Henry County to GEORGE HAIRSTON of the same for the sum of Thirty five pounds sells land on Mill, one line the Ridge Path contains 50 acres. Wit: JOHN (X) BROWN, ROBERT HAIRSTON, GEORGE HAIRSTON. Signed: JOHN DEMPSEY. Proved: 25 Nov. 1799.

Pages 200-201. Aug. Court 1799. Inquest. JOSEPH HOBSON desires to build a water grist mill on Ralph's Branch of Leatherwood Creek, and a jury called to ascertain the safety of same: BRICE MARTIN, JR., JOHN ALEXANDER, DA. REAMEY, JOHN CREASEY, FRANCIS COX, JO. BURGESS, WILLIAM STOKES, BENJAMIN JONES, CHARLES PHILPOTT, JAMES HOWARD, SAMUEL ELLIOTT, WILLIAM DILLIAN. They state that the lands of THOMAS JETT would be damaged by such a Mill. Proved: 25 Nov. 1799.

Pages 202-203. Sept. Court 1799. PETER PERKINS desires to build a water grist mill on a cannal taken out of the Mayo River at his Iron Works, known by the name of Bouldin & Perkins Irons Works, whereof THOMAS BOULDIN and PETER PERKINS are proprietors. Jury to ascertain safety: WILLIAM SHELTON, THOMAS OAKLEY, LEGAN MAYS, EDWARD DANIEL, JESSE MURPHY, THOMAS JAMISON, ARCHIBALD FARRIS, AMBROSE WHITE, GARROT WILLIAMS, WILLIAM HILL, JOHN WEAVER, JESSE ATKISSON...do declare that no damage would be done. Proved: 25 Nov. 1799.

Pages 203-204. 30 Dec. 1799. DAVID LANIER of Henry County to GEORGE HAIRSTON of the same for the sum of One hundred ninety pounds sells land on the waters of Marrowbone Creek joins lines of WILLIAM DANDRIDGE, STOVALL and HICKS, 273 acres by estimate. No wit. Signed: DAVID LANIER. Proved: 30 Dec. 1799.

Pages 204-205. 21 Dec. 1799. I, MILLICENT FARGUSON, widow of ROBERT FARGUSON, deceased and me hereunto moving appoint TUNSTALL COX attorney to recover my dower and 200 acres more or less the land whereon JOHN LUMPKIN formerly lived in the County of King & Queen, it being land my deceased husband sold and conveyed to JOHN LUMPKIN by deed which I never released my right of dower. Wit: JOHN FRENCH, JOHN COX. Signed: MILLICENT FARGUSON. Proved: 30 Dec. 1799.

Pages 205-206. 18 Dec. 1799. JOHN BOOTH of the state of Georgia to GEORGE HAIRSTON of Henry County for the sum of Two hundred pounds sells a parcel of land in Henry County contains 854 acres on both sides of Sandy River joins ROBERTS lines. Wit: FREDERICK ECKHOLS, JOHN ROWLAND, JR., THOMAS C. BOULDIN. Signed: JOHN BOOTH. Proved: 30 Dec. 1799.

Pages 207-208. 1 Nov. 1799. JOHN NANCE and MARY NANCE his wife of Henry County to JOHN WILLS of Brunswick County for a sum of money convey a tract of land containing 240 acres in Henry County on a branch of Leatherwood Creek, joins the lines of GEORGE KING, a branch called Burnett's Spring Branch, NIXON, STOCKTON, HAILE and GARLAND. Wit: JOHN KING, JR., JOSEPH NIXON, WILLIAM DESHAZO, JOHN KING, CHARLES JONES. Signed: JOHN NANCE, MOLLY NANCE. Proved: 27 Jan. 1800.

Pages 208-209. 7 Sept. 1799. WILLIAM ROBISON (ROBERSON) of the county of Henry to JOHN HAMMONDS of the same for the sum of One hundred pounds sells 54 acres begins on Smith River, Wilson's line to Leatherwood Creek. Wit: WILLIAM COLLINS REA, HEZEKIAH (X) DUNN, WILLIAM (X) DUNN. Signed: WILLIAM ROBERSON, HESTER (X) ROBERSON. Proved: 25 Nov. 1799 & 27 Jan. 1800.

Page 210. 23 Apr. 1799. BLIZARD MAGRUDER of Henry County to OZBURN WILLIAMS of the same for the sum of Thirty dollars, by survey 30 acres more or less on the waters of the Mayo River joins COL. JOHN DILLARD, GARROTT WILLIAMS. Wit: RICHARDSON HERNDON, JOSEAH LEAK, GARROT WILLIAMS. Signed: BLIZARD MAGRUDER. Proved: 26 Aug. 1799.

Page 211. 15 Jan. 1800. MARY HICKEY of Henry County to ALEXANDER HUNTER of the same for the sum of Fifteen pounds sells 120 acres by survey on the waters of Buttron Town Creek. No wit. Signed: MARY

HICKKEY. Proved: 27 Jan. 1800.

Pages 212-213. 6 Jan. 1796. WILLIAM JOHNSON of Franklin County, Virginia to SAMUEL PHILPOTT of Patrick County, Virginia for Twenty pounds sells land in Henry and Patrick County on the north side of Smith River, 50 acres more or less. Wit: JOHN PHILPOTT, WILLIAM THOMPSON, RICHARD (X) MAYNOR. Signed: WILLIAM (X) JOHNSON. Proved: 29 Feb. 1796 & 27 Jan. 1800.

Pages 213-214. 8 June 1799. GEORGE REAVES and MARY REAVES, his wife, of Patrick County to JOHN PHILLIPS of Henry County for Fifty pounds sells part of a certain tract in Henry County on Hicks Mill Creek, being 30 acres. Wit: JOHN PHILPOTT, WILLIAM MILLER, WILLIAM DEMEY, JOEL DEMEY. Signed: GEORGE REEVES. Proved: 24 June 1799 & 27 Jan. 1800.

Pages 214-215. 3 Jan. 1800. ALEXANDER HUNTER of Henry County to ROBERT H. HUNTER of the same for the sum of Ninety pounds sells land on both sides of Smith River, 300 acres, begins on the south side of the River to my upper cross fence in the Horseshaw tract, STEPHEN STONE'S, cross the river to JOHN PELPHREY'S corner, PHILPOTT and Back Branch. Wit: JOHN HORD, RUTH HORD. Signed: ALEXANDER HUNTER. Proved: 27 Jan. 1800.

Pages 215-216. 27 Jan. 1800. JOHN PACE, attorney for JOHN BOLT to SAMUEL ELLIOTT for Thirty three pounds sells by estimate 100 acres more or less on a branch of Muster Branch on the West side joining DANIEL REAMEY. No wit. Signed: JOHN PACE, attorney for JOHN BOLT. Proved: 27 Jan. 1800.

Pages 216-217. 30 Dec. 1799. Trustees of Martinsville to JACOB DEAN (DAINES) Twenty pounds for a lot of land in the town of Martinsville, Eleven pounds agreeable to the plan of the Town, it being land THOMAS JAMESON purchased of the Commissioners appointed by an Act of Assembly for the purpose and we GEORGE WALLER, JOSEPH ANTHONY, JOHN REDD and GEORGE HAIRSTON warrant and defend the title. Wit: AARON MILLS, EDM. WALLER. Signed: Trustees for the Town of Martinsville: GEORGE WALLER, JOSEPH ANTHONY, JOHN REDD, GEORGE HAIRSTON. Proved: 24 Feb. 1800.

Pages 217-218. 25 Feb. 1800. Apprentice Bond. FREDERICK ECHOLS of Henry County, Tanner and Curryer, to JAMES INNES of Patrick County.

The said JAMES INNES has bound himself to FREDERICK ECHOLS for a term of three years from 1 Jan. 1800. He shall keep his masters secrets, his lawful commands gladly obey, shall not hurt his master or let it be done by others to his goods. Shall not purloin at cards, dice or any other unlawful game, shall not frequent Taverns or Tipling Houses nor contract matrimony. FREDERICK ECHOLS will teach JAMES INNES the art of tanning and currying business of leather. Will provide clothing, washing and lodging. Shall also provide one suit of Sunday clothes. Wit: JOHN SALMON, SENR., GEORGE WALLER, SENR. Signed: JAMES J. INNES, FREDERICK ECKHOLS. Proved: 25 Feb. 1800.

Pages 218-220. 11 Sept. 1798. An agreement between JOHN SPENCER and WILLIAM SPENCER, sons and legatees of JAMES SPENCER, deceased to JOHN DILLARD executor of the said JAMES SPENCER, deceased for and in behalf of GEORGE WASHINGTON SPENCER and JAMES SPENCER under age sons of JAMES SPENCER, deceased. That by the will of their deceased father the lands he was possessed willed to JOHN & WILLIAM SPENCER and willing that their other two brothers should share equally in the land, slaves, etc., also an equal division of the land obtained by their Mother MARGARET BASSETT for her two sons JAMES SPENCER and GEORGE WASHINGTON SPENCER and by NATHANIEL BASSETT. Given up to equally divide agreeable to the true intent and meaning of the agreement. Each party agrees to be lair off in 4 lots to be divided and lotted by SAMUEL JENNINGS, WILLIAM SHELTON, NATHANIEL BASSETT and WILLIAM HILL. To be done by the last of October next, and to draw lotts by choice. Wit: ROBERT ALLEN, REUBEN WADE, JOHN H. ROWLAND. Signed: JOHN SPENCER, WILLIAM SPENCER, JOHN DILLARD. Proved: 25 Feb. 1800.

Pages 220-221. 21 Sept. 1799. BENJAMIN MITCHELL of Henry County to WILLIAM CUNNINGHAM of the same for the sum of Twenty pounds sells 100 acres of land that joins CALLAY'S. Wit: JOSEPH JONES, SAMUEL (X) SHOMATE, FRANCIS COX. Signed: BENJAMIN MITCHELL. Proved: 31 Mar. 1800.

Pages 221-222. 25 Mar. 1800. JOHN MINTER of the county of Henry to THOMAS WILKINS of the same for the sum of Fifty pounds sells and conveys land on the waters of Leatherwood Creek, 138 acres. No wit. Signed: JOHN MINTER. Proved: 31 Mar. 1800.

Pages 222-223. 25 Mar. 1800. JOHN MINTER of Henry County to THOMAS STEWART of the same for the sum of Fifty pounds sells and conveys a parcel of land, 111 acres on the waters of Leatherwood Creek. No wit. Signed: JOHN MINTER. Proved: 31 Mar. 1800.

Pages 223-224. 31 Mar. 1800. JOHN WALLER of Henry County to GEORGE WALLER, JR. of the same for the sum of Sixty pounds sells 182 acres more or less joins line of Randolph & Company where it crosses a branch on the south side of Smith River, up the branch to Salmon's corner. Wit: JOHN SALMON, WILLIAM STOKES. Signed: JOHN WALLER. Proved: 31 Mar. 1800.

Pages 224-225. 31 Mar. 1800. PETER GARLAND of Henry County to THOMAS ALEXANDER of the same for the sum of One hundred fifty pounds sells one certain tract with all buildings and part of that massuage tenement and tract purchased of PETER HAIRSTON, contains 150 acres, joins GARLAND'S back line under the Mountain, GRAVES and JAMES REA. Lines agreeable to an agreement dated 26 Oct. 1797. No wit. Signed: PETER GARLAND. Proved: 31 Mar. 1800.

Pages 226-227. March Court 1800. PETER GARLAND desires to build a water grist mill on the south fork of Little Marrbone Creek, he owns the land on both sides. Court summons twelve freeholders to inspect the said property to ascertain if there would be damage to other property owners. Jurors: BRICE MARTIN, THOMAS OAKLEY, ALEXANDER MOORE, GOODWIN MAYSE, WILLIAM FRANCIS, DANIEL REAMEY, EDWARD, DANIEL DAVID EPPERSON, DAVID MAYSE, SANDFORD RAMEY, REUBEN PAYNE, WILLIAM PACE find no cause for damage. 4 April 1800. Proved: 28 Apr. 1800.

Pages 228-229. 28 Apr. 1800. WILLIAM JONES of Patrick County and ZACKERIAH PHILPOTT of Henry County to GEORGE HAIRSTON of Henry County for the sum of One hundred pounds sells land on the branches of Beaver Creek (in Henry County), by estimate 150 acres joins AMBROSE JONES, PHILPOTT (formerly BRETHEART), WILLIAM JONES' old line. No wit. Signed: WILLIAM JONES, ZACKERIAH PHILPOTT. Proved: 28 Apr. 1800.

Pages 230-231. 29 Mar. 1800. JOHN WELLS of Henry County to THOMAS DICKERSON of the same for the sum of Fifty pounds sells land on the north side of Turkey Cock Creek, in all 50 acres more or less and part of the said tract that JAMES HUNT now owns and bounded by STANDFIELD HARDWAY, WILLIAM HANKINS and JAMES HUNT. No wit. Signed: JOHN WELLS. Proved: 28 Apr. 1800.

Page 231. 30 Apr. 1800. GEORGE HAIRSTON of Henry County to FREDERICK ECKHOLS of the same gives and grants 1 acre of land where FREDERICK ECKHOLS hath erected a tanyard adjoining the town of Martinsville on the following terms: as long as ECKHOLS continues the tanyard on the said one acre, but should he discontinue the tanyard, the land is to revert back to GEORGE HAIRSTON. No wit. Signed: GEORGE HAIRSTON. Proved: 30 Apr. 1800.

Pages 232-233. 24 Apr. 1799. HENRY VAUGHAN of the county of Halifax to NATHAN MASON of the county of Franklin, for the sum of Thirty pounds sells and conveys a tract of land in Henry County on the branches of Read Creek, joins GOODE by estimate to be 150 acres. Wit: BENNET HANCOCK, WILLIAM WHITTAKER, THOMAS CAMPBELL. Signed: HENRY (X) VAUGHAN. Proved: 25 Nov. 1799 & 26 May 1800.

Pages 233-234. 26 May 1800. JOHN GROGEN and MARY GROGEN his wife of Henry County to JOHN PRICE of the same for the sum of Fifty pounds sells a parcel of land being part of the same tract that CHARLES COX now lives on, on by estimate 134 acres. No wit. Signed: JOHN GROGEN. Proved: 26 May 1800.

Pages 234-235. 26 May 1800. JOHN GRIGGS of Henry County to PRESLEY SIMSON of the same for the sum of One hundred dollars sells land on the branches of Leatherwood Creek, 236 acres more or less joins HENRY SHACKLEFORD, GORD, LOMAX & Company. No wit. Signed: JOHN (X) GRIGGS. Proved: 26 May 1800.

Pages 235-236. May 1800. GEORGE WALLER, GEORGE HAIRSTON, JOS. MARTIN, JOHN REDD, JOSEPH ANTHONY, JOSEPH BOULDIN and DAVID LANIER trustees for the Town of Martinsville to GEORGE WALLER, JR. for the sum of Twenty pounds 2 shillings, sells one lott in the town of Martinsville, Lott #2, agreeable to a plan of the said town, the lot whereon HARRISON BOYD formerly live. No wit. Signed: (All of trustees). Proved: 26 May 1800.

Pages 236-237. 31 Mar. 1800. WILLIAM HAYS, SENR. and SALLY HAYS his wife of Henry County to WILLIAM HAYS, JR. for the sum of Fifty pounds sells a tract of land on the Mayo River being 125 acres more or less begins on the south side of the Mayo River up the River to JOHN DILLARD'S. No wit. Signed: WILLIAM HAYS, SENR. Proved: 30 June 1800.

Pages 238-239. 11 Jan. 1792. JAMES EDWARDS, SENR. of Henry County to JACOB CAYTON of the same for the sum of Sixty pounds sells land on the south side of Smith River, 400 acres more or less joins JAMES ROBERTS, Middle Island Branch. Wit: DUTTON LANE, WILLIAM HANNAH, JAMES (X) EDWARDS, JR. Signed: JAMES EDWARDS, SENR., LUCEY (X) EDWARDS. Proved: 29 Apr. 1792 & 30 June 1800.

Pages 239-240. 5 Mar. 1800. GEORGE F. HARRIS of Pittsylvania County to NATHANIEL DURHAM of Henry County for the sum of Twenty dollars sells a tract of land by estimate 100 acres in Henry County on the waters of Home Creek, joins lines of JOHN HAMMON, JOSEPH AMBROSE, MOSES WILSON and JOHN STEVENS. No wit. Signed: GEORGE FULLER HARRIS. Proved: 30 June 1800.

Pages 240-241. No date. Inquest at JOHN CREASEY'S 11 July 1800 before HENRY LYNE, Coroner upon the viewing of the body of the deceased OBEDIENCE CREASEY then and there lying dead, the following are inquiring as to the manner of her death: HENRY JONES, CHARLES ROYSTER, SAMUEL SHOEMATE, THOMAS BARTON, THOMAS JETT, THOMAS WILKINS, JOSEPH HOPSON, FRANCIS COX, JOHN ALEXANDER, SAMUEL ELLIOTT, DUDLEY STEPHENS, GRIFFIN GRIFFITH. It is determined that one negro man named Tom, property of JOHN CREASEY, we believe was the murderer by force of arms in the water. There were wounds of bruises on arms and the back of hips, which appeared like being held by force of arms in the water and murder committed on 10 July 1800. Proved: 28 July 1800.

Pages 242-243. 31 Dec. 1799. JOHN CROUCH of the county of Henry to JOHN ALEXANDER of the same for the sum of One hundred twenty five pounds sells and conveys a tract of land 159 acres by survey dated 19 Apr. 1798 on the waters of Smith River joins JOHN ROWLAND, formerly WILLIAM ALEXANDER. Wit: JOHN PACE, INGRUM ALEXANDER, REUBEN PAYNE. Signed: JOHN CROUCH. Proved: 28 July 1800.

Page 243. 29 Apr. 1800. JOHNE FEE, Complainant against WILLIAM FEE, Defendant. It is ordered that the Defendant convey to the Complainant the part of the tract on the south side of the South Mayo River in Henry County...to be layed off of a tract conveyed to the Defendant by GEORGE WALLER for 195 acres dated 11 Aug. 1784 by a dividing line 10 to 15 polls above the Waggon Ford on the Mayo River, straight until it strikes the Waggon Road. The Complaintant to recover from the Defendant his costs. Clerk cost 9 dollars, 18 cents; Sheriff cost 1 dollar, 23 cents; Lawyer fee 5 dollars; total 15 dollars, 41 cents. Proved: 29 Apr. 1800.

Page 244. 29 July 1800. Bond of THOMAS BARTON who is to be Surveyor for the County of Henry. His securities GEORGE HAIRSTON and JOHN ALEXANDER. Proved: 29 July 1800.

Pages 244-245. 29 July 1800. WILLIAM FEE of Henry County to JOHN FEE in consideration of an Order of the Court of Henry County, conveys and assigns one tract of land on the south side of the Mayo River, 80 acres being part of a 195 acre tract deeded from GEORGE WALTON to WILLIAM FEE 11 Aug. 1787. No wit. Signed: WILLIAM FEE. Proved: 29 July 1800.

Pages 245-246. 27 Sept. 1800. STEPHEN CARTER and PEGGY CARTER his wife of Henry County to JOHN PASSLY of the same for the certain sum of money sells 200 acres more or less on the waters of Beaver Creek, Crab Tree Branch and the lines of GEORGE HAIRSTON. Wit: JOHN KING, JR., SOLLOMAN POSTON, ELISHA PEDIGO. Signed: STEPHEN (X) CARTER, PEGGY (X) CARTER. Proved: 29 Sept. 1800.

Pages 247-248. 27 Sept. 1800. JOHN HALEY and MARTHA HALEY his wife of Henry County to JOHN KING of the same for a certain sum of money sells 212 acres on the south side of Leatherwood Creek, includes part of a North Creek of the said waters joins PETER GARLAND, JOHN WELLS, GEORGE HAIRSTON. No wit. Signed: JOHN HALEY. Proved: 29 Sept. 1800.

Pages 248-249. 29 Sept. 1800. ROBERT STOCKTON of Kentucky to WILLIAM MITCHELL executor of GEORGE KEY, deceased...ROBERT STOCKTON in consideration of the sum of One hundred thirty pounds paid by the said WILLIAM MITCHELL sells 300 acres of land more or less on Middle Creek joins WILLIAM BARNARD, Smith River, THOMAS WILSON. Wit: THOMAS JETT, JAMES HOWARD, GEORGE WALLER, JR. Signed: ROBERT STOCKTON. Proved: 29 Sept. 1800. . . .Memo. ROBERT STOCKTON and WILLIAM MITCHELL do agree should any land be lost by prior claim the said STOCKTON shall refund according to quantity received.

Pages 250-251. 25 Aug. 1800. JAMES MASTIN and SALLY MASTIN his wife of Henry County to HENRY CLARK and GEORGE WALLER, JR. of the same for the sum of Forty pounds sells 100 acres more or less on the waters of Mulberry Creek, crosses the road from the Henry Court House to Leatherwood. Wit: JAMES HOWARD, SHD. DENT, JONATHAN CLARK. Signed: JAMES MASTIN, SALLY MASTIN. Proved: 29 Sept. 1800.

Pages 251-252. 29 Sept. 1800. GEORGE HAIRSTON, JOSEPH MARTIN, JOSEPH ANTHONY, JOHN REDD, JOSEPH BOULDIN, Trustees of the Town of Martinsville to HENRY CLARK for the consideration of Fifty five dollars sell Lots #3 and #4. No wit. Proved: 29 Sept. 1800.

Pages 252-253. 16 June 1800. URIAH CAMERON of Pittsylvania County to ALLEN WOMACK of the same for the sum of Twenty seven pounds sells a tract of land 281 acres more or less in Henry County on Turkey Pen Branch, joins JAMES STRONG, JOHN MAY, EDMOND EDWARDS. Signed: URIAH (X) CAMERON. Proved: 27 Oct. 1800. . . .At a Court held for Pittsylvania County 16 June 1800 URIAH CAMERON acknowledged this to be his act and deed.

Pages 254-255. 18 Oct. 1800. JOHN FEE of Henry County to AUGUSTINE THOMAS of Patrick County for the sum of One hundred pounds sells a parcel of land on the south side of the South Mayo River in Henry County being 80 acres more or less, a part of 195 acres formerly the property of WILLIAM FEE, above the Waggon Road. Wit: GEORGE TAYLOR, JOHN B. PITTMAN. Signed: JOHN FEE. Proved: 27 Oct. 1800.

Pages 255-256. 25 Mar. 1800. JOSEPH MARTIN of Henry County to BRICE MARTIN, JR. of the same for the sum of One hundred pounds sells land on the waters of Leatherwood Creek bounded by lands formerly LOMAX & Company on the west by unknown land on all other sides, 96 acres known by the name of DONELSON'S land. It is the tract purchased from WILLIAM TUNSTALL of Pittsylvania County. No wit. Signed: JOSEPH MARTIN. Proved: 28 Oct. 1800.

Pages 256-257. No date. ROBERT PEDIGO, for the love, goodwill and affection I bear towards my sons and daughter, ROBERT PEDIGO, JR., ELIJAH PEDIGO and PHEBEY PEDIGO give, grant, etc. all my right and title to a certain tract of land in Henry County on both sides of Ralphs Branch of Leatherwood Creek, 282 acres. No wit. Signed: ROBERT PEDIGO. Proved: 28 Oct. 1800.

Pages 257-258. 18 Dec. 1799. JAMES OFFICER of Henry County to PETER LEAK of the same for the sum of Sixty pound sells 68½ acres of land that joins JOSEPH MORRIS and the JORDON'S. Wit: SAMUEL C. MORRIS, CHARLES FOODRILL, JAMES SHELTON, THOMAS OFFICER, GREG. DURHAM. Signed: JAMES OFFICER, MARGET OFFICER. Proved: 24 June 1800.

Page 258. No date. Bond of JOHN WELLS is to be Sheriff of Henry County and to Collect the Tax, etc. His securities: GEORGE HAIRSTON, JOHN COX and JOHN SALMON. Proved: 24 Nov. 1800.

Page 259. 24 Dec. 1800. HENRY LYNE of Henry County, one of the legatees of EDMOND LYNE, deceased of Bourbon County, Kentucky. Me, hereunto moving appoint WILLIAM STARLING of Mercer County, Kentucky my attorney to convey in fee simple unto ALEXANDER DORR of Mason County, Kentucky a tract of land in the Northwest Territory on the Ohio River near the mouth of Eagle Creek by estimate 1,000 acres and to receive from ALEXANDER DORR a certain sum of money. Wit: JOHN REDD, REUBEN PAYNE, JOSEPH MARTIN. Signed: HENRY LYNE. Proved: 29 Dec. 1800.

Page 260. No date. MARGARET CRUM, for all the good deeds done for me by my son WILLIAM CRUM and for the love and affection I bear unto him, give the following goods and chattels: 1 red cow, 1 calf, 2 yearlings, 4 pigs, 2 featherbeds and furniture, 1 chest and table with all other household and kitchen and plantation tools. MARGARET CRUM to have the benefit of the above until her decease. Wit: JOHN HARRISON, JOSEPH THOMAS, JOSEPH BARRINGTON. Signed: MARGARET (X) CRUM. Proved: 26 Jan. 1801.

Page 261. 27 Oct. 1800. PARTHENA FEE the wife of JOHN FEE releases her right of dower to a deed from her husband to AUGUSTINE THOMAS. Proved: 26 Jan. 1801.

Pages 262-263. 28 July 1800. BLIZARD MAGRUDER of Henry County to CHARLES WHITLOCK of the same for the sum of One hundred dollars...a parcel of land (no acreage given) joins the land of Bouldin and Perkins Iron Works. Wit: JOHN DILLARD, WILLIAM MOORE, SAMUEL ANTHONY, PHILLIP (X) ANGLIN. Signed: BLIZARD MAGRUDER. Proved: 24 Nov. 1800.

Pages 263-264. 26 Jan. 1801. JOSEPH GRAVELY, JR. and HEALIN GRAVELY his wife of Henry County to MICHAEL AKIN of the same for the sum of Sixteen pounds sells a parcel of land in Henry County on Grassy fork of the fishing fork of Leatherwood Creek 80 acres more or less. No wit. Signed: JOSEPH GRAVELY, JR. Proved: 26 Jan. 1801.

Pages 264-265. 26 Jan. 1801. Bond. HENRY CLARK has undertaken to build a bridge across Beaver Creek for the use of the said County where the present bridge now stands or a small distance below, to be build of good hewed oak timber the post sills to 12" sq., 2" higher than the present bridge from the low water mark and covered with good oak or pine plank 2½" thick, good and substantial railing on each side. Bridge to be fit for waggons and complete by 1 June next and to be mainted for 7 years. Wit: JOHN COX, THOMAS EAST. Signed: HENRY CLARK, JOHN WELLS. Proved: 26 Jan. 1801.

Pages 265-266. 5 Oct. 1898. PETER PERKINS of Pittsylvania County to GEORGE HAIRSTON of Henry County for the sum of Seventy five pounds sells all that messuage, plantation and tract of land on the branches of Leaterwood Creek in Henry County by deed 175 acres, joins LOMAX & Company, JOHN CONWAY deed to PERKINS, ALEXANDER MCCULLOCK, REUBEN NANCE. Wit: JOSEPH MARTIN, JOHN REDD, JOHN MARR, JOHN COX. Signed: PETER PERKINS. Proved: 26 Nov. 1798 & 26 Jan. 1801.

Pages 266-267. 20 Mar. 1794. WILLIAM MULLINS of the county of Franklin to MARTHA CARTER of Henry County for the sum of Seven pounds sells 50 acres in Henry County on Little Read Creek, joins HENRY VAUGHAN, JOHN BURCHETT. Wit: WILLIAM HEARD, BALDWIN ROWLAND, BRADLEY (X) MEREDITH. Signed: WILLIAM (X) MULLINS. Proved: 26 Sept. 1794 & 26 Jan. 1801.

Pages 268-269. 4 Oct. 1800. THOMAS WHITE RUBLE of Henry County to JOHN REDD of the same for the consideration of Three hundred pounds sells and conveys all that tract on both sides of Town Creek containing 100 acres joining DANIEL SMITH, SHADRACK TURNER. Wit: JOHN ROWLAND, L. ADAMS, JOHN ALEXANDER, WILLIAM MITCHELL. Signed: THOMAS WHITE RUBLE.

Proved: 26 Jan. 1801.

Pages 269-270. 23 Feb. 1801. JOHN DOWDIE and MARY DOWDIE of Bedford County to WILLIAM DESHAZO of Henry County for the sum of One hundred twenty pounds sells 450 acres on the branches of Leatherwood Creek beginning at JANET BURCHE'S corner, LOMAX & Company, also part of another tract where WILLIAM BRETHEART did own, the land conveyed by DAVID WATSON to WILLIAM BRETHEART and returned in the Courts of Henry County. Signed: JOHN (X) DOWDIE. Proved: 23 Feb. 1801.

Page 271. 24 Feb. 1801. RUTH HAIRSTON of Franklin County for the natural live and affection I bear ROBERT HAIRSTON of Henry County, son of GEORGE HAIRSTON, give, grant unto the said ROBERT HAIRSTON a negro girl named Janty about 12 or 13 years old, which said slave was sold by GEORGE HAIRSTON some years back to RUTH HAIRSTON. No wit. Signed: RUTH HAIRSTON. Proved: 24 Feb. 1801.

Page 272. 25 May 1799. Deed of Trust. JAMES HENDERSON of Henry County to PETER GARLAND, the following furniture: 1 bed and furniture, loom and geese, 2 chairs, 1 table, 5 pewter plates and 1 dish, total 9 pounds 2 pence. Wit: THOMAS ALEXANDER. Signed: JAMES HENDERSON. Proved: 24 Feb. 1801. . . . The Condition is that if the said JAMES HENDERSON should pay the debt due WILLIAMSON & GARLAND on or before 25 December next, the said property will be released.

Page 273. 13 Mar. 1801. THOMAS WILKINS of Henry County to THOMAS FOSTER of the same for the sum of Thirty pounds sells and conveys a parcel of land containing 52 acres on the waters of Leatherwood Creek. Signed: THOMAS WILKINS. Proved: 30 Mar. 1801.

Page 274. 30 Mar. 1801. GEORGE HAIRSTON of Henry County to JOHN DAVIS of the same for the sum of Fifteen pounds sells and conveys 50 acres on the Reedy branch of the fishing fork of the Leatherwood Creek that joins DAVIS' own land. No wit. Signed: GEORGE HAIRSTON. Proved: 30 Mar. 1801.

Page 275. 28 Mar. 1801. DAVID MAYS and MILLEY MAYS, his wife, of Henry County to JESSE MAYS of the same for the sum of Fifty pounds sells 100 acres more or less on Marrowbone Creek, to the mouth of Hurricane Branch, joins DAVID EPPERSON, GEORGE HAIRSTON.

No wit. Signed: DAVID MAYS. Proved: 30 Mar. 1801.

Pages 276-277. 13 Mar. 1801. JACOB CAYTON of Henry County to DUTTON LANE of the same for the sum of Twenty pounds sells land on the south side of Smith River, by estimate 61 acres joins Morgan's Road, COX and WHITTON. Wit:JOSEPH GOODWIN. Signed: JACOB (X) CAYTON. Proved: 30 Mar. 1801.

Page 277. 30 Mar. 1801. JOSEPH MARTIN of Henry County to WILLIAM LARRANCE of the same for a certain sum sells 26 acres on the east side of the north fork of Leatherwood Creek. No wit. Signed: JOSEPH MARTIN. Proved: 30 Mar. 1801.

Page 278. 13 Mar. 1801. JOSEPH MARTIN, SENR. of Henry County to INGRUM ALEXANDER of the same for the sum of Seventy pounds sells land on the north fork of Leatherwood Creek, 120 acres by survey joins SAMUEL SOUTHERLAND'S corner in LOMAX & Company's order line. No wit. Signed: JOSEPH MARTIN. Proved: 30 Mar. 1801.

Page 279. 30 Mar. 1801. JOSEPH MARTIN of Henry County to GEORGE HILL of the same for the sum of $452.00 sells land on both sides of the north fork of Leatherwood Creek containing 226 acres, begins on the west side of the said Creek, with MORRIS' and LARRANCE, crosses creek to the Leatherwood Road to MORRIS' line at the Old Meeting House on the north east side of the Road. No wit. Signed: JOSEPH MARTIN. Proved: 30 Mar. 1801.

Page 280. 30 Mar. 1801. JOSEPH MARTIN of Henry County to FREDERICK UHLES of the same for the sum of $500.00 sells 200 acres on the east side of the north fork of Leatherwood Creek, to Leatherwood Road. No wit. Signed: JOSEPH MARTIN. Proved: 30 Mar. 1801.

Page 281. 30 Mar. 1801. JOSEPH MARTIN of Henry County to BARNABA WELLS of the same for One hundred and twelve pounds sells land on the west side of the north fork of Leatherwood Creek, 100 acres. No wit. Signed: JOSEPH MARTIN. Proved: 30 Mar. 1801.

Page 282. 30 Mar. 1801. JOSEPH MARTIN of Henry County to SAMUEL SUTHERLAND of the same for the sum of One hundred twelve pounds on the west side of the north fork of Leatherwood Creek, 100 acres. No wit. Signed: JOSEPH MARTIN. Proved: 30 Mar. 1801.

Page 283. 28 Mar. 1799. WILLIAM CAYTON to JOHN COATES COX both of Rockingham County, North Carolina for the sum of One hundred dollars sells land in Henry County, on the Stuart and Daug Creeks, being part of a tract given by JACOB CAYTON to WILLIAM CAYTON...lines: Morgan's Road, Gilley's, WATSON. By estimate 300 acres. Wit: JOHN LEAK, LUKE ADAMS, J. CHATTERS. Signed: WILLIAM CAYTON. Proved: 25 Feb. 1799 & 30 Mar. 1801.

Page 284. 30 Mar. 1801. GREEN BOULDIN of Henry County to ROBERT ANDERSON of the same for the sum of Ten pounds sells by estimate 53 acres joins BRICE MARTIN on Grassy Creek. Wit: WILLIAM SHELTON, GEORGE WALLER,JR., SAMUEL CARR. Signed: GREEN BOULDIN. Proved: 30 Mar. 1801.

Pages 285-286. 11 March 1801. Deed of Trust. BENJAMIN HARRISON of Henry County to JOHN ALEXANDER and SANFORD REAMEY of the same, guardians of SAMUEL COLE. BENJAMIN HARRISON has agreed to a division of the estate of WALTER KING COLE, deceased between the said SAMUEL COLE and BENJAMIN HARRISON in right of his wife and delivered the full 2/3 thereof to JOHN ALEXANDER and SANDFORD REAMEY guardians, without reserving any part for payment of debts that JOHN ALEXANDER and REAMEY have undertaken and assumed, thereby lying themselves to become bound to pay all debts. BENJAMIN HARRISON being desirous of keeping them from being responsible does hereby exonerate them. Places in trust the land whereon he now lives 290 acres more or less, land his wife holds dower, also negro fellow Ned he holds in his own right and Bower, Joe, Brown, Ruth, Andrew, Jenny, Charlotte, Anne, Cele, Watt, Sinda, 4 horses, 5 cows and household furniture. Wit: P. H. FONTAINE, P. GARLAND, WILLIAM MITCHELL. Signed: BENJAMIN HARRISON. Proved: 30 Mar. 1801.

Page 287. 30 Mar. 1801. GEORGE HAIRSTON of Henry County to THOMAS CHAPMAN of the same for the sum of One hundred pounds sells by survey 100 acres on the waters of the south fork of Leatherwood Creek, joins REUBEN NANCE. No wit. Signed: GEORGE HAIRSTON. Proved: 30 Mar. 1801.

Page 288. No date. Bill of Sale. JEREMIAH STONE of Henry County to JAMES BAKER of the same for the sum of One hundred forty four pounds sells: one negro woman Gean for one hundred pounds, 3 feather beds and furniture, Thirty six pounds; 6 hd cattle

Fifteen pounds, 1 iron pot, 1 dutch oven 12 shilling, 12 pewter plates, 2 dishes, 4 basins for Three pounds. Wit: DAVID BAKER, ISAAC (X) HOLLANDSWORTH. Signed: JEREMIAH STONE. Proved: 30 Mar. 1801.

Pages 288-289. 27 Apr. 1801. PETER GARLAND of Henry County to JOHN WILLS of the same for a certain sum sells 100 acres on the waters of Leatherwood Creek joins GEORGE KING, MARSHALL, TOOMES ....., this is the tract PETER GARLAND purchased of JOHN HAILEY. No wit. Signed: PETER GARLAND. Proved: 27 Apr. 1801.

Pages 289-290. 17 Jan. 1801. JOHN BARKSDALE of Henry County to WILLIAM BARKSDALE of the same, for the natural love and affection he bears unto his son, does give and bequeath unto him all that divided tract on the north side of Smith River being part of a tract whereon JOHN BARKSDALE now lives, by estimate 150 acres begins at the Waggon Road, joins THOMAS NUNN. Wit: STANWIX HORD, WILLIAM DRAPER, WILLIAM WALLER. Signed: JOHN BARKSDALE. Proved: 25 May 1801.

Page 291. 10 Jan. 1801. PETER LARK of Henry County to JOSHUA WALLER of the same for the sum of Seventy five pounds sells by estimate 60 acres on the waters of Horsepasture Creek joins the said WALLER and MAGRUDER. Wit: WILLIAM WALLER, JACOB LINDSAY, THOMAS STARLING, E. WALLER. Signed: PETER LEAK, HANNAH LEAK. Proved: 25 May 1801.

Page 292. 10 Jan. 1801. JOHN WALLER of Henry County to PETER LEAK of the same for the sum of Fifteen pounds sells 8 acres on the waters of Horsepasture Creek joins LEAK'S own land. No wit. Signed: JOHN WALLER, MARY WALLER. Proved: 25 May 1801.

Page 293. 10 Mar. 1801. ALEXANDER MCCULLOCK and LYDIA MCCULLOCK his wife to REUBEN NANCE for the sum of Eighty pounds sells land on the Rocky Branch of the south fork of Leatherwood Creek, 40 acres that joins NANCE. No wit. Signed: ALEXANDER (X) MCCULLOCK. Proved: 25 May 1801.

Page 294. 25 May 1801. GEORGE HAIRSTON of Henry County to JOHN WEAVER of the same for the sum of Seven pounds ten shillings sells 100 acres that joins WEAVER and BOULDIN. No wit. Signed: GEORGE HAIRSTON. Proved: 25 May 1801.

Page 295. No date. Dower release. DAVID LANIER and JOHN WELLS conveyed unto HENRY MORRIS, SENR. two tract of land by estimate 100 acres, their wives hereby relinquish their right of dower...JUDITH WELLS wife of JOHN WELLS and MARY LANIER wife of DAVID LANIER. Proved: 29 June 1801.

Page 296. No date. DAVID LANIER, JOHN WELLS and MATHEW WELLS conveyed unto HENRY MORRIS 132 acres and TABITHIA WELLS the wife of MATHEW WELLS releases her right to dower. Proved: 29 June 1801.

Page 297. 17 Dec. 1800. RICHARDSON HERNDON of Henry County to ARCHIBALD FARRIS of the same for One hundred pounds sells land on the waters of the Mayo River joins FARRIS' own land. Wit: WILLIAM F. MILLS, REUBEN WADE, DAVID MULLINS, R. A. DANES, SAMUEL C. MORRIS. Signed: RICHARDSON HERNDON. Proved: 29 June 1801.

Page 298. 2 Apr. 1801. Deed of Trust. MARTEL LASUEUR of Henry County to GEORGE HAIRSTON of the same...in order to secure payment of a debt of Five hundred dollars due unto GEORGE HAIRSTON, LASUEUR secures with the following negros: Will, Webb, Samuel, Phillis, Rachel, Isham, Daniel, household furniture, plantation tools and livestock. Wit: POLLY LASEURE. Signed: MARTEL LASUEUR. Proved: 29 June 1801.

Pages 299-300. 24 Apr. 1801. MARTHA FONTAINE of Henry County to JOSEPH MARTIN of the same for the sum of Five pounds sells and conveys land by survey 125 acres on the waters of Mulberry and Rug Creek joins JOSEPH BOULDIN. Wit: P. H. FONTAINE, THOMAS STARLING, NATHANIEL DANDRIDGE. Signed: MARTHA FONTAINE. Proved: 24 May 1801.

Pages 300-301. 10 Mar. 1801. ALEXANDER MCCULLOCK and LYDIA MCCULLOCK his wife of Henry County to REUBEN NANCE of the same for the sum of Eighty pounds sells land on the waters of Leatherwood Creek and Rockey Branch. No wit. Signed: ALEXANDER (X) MCCULLOCK. Proved: 24 May 1801.

Page 302. 17 Feb. 1801. EPHRAIM WILSON of Henry County to STANWIX HORD of the same for the sum of Four pounds sells: 1 sow, 9 piggs, 1 pail and tub, 1 piggin, 1 4-gal. pot, 1 double oven, 1 flat iron, gridle, spinning wheel, 1 blanket, 1 bed stead, 1 cupboard. Wit: WILLIAM BARKSDALE, JOHN M. BOWLES, WILLIAM BURRIS. Signed: EPHRAIM WILSON. Pr:28 July 1801.

Pages 302-304. 14 Jan. 1800. ALEXANDER BRYDIE, Attorney for PATRICK HART of the city of Richmond to MARTHA WALLER of Henry County for the sum of One hundred fifty eight pounds sells and conveys 317 acres in Henry County, it being the whole of a tract whereon SAMUEL TARRANT lately lived and was by indent of mortgage dated 22 Feb. 1788 conveyed by SAMUEL TARRANT to DAVID ANDERSON, foreclosure decreed July 1790, now PATRICK HART'S. Wit: JOSEPH MARTIN, BENJAMIN COOK, JOHN REDD. Signed: ALEXANDER BRYDIE. Proved: 26 Feb. 1800 & 26 Mar. 1800.

Page 304. 27 Dec. 1800. Deed of Trust. BARNA WELLS of Henry County to FRANCIS NORTHCUTT of the same, sells 1 negro man slave named Caddiff for One hundred pounds. BARNA WELLS borrowed One hundred pounds from NORTHCUTT and payment is due by 25 Dec. 1801. Wit: THOMAS WILKINS, JAMES (X) BRANS. Signed: BARNA WELLS. Proved: 27 July 1801.

Pages 305-306. 27 July 1801. JOHN FRENCH of Henry County to WILLIAM SHARP of Petersburg for the sum of Two hundred twenty pounds sells land on the south side of Smith River in Henry County, it being the tract JOHN FRENCH purchased of WILLIAM HEATH, by estimate 100 acres, joins THOMAS JARVIS, JAMES COOK and JOHN TRAVERS. No wit. Signed: JOHN FRENCH. Proved: 27 July 1801. . . .Memo: JOHN FRENCH is to have possession of the land until 25 Dec. 1801.

Pages 306-308. 25 Nov. 1799. MARTHA FONTAINE and JOSEPH MARTIN to JOSEPH BOULDIN, all of Henry County, for the sum of Three pounds four shillings sells land that joins BOUDLIN, it being 307 acres. Wit: NATHANIEL W. DANDRIDGE, CHARLES FONTAINE, JOHN REAMEY. Signed: MARTHA FONTAINE, JOSEPH MARTIN. Proved: 25 Nov. 1799 & 25 July 1801.

Pages 308-309. 17 Jan. 1801. DAVID MEADE RANDOLPH of the city of Richmond in capacity of surviving partner of BENJAMIN HARRISON and DAVID M. RANDOLPH and also for the heirs of BENJAMIN HARRISON, deceased to JOSEPH MARTIN. DAVID MEAD RANDOLPH and BENJAMIN HARRISON had a tract in Henry County on the waters of Leatherwood Creek 2,799 acres...lines: north fork of Leatherwood Creek, LOMAX & Company. Plat was made by JOHN FONTAINE 5 May 1789 whereas Gen. JOSEPH MARTIN purchased of BENJAMIN HARRISON 1210 acres of the above lands...now this indenture for Eight hundred fifty eight pounds 9 shillings sells the whole of the residue of the said tract, 1589 acres more or less. Wit: GEORGE WALLER, JR., THOMAS ALEXANDER, B. MARTIN. Signed: DAVID MEADE RANDOLPH. Proved: 23 Feb. 1801.

Page 310. 8 Aug. 1801. Deed of Gift. LITTLEBERRY HURT of Adams County, Territory of Louisiana for the good will and affection I bear for my nephew LITTLEBERRY HURT STONE and my niece MARY NUNN wife of JOSEPH NUNN both of Henry County, give and grant to them all my right and title of my father's estate which will be coming to me at the decease of my father and mother. Wit: BALDWIN ROWLAND, JAMES HEARD, WALLER REDD. Signed: LITTLEBERY HURT. Proved: 31 Aug. 1801.

Pages 310-311. 20 Feb. 1801. HENRY SHACKLEFORD and POLLY SHACKELFORD his wife of Henry County to ADRON ANGLIN of Pittsylvania County for the sum of Thirty pounds sells a parcel of land on Grasy fork of the fishing fork of Leatherwood Creek by estimate 40 acres. Wit: THOMAS BURNET, JAMES BRADFIELD, CALEB ANGLIN. Signed: HENRY SHACKLEFORD. Proved: 31 Aug. 1801.

Pages 311-312. 1798. SHADRICK DENT of Henry County to CHARLES DAVIS of the same for the sum of Four pounds thirteen shillings nine pence sells 6¾ acre on the branch of Reedy Creek. No wit. Signed: SHADRICK DENT. Proved: 31 Aug. 1801.

Pages 313-314. 5 Aug. 1801. ROBERT PEDEGO of Henry County to CHARLES AGEE of the same for One hundred dollars sells land on the waters of Mulberry Creek by estimate 100 acres more or less on Pole Bridge Branch. Wit: ELIJAH PEDIGOE, HENRY PEDIGOE, JACOB AGEE. Signed: ROBERT PEDEGO. Proved: 31 Aug. 1801.

Page 315. 31 Aug. 1801. BARTLETT WADE of Henry County to JOHN P. PYRTLE of the same for the sum of One hundred fifty pounds sells land on both sides of Big Reedy Creek by estimate 250 acres near the Old Meeting House. No wit. Signed: BARTLET WADE. Proved: 31 Aug. 1801.

Pages 316-317. 8 Aug. 1801. THORNTON BERNARD of King George County to JOHN CREASEY of Henry County for the sum of One hundred sixty six pounds ten shillings land in Henry County, a part of BERNARD'S order on Fall and Middle Creeks...line between WILLIAM BERNARD and THORNTON BERNARD, JOHN SMITH, TITUS HUNTER, 166½ acres by survey. Wit: THOMAS BARTON, JOHN ALEX-

ANDER, JAMES ALEXANDER, PETER GEARHEART, NATHANIEL W. DANDRIDGE. Signed: THORNTON BERNARD. Proved: 31 Aug. 1801.

Page 317. 31 Aug. 1801. PRESLEY SIMPSON of Henry County to SAMUEL ANGLIN of the same for One hundred dollars land on the branches of fishing fork of Leatherwood Creek 100 acres more or less joins MICHAEL AKINS, HAIRSTON, GRAVELY. No wit. Signed: PRESLEY (X) SIMPSON. Proved: 31 Aug. 1801.

Page 318. 31 Aug. 1801. MICHAEL MCDANIEL of Henry County to JOHN C. PYRTLE of the same for Forty five pounds sells land on both sides of Little Reedy Creek, by estimate 50 acres more or less. Land conveyed to MCDANIEL by JOSEPH KING, see that deed for more details. No wit. Signed: MICHAEL MCDANIEL. Proved: 31 Aug. 1801. . . .AUIRILLA MCDANIEL release her right of dower.

Page 319. 31 Aug. 1801. SALLY BARKSDALE, WILLIAM BARKSDALE and STANWIX HORD Administrators of the estate of JOHN BARKSDALE, deceased are to make an inventory and administer the estate. Should a Will be found it will be exhibited. Securities: JOSEPH MARTIN, GEORGE HAIRSTON. Signed: SALLY (X) BARKSDALE, WILLIAM BARKSDALE, STANWIX HORD. Proved: 31 Aug.1801.

Page 320. 15 Sept. 1801. SAMUEL WATSON and PHEBE WATSON, his wife of Henry County to AMEY PEDIGO of the same for the sum of Sixteen pounds sells a parcel of land, 45 acres, on Ralph's Branch of Leatherwood Creek, joins the south fork of SAMUEL WATSON'S spring branch. No wit. Signed: SAMUEL WATSON, PHEBE WATSON. Proved: 28 Sept. 1801.

Page 321. 28 Sept. 1801. Bond of GEORGE HAIRSTON who is appointed Sheriff to collect and receive all fees and dues. His securities are: JOHN ALEXANDER, JOSEPH BOULDIN, JOHN PACE, JOHN ROWLAND. Proved: 30 Sept. 1801.

Page 322. A duplicate of page 321.

Page 323-324. 30 Aug. 1801. THORNTON BERNARD of King George County to REUBEN PAYNE of Henry County for the sum of Two hundred ninety nine pounds fourteen shillings sells by survey 333 & 1/3 acres on Fall Creek joins JOHN CREASEY, JONATHAN STONE, splitting the line between JOHNATHAN STONE and THORNTON BERNARD'S lot 333 1/3 acres called a reserve, through a second 666 2/3 acres lot lately laid off by THORNTON BERNARD near MOSES SMITH and NORTON'S Road. Wit: T. P. GARLAND, THOMAS DIX, ROBERT G. PAYNE. Signed: THORNTON BERNARD. Proved: 31 Aug. 1801. . . .13 Aug. 1801. Possession was granted this date, and the payment of the above was received.

Page 325. 22 Oct. 1798. ROBERT STOCKTON and his wife CATHERINE STOCKTON of Henry County to PHILIP RYAN of the same for the sum of Two hundred pounds sells and conveys a tract of land, 200 acres more or less on the Rockey Branch of Leatherwood Creek joins REUBEN NANCE'S old line. Wit: WILLIAM BROWN, ANN STOCKTON, DORICS STOCKTON. Signed: ROBERT STOCKTON, CATHERINE STOCKTON. Proved: 29 Sept. 1801.

Page 326. 14 Sept. 1801. WILLIAM SPENCER of Henry County to WILLIAM HILL of the same for the sum of One thousand dollars sells land on Horsepasture Creek, joining the land of the said HILL, JOHN STONE, GEORGE W. SPENCER, JOHN SMITH and JOHN STAPLES. By estimate 233 acres, it being the land that WILLIAM SPENCER was entitled to of his father's estate as allotted to him by a Division Agreement. Wit: JOHN HARRIS, THOMAS HILL, JOHN DILLARD, JAMES BOHANNON. Signed: WILLIAM SPENCER. Proved: 14 Sept. 1801.

Page 327. 8 Aug. 1801. THORNTON BERNARD of the county of King George to JONATHAN STONE of Henry County for the sum of One hundred sixty six pounds ten shillings sells a part of Bernard's Order on Fall and Middle Creek, joins lines of JOHN CREASEY, WILLIAM BERNARD, JOHN SMITH and HUNTER'S field by survey 166½ acres. Wit: THOMAS BARTON, JOSEPH ALEXANDER, JOHN ALEXANDER, PETER GEARHEART. Signed: THORNTON BERNARD. Proved: 29 Sept. 1801.

Page 328. 10 Feb. 1801. JONATHAN STONE of Henry County to JAMES DYER of the same for the sum of Sixty six dollars sells land on the waters of Leatherwood Creek, 66 acres joins JESSE DELOZER, NICKOLAS AIKEN and DICKERSON. No wit. Signed: JONATHAN STONE. Proved: 29 Sept. 1801.

Pages 329-330. 18 April 1801. Deed of Trust. JOHN PURCELL to JOHN HOPSON in the amount of Forty pounds nine shillings two pence indebted to LANIER, SHELTON and COOKE and for and in further consideration of Twenty three pounds with interest indebted to CALEB TATE of Lynchburg (cost more fully appear in a suit in courts of Henry County)...secures with slave James. Wit: JOHN H. HANIER, THOMAS STARLING, JOSEPH BOULDING. Signed: JOHN PURCELL, JOHN HOPSON. Proved: 28 Sept. 1801.

Page 331. Sept. 1801. CARTER DILLEN of Henry County to WILLIAM F. MILLS of the same for the sum of One hundred fifty pounds sells 278 1/3 acres it being one-third part of 835 acres willed to CARTER DILLEN, HENRY DILLEN and WILLIAM DILLEN by HENRY DILLEN. Joins lines of WILLIAM DILLEN. Wit: BALLENGER WADE, THOMAS STARLING. Signed: CARTER (X) DILLEN. Proved: 29 Sept. 1801.

Page 332. 26 Oct. 1801. WILLIAM JOSEPH of Henry County to SPENCER GROGAN of the same for Fifty pounds sells land on the south side of Smith River by estimate 200 acres more or less joins JOHN GROGAN, Hind's Branch, County Line and COCKRAM. No wit. Signed: WILLIAM (X) JOSEPH. Proved: 26 Oct.1801.

Page 333. 26 Oct. 1801. I, FRANCIS COX, in consideration of the love, affection and good will I have towards my daughter ELIZABETH OLDHAM widow, the land whereon she now lives, my negro woman Senor and her child Hannah. No wit. Signed: FRANCIS COX. Proved: 26 Oct. 1801.

Pages 333-334. 29 Sept. 1801. ROBERT STOCKTON of the state of Kentucky to GEORGE HAIRSTON of Henry County for the sum of Five hundred dollars, land on the west fork of Leatherwood Creek, which land was decreed by the High Court to ROBERT STOCKTON, 300 acres by a claim of JOHN CALLAHAM against LOMAX & Company for improving the said LOMAX lands on Leatherwood Creek, which decree was made to ROBERT STOCKTON 10 Mar. 1795; 200 acres only of the 300 acres is only sold to GEORGE HAIRSTON, the other 100 acres still remains which is to divide by a line to be run from pointers in the old line just above the Mill Pond, joins JAMES HOWARD. Wit: JOSEPH ANTHONY, HENRY CLARK, JAMES HOWARD. Signed: ROBERT STOCKTON. Proved: 28 Oct. 1801.

Pages 335-336. 28 Mar. 1801. JOHN KELLY of Henry County to MASON KELLY of the same, for the consideration of Thirty pounds sells and conveys a tract of 300 acres begining at the mouth of Drag Creek to the north fork to JOHN KELLY'S back line to JACOB CATON'S line to the old Survey thence to Smith River. Wit: JACOB (X) CAYTON, DUTTON LANE, JR., WILLIAM NORMAN. Signed: JOHN KELLY. Pr: 30 Mar.1801.

Pages 336-337. 29 Oct. 1801. Bond of GEORGE HAIRSTON, with his security FRANCIS COX, who has been appointed Sherif of Henry County to collect levies and accounts as by Law. No wit. Signed: GEORGE HAIRSTON, FRANCIS COX. Proved: 30 Nov. 1801.

Page 337. 30 Nov. 1801. HANNAH DILLEN, wife of CARTER DILLEN, releases her right to dower in a deed to WILLIAM F. MILLS, 278 1/3 acres.

Pages 338-339. 7 Nov. 1801. WILLIAM MITCHELL, executor of GEORGE KEY, deceased of Henry County to JAMES SMITH of Surry County, North Carolina for the sum of One hundred eighty dollars sixty seven cents sells land in Henry County on Smith River, Fall and Middle Creeks 300 acres more or less joins WILLIAM BERNARD and THOMAS WILLIAMS. Signed: WILLIAM MITCHELL. Proved: 30 Nov. 1801.

Pages 340-341. 30 Nov. 1801. MARTHA FONTAINE of Henry County to GEORGE HAIRSTON of the same for the sum of One hundred thirty seven pounds ten shillings sells land on the waters of Mulberry Creek, Smith River, Beaver Creek (land was patented to PATRICK HENRY in 1785 and contained 2,125 acres) of which MARTHA FONTAINE has sold: 250 ac. to JAMES MASTERS (see deed), 307 ac. to JOSEPH BOULDIN by deed; 125 ac. to GEN. JOSEPH MARTIN by deed, with these taken out leaves 1,443 acres, see patent and other deeds for descriptions. Wit: P. H. FONTAINE, THOMAS J. W. LARRIMORE, NATHANIEL W. DANDRIDGE. Signed: MARTHA FONTAINE. Proved: 30 Nov. 1801.

Pages 341-342. 22 Nov. 1801. JAMES MURPHY, SENR. and ELIZABETH MURPHY, his wife to JAMES MURPHY, JR. all of Henry County, for the sum of Thirty pounds sells by estimate 70 acres on the branches of Donalds Creek, joins JAMES MURPHY, SENR. No wit. Signed: JAMES (X) MURPHY. Proved: 30 Nov. 1801.

Page 343. 30 Nov. 1801. THOMAS BOULDIN and his wife MARTHA BOULDIN of Henry County to PETER PERKINS of Pittsylvania County for the sum of $440.00, sells ½ or all the fee simple right and title that THOMAS BOULDIN has to a tract containing 154 acres on the north side of the north fork of Mayo River, being a tract purchased by BOULDIN and PERKINS in partnership of JOHN DILLARD. No wit. Signed: THOMAS BOULDIN, MARTHA BOULDIN. Proved: 30 Nov. 1801.

Page 344. 14 Oct. 1801. THOMAS COX of Charlotte

County to JOHN COX of the same, sells 180 acres in Henry County on the Muster Branch of Leatherwood Creek for the sum of Fifty pounds joins the lines of STEPHEN, BARNARD and FRANCIS COX. Wit: THOMAS BOULDIN, MARTHA BOULDIN, WILLIAM BADEN (?). Signed: THOMAS COX. Proved: 31 Nov. 1801.

Page 345. 5 Oct. 1801. JAMES SPENCER,JR. of Henry County to JONADAB WADE of the same for the sum of Two hundred fifty five pounds sells two tract of land contains 214 acres more or less on Marrowbone Creek and branches thereof adjoining the lands of JONADAB WADE, DAVID MULLINS and ALEXANDER MOORE, it being the whole of the land assigned JAMES SPENCER by dividing of his father's estate. One tract is 100 acres conveyed by deed from JESSE CHANDLER to JAMES SPENCER, deceased heirs joins JAMES TAYLOR. The other tract of 114 acres joins the former and is now in the possession of JONADAB WADE. Wit: JOSIAH LEAKE, HUBBARD (X) HATCHER, JOHN DILLARD. Signed: JAMES SPENCER, JR. Proved: 30 Nov. 1801.

Page 346. 15 July 1801. Bill of Sale. JEREMIAH STONE of Henry County to JAMES BAKER of the same for the sum of Ninety pounds sells and conveys one negro woman named Jane. Wit: BARTLET WADE, THOMAS BAKER, DANIEL BAKER, JO. WITT. Signed: JEREMIAH STONE. Proved: 25 Jan. 1802.

Pages 347-348. 10 Oct. 1801. SARAH CLIFT of Pittsylvania County to WILLIAM HANKINS of the same for the sum of One hundred fifty pounds sells land in Henry County and Pittsylvania County on Crooked Run Creek, 150 acres more or less being part of the land SARAH CLIFT bought of DANIEL HANKINS, whereon she now lives. Wit: D. LANIER, STEPHEN AUSTIN, JAMES COX, JOSEPH CLIFT. Signed: SARAH (X) CLIFT. Proved: 25 Jan. 1802.

Pages 348-349. 23 Dec. 1801. JOHN ROWLAND of Henry County to BRICE MARTIN of the same sells 6 acres that joins BRICE MARTIN and JOHN ALEXANDER. Proved: 25 Jan. 1802.

Pages 349-350. 25 Jan. 1802. JAMES MURPHEY, SENR. of Henry County to FRANCIS MURPHY of the same for the sum of $500.00 sells the balance of a tract where I formerly lived, also another tract joining the same on both sides of Daniels Creek, it being 239 acres more or less joins PETER COPLAND, JAMES DONALD and REDD. No wit. Signed: JAMES (X) MURPHY.

Proved: 25 Jan. 1802.

Pages 350-351. 13 Dec. 1801. Deed of Gift. SANFORD REAMEY of Henry County to ROBERT FINCH and POLLY FINCH, natural children of SUSANNAH FINCH of the State of Georgia...for the love and affection for ROBERT FINCH and POLLY FINCH and for better maintainance and livelyhood of the said, gives, grants and conveys to them one negro girl slave named Polly. Should either ROBERT or POLLY FINCH die without issue, the slave shall return to the children begotten by me of the body of ELIZABETH REAMEY my present wife. Wit: JOHN WASH. Signed: SANFORD REAMEY. Proved: 25 Nov. 1802.

Page 352. No date. Dower release. SIDNEY FRENCH wife of JOHN FRENCH hereby releases her right of dower to the land sold to WILLIAM SHARP of Peterburgh, County of Dinwiddie, 100 acre tract. Proved: 25 Jan. 1802.

Pages 351-352. 27 Jan. 1801. Power of Attorney. HARDIN WEATHERFORD of the county of Pittsylvania being by the last Will and Testament of DAVID WEATHERFORD the executor of his estate in Henry County...Whereas I live a distance and cannot conveniently travel to attend the business as it needs. appoint FRANCIS COX of Henry County my attorney to transact all business. Wit: SAMUEL ELLIOTT, SARAH (X) PEARSON. Signed: HARDIN (X) WEATHERFORD. Proved: 25 Jan. 1802.

Pages 352-353. 11 May 1801. Deed of Trust. DAVID LANIER Of Henry County to GEORGE HAIRSTON of the same, in order to secure payment of a debt of Two hundred three pounds with interest from the 13th of April last which GEORGE HAIRSTON has in time been security for DAVID LANIER, owed to CHARLES DUNCAN of Chesterfield County, due from 13 April. LANIER secures this with the following slaves: Targe, Reubin, Easter, Cate, Plott, and Chaney. Wit: DAVID LANIER, JR. Signed: DAVID LANIER. Proved: 25 Jan. 1802.

Pages 354-355. 28 Dec. 1801. JOHN NIXON of Henry County to GEORGE HAIRSTON of the same for the consideration of One hundred pounds sells all that plantation, tenement and parcel of land on the north west branch of Leatherwood Creek, by deed from BIRD and MARY NANCE to JOHN NIXON, 100 acres more or less joins CHARLES BURNET'S spring branch, and ROBERT

STOCKTON. Wit: WASHINGTON ROWLAND, HARDIN HAIRSTON, JOHN PURCELL. Signed: JOHN (X) NIXON. Proved: 25 Jan. 1802.

Page 356. 16 Jan. 1802. JOHN OAKES of Henry County to BENJAMIN SMITH of the same for Fifty pounds sells by estimate 100 acres more or less on Smith River to the County Line. Wit: WILLIAM WATSON, CORNELIUS CAYTON, RODAY (X) CAYTON. Signed: JOHN OAKES. Proved: 22 Feb. 1802.

Page 357. 31 Mar. 1802. JOHN SMITH and SALLY SMITH his wife of Henry County to HENRY CLINTON of the same for Thirty pounds sells land on the waters of Horsepasture Creek, 65 acres joining JOHN NICHOLDS and JOHN STONE. No wit. Signed: JOHN SMITH, SALLY SMITH. Proved: 29 Mar. 1802.

Page 358. 16 Jan. 1802. JOHN HUTCHENS, SENR. of Stokes County, North Carolina to JOSIAH TAYLOR of Henry County for Forty five pounds sells 50 acres more or less on the south side of the South Mayo River at the mouth of a branch below the plantation of FREDERICK HUTCHENS on the other side. No wit. Signed: JOHN HUTCHENS. Proved: 29 Mar. 1802. . . .MOLLY HUTCHENS, wife of JOHN HUTCHENS, releases her right of dower to the above.

Page 359. 20 Mar. 1802. JOSEPH MARTIN of Henry County to HENRY SHACKLEFORD, SENR. of the same for the sum of Eighty two pounds ten shillings sells 150 acres by survey on Leatherwood Creek, joins LOMAX & Company...it being part of the LOMAX & Company order land purchased by JOSEPH MARTIN some years ago. No wit. Signed: JOSEPH MARTIN. Proved: 29 Mar. 1802. . . . .SUSANAH MARTIN wife of JOSEPH MARTIN, releases her right of dower to the above.

Page 360. 23 Mar. 1802. JOSEPH MARTIN of Henry County to GEORGE TAYLOR of the same for the sum of Five hundred pounds sells 296 acres on Smith River, joins THOMAS GRAVES' fish trap on Smith River, it being the tract JOSEPH MARTIN purchased of THOMAS GRAVES. Signed: JOSEPH MARTIN. Proved: 29 Mar. 1802. . . . .Memo: JOSEPH MARTIN reserves the right forever to the fishery he now occupys (sic) in the Big Shoals. . . . .SUSANAH MARTIN wife of JOSEPH MARTIN, releases her right of dower to the above.

Page 361. 25 Nov. 1789. THOMAS MAN RANDOLPH of the county of Goochland to JAMES ROBERTS and

JOSEPH ROBERTS sons and heirs of JOSEPH ROBERTS, deceased of Henry County for the sum of Two hundred pounds paid by the said JOSEPH ROBERTS deceased, sells 2 tracts on both sides of the north fork of the Mayo River contains by estimate 179 acres (each tract) and joins each other, also joins a tract of 130 acres formerly part of the same now to JOHN STAPLES. By their father's will this is their lotts..allotted by the Henry County Court. Wit: ABRAM PENN, THOMAS COOPER, GEORGE PENN. Signed: THOMAS M. RANDOLPH. Proved: 21 Mar. 1802.

We, JOSEPH ROBERTS and JAMES ROBERTS do assign our rights and title to the within deed to JOHN STAPLES as we have full satisfaction for the same. Wit: NATHAN SHELTON, MICAJAH HUGHRES, NATHANIEL W. SHELTON. Signed: JAMES ROBERTS, JOSEPH ROBERTS.

Page 362. 29 Mar. 1802. Bond. GEORGE HAIRSTON has undertaken to build a bridge for the use of the public highway across Marrowbone Creek about ½ mile below his Mill, near his Marrowbone Store to be completed by 20 April next. To keep same in repair so that carriages and passengers can pass in safety for a term of seven years. Signed: GEORGE HAIRSTON, REUBEN PAYNE. Proved: 29 Mar. 1802.

Pages 362-363. 16 Apr. 1802. Inquist at the house of HENRY JONES on the waters of Leatherwood Creek where he intends to build a water grist mill, owns the land on both sides of the creek, REUBEN NANCE, THOMAS (X) CHAPMAN, ALEXANDER (X) MCCULLOCK, WILLIAM (X) LARRANCE, HENRY LARRANCE, BENJAMIN JONES, GEORGE WALLER, JR., JAMES MASTERS, THOMAS JETT, CHARLES ROYSTER and JOHN (X) CREASEY, HENRY (X) HEFFLEFINGER have examined the lands and affirm that no damage would be caused by overflowing. HENRY (X) HEFFLEFINGER gives his affirmation not oath. Proved: 26 Apr. 1802.

Pages 363-364. 26 Apr. 1802. THOMAS NUNN of Henry County to MICHAEL MCDANIEL of the same for Thirty pounds sells all that dividend tract on Little Rock Run by estimate 200 acres more or less. One of the lines is Town Creek Road. No wit. Signed: THOMAS NUNN. Proved: 26 Apr. 1802.

Pages 364-365. 26 Apr. 1802. THOMAS NUNN, SENR. of Henry County to THOMAS NUNN, JR., JOHN NUNN and JOSEPH NUNN for the natural love and affection he bears unto his sons gives unto them all that tract on both sides of Little Rock Run, 150 acres more or less, being part of a greater tract granted THOMAS NUNN, SENR. by patent dated 29 May 1797 at Richmond.. reference thereunto for fuller description. No wit. Signed: THOMAS NUNN, SENR. Proved: 25 Apr. 1802.

Pages 365-366. 16 Dec. 1801. Deed of Trust. MICHAEL ROWLAND to GEORGE HAIRSTON both of Henry County - debt to GEORGE HAIRSTON in the amount of Fifty four pounds nine shillings, secures with five head horses, one wagon and his household furniture. To be paid by 25 Dec. 1802. Wit: GEORGE HAIRSTON, JR., JAMES DILLARD, JOHN ROWLAND, JR., HUBBARD (X) HATCHER. Signed: MICHAEL ROWLAND. Proved: 26 Apr. 1802.

Page 367. 10 Jan. 1802. Deed of Trust. JOHN PURCELL to GEORGE HAIRSTON both of Henry County - debt Ninety four pounds, eighteen shillings, eight and one-half pence, secures with one negro man Jim, his cattle, horses, household furniture and plantation tools. Due 1 January next. Wit: HARDIN HAIRSTON, WASHINGTON ROWLAND. Signed: JOHN PURCELL. Proved: 26 Apr. 1802.

Pages 368-369. 2 Mar. 1802. WILLIAM PORTER of Powhatan County to GEORGE HAIRSTON of Henry County for Two hundred seventy five pounds sells land in Henry County on the waters of Beaver Creek by survey 200 acres which land is part of a tract sold by ROBERT STOCKTON to JOHN ST. WOODSON, lines of ZACKERIAH PHILPOTT. Wit: THOMAS BARTON, BARTLET JONES, HARDIN HAIRSTON, BENJAMIN WOODSON. Signed: WILLIAM PORTER. Proved: 26 Apr. 1802.

Page 369. 26 Apr. 1802. GEORGE HAIRSTON and ELIZABETH HAIRSTON his wife, of Henry County to REES HUGHES of the same for the sum of $302.00 sells 150 acres more or less on Middle Creek joins lines of DANIEL WILSON and LOMAX & Company. No wit. Signed: GEORGE HAIRSTON. Proved: 27 Apr. 1802.

Page 370. 19 Mar. 1802. Inquist at General JOSEPH MARTIN'S in Henry County. HENRY LYNE, Coroner, to view the body of an infant child suposed to be the child of NANCY ARNOLD then and there lying dead and upon the oath of: BENJAMIN JONES, CAR WALLER, WILLIAM STOKES, CHARLES PHILPOTT, JAMES HOWARD, WILLIAM DESHAZO, JOHN WELLS, JOHN ST. WOODSON, ZACKERIAH PHILPOTT, THOMAS ALEXANDER, JOHN HAMONS and JOSEPH ANTHONY to inquire the when, where and how and after what manner the said infant came to his death. They do say that NANCY ARNOLD not having the fear of God before her eyes but being moved and seduced by the devil on 15 Mar. 1802 choked with a string, with malice and aforethought the child who instantly died. he has no goods or land and only 1 horse. Proved: 27 Apr. 1802.

Pages 371-372. 27 Apr. 1802. GEORGE HAIRSTON and ELIZABETH HAIRSTON his wife of Henry County to ADAM STULTS of the same for Forty five pounds sells land on the headwaters of Leatherwood Creek, 200 acres joins lines of FRANCIS NORTHCUTT, WILLIAM BROWN and MAGRUDER. No wit. Signed: GEORGE HAIRSTON. Proved: 29 Apr. 1802.

Pages 372-373. 31 May 1802. MOSES WILSON to THOMAS WILSON both of Henry County for Fifty five pounds sells land on Leatherwood Creek and Smith River 246 acres, joins THOMAS WILSON'S tract purchased of JAMES WILSON. No wit. Signed: MOSES (X) WILSON. Proved: 31 May 1802.

Pages 373-374. 31 May 1802. SAMUEL ROSE, attorney in fact for PATRICK ROSE and WILLIAM CABALL executors of the last will and testament of Col. HUGH ROSE late of Amherst County, deceased and CAROLINE M. ROSE, widow of HUGH ROSE to HENRY LYNE of Henry County for Five shillings sells 50 acres in Henry County on Ramsey's Creek. Signed: SAMUEL ROSE, attorney for PATRICK ROSE and WILLIAM CABALL and CAROLINE ROSE. Proved: 31 May 1801.

Pages 374-375. 31 May 1802. SAMUEL ROSE attorney for PATRICK ROSE and WILLIAM CABALL executors of the last will and testament of Col. HUGH ROSE late of Amherst County, deceased, and CAROLINE M. ROSE widow of HUGH ROSE to JOHN SALMON of Henry County for the sum of Five shillings 25 acres on the south side of Jordon's Creek...to a creek which HENRY LYNE lives on to a great fall of water, otherwise the Mill Seat and part of a tract formerly SAMUEL JORDON'S. Signed: SAMUEL ROSE, attorney for PATRICK ROSE, WILLIAM CABALL, and CAROLINE ROSE. Proved: 31 May 1802.

Page 375. 8 Nov. 1801. JOSEPH BAILEY and PATTY BAILEY his wife formerly PATTY BROSHEARS to CREASSEY KEY for Fifteen pounds sells what she has or may have to 1/7th part of PATTY'S father PHILIP BRASHEARS deceased, under his will consisting of land and personal property willed to her after her mother NANNY BRASHEAR'S death, said land in the possession of

NANNY BRASHEARS. Wit: JOHN PACE, THOMAS (X) WILSON, ISABEL (X) KEY. Signed: JOSEPH (X) BAILEY, PATTY (X) BAILEY. Proved: 31 May 1802.

Pages 376-378. 10 Mar. 1798. Deed of Trust. THOMAS WHITE RUBLE to GEORGE WALLER, JR., WILLIAM WALLER and EDMOND WALLER. THOMAS WHITE RUBLE has executed to JOHN REDD Bonds (1) Two hundred pounds in cash with a condition thereunder written for payment of One hundred pounds in cash or in bar iron at cash price at the Iron Works of the said RUBLE on or before 1 July 1799. (2) Two hundred pounds with the condition written for payment $100.00 cash or in bar iron at the Iron Works on or before 1 July 1800. (3) Two hundred pounds with payment One hundred pounds or bar iron dated 1 July 1801. (4) Two hundred pounds, to be paid One hundred pounds cash or bar iron 1 July 1802. All will more fully appear in the said Bonds. THOMAS WHITE RUBLE assigns lands in Henry and Patrick County on Town Creek joins DANIEL SMITH, SHADRACK TURNER (for more detail see his will), also one other tract in Patrick County on both sides of Goblington Creek joins ADAMS order line, LUKE FOLEY, two other tracts in Henry County, and one in Patricks (see Bonds). To include the Iron Works, houses, homes, improvements and all belongings. Wit: GEORGE FRASHER, WILLIAM WITT, JOHN TURNER, SR. Signed: THOMAS WHITE RUBLE, GEORGE WALLER, JR., WILLIAM WALLER, EDMOND WALLER. Proved: 26 Mar. 1798.

Pages 379-380. 17 Sept. 1801. BENJAMIN HARRISON, JR. to P. H. FONTAINE sells all interest in a tract of land where the said HARRISON now lives and in the land layed off and lotted him for his wife's dower and also personal property which he holds by virtue of his marriage to the present SALLY HARRISON formerly SALLY COLE widow and relict of WALTER KING COLE deceased as follows, slaves: Bouzer, Rachel, Jenny, Andrew, Joe, Amy, Charles, Lindy and Charlotte, all stock of every kind, my part of the present crop now growing and the furniture and all else I enjoy and hold of the above marriage. P. H. FONTAINE is to hold all the aforesaid for the use and benefit of my wife SALLY HARRISON and for my daughter ELIZABETH HARRISON and them only for the lifetime of my wife, and so much of the property as shall be left to be conveyed to my daughter ELIZABETH HARRISON for her use. Wit: NATHANIEL W. DANDRIDGE, THOMAS STARLING, JOHN M. LANIER. Signed: BENJAMIN HARRISON. Proved: 28 June 1802.

Pages 380-381. 26 July 1802. JOHN GRIGGS, SENR. of Henry County to ABNER STULTS of the same for Sixty pounds sells 128 acres more or less on Beaver Creek joins DAVID BUNCH, HICKS and MAGRUDER. Wit: ADAM STULTS, GABRIE (X) STULTS, SAMUEL MARSHALL. Signed: JOHN (X) GRIGGS. Proved: 26 July 1802.

Pages 381-382. 29 June 1802. Deed of Trust. BENJAMIN DILLEN to JOHN REDD, debt of Eighteen pounds 11 shilling and 4 pence with legal interest from 5 Sept. 1801 until paid. Secures with furniture, cattle and household effects. To be sold after 1 October. Wit: WALLER REDD. Signed: BENJAMIN DILLEN. Proved: 26 July 1802.

Pages 382-383. 29 Mar. 1802. Received of JOHN REDD Sixteen pounds one shilling four pence leaving a balance due him on a settlement and in order to secure the same to him I give the following: 1 yoke oxen, oxen cart and cattle. Wit: WALLER REDD. Signed: AUGUSTINE WOODLIFF. Proved: 26 July 1802.

Pages 383-384. 27 Jan. 1802. Deed of Trust. WILLIAM CRUM of Henry County to WILLIAM GRATSY of Pittsylvania County...in order to secure the payment of Seventeen pounds six shillings nine pence due to DAVID PANNILL of Pittsylvania County by note gives deed to WILLIAM GRATSY as follows: the land in Henry County whereon WILLIAM CRUM now lives, joins JOSEPH BARRINGTON, JOSEPH JONES and GEORGE HAIRSTON by estimate 243 acres. If the debt is not paid by 1 May 1803, the land to be sold to the highest bidder. Wit: JOHN CARTER, EDWARD JABY, JACOB REIGER, SR., RICHARD REIGER. Signed: WILLIAM (X) CRUM. Proved: 26 May 1802.

Page 384. 28 May 1802. SARAH WATSON, JOHN W. WATSON, THOMAS H. WATSON, MARY ANN WATSON, HENRY S. WATSON of Henry County to WILLIAM HEATH of Campbell County, town of Lynchburg, for a certain sum sells land in Henry County on the waters of Horsepasture Creek, reference to the patent will show issued to Doct. JOHN WATSON 20 Mar. 1801 for 102½ acres. Wit: WILLIAM FRENCH, JOHN BAILEY, JOHN (X) TRAVIS, JOSIAH LEAK, PINES ALLEN. Signed: SARAH WATSON, JOHN W. WASON, THOMAS H. WATSON, MARY ANN WATSON, HENRY S. WATSON. Proved: 26 July 1802.

Page 385. 28 May 1802. SARAH WATSON, JOHN W. WATSON, THOMAS H. WATSON, MARY ANN WATSON and HENRY S. WATSON of Henry County to JOHN BAILEY for value received land on the waters of Jourdon Creek joins HENRY DILLEN'S first and second survey lines... no acreage given. Wit: WILLIAM FRENCH, JOHN TRAVIS (X), PINES ALLEN, JOSIAH LEAK. Signed: SARAH WATSON, JOHN W. WATSON, THOMAS H. WATSON, MARY ANN WATSON, HENRY S. WATSON. Proved: 26 July 1802.

Pages 386-387. 26 July 1802. GEORGE HAIRSTON of Henry County to JOHN PRICE of the same for Forty pounds sells land on the waters of Matrimony Creek, the said tract surveyed 5 April 1798 and by that survey 394 acres. No wit. Signed: GEORGE HAIRSTON. Proved: 26 July 1802.

Pages 387-388. 24 July 1802. KINNEY MCKINNEY for the love and affection he bears unto JEAN HENSLEY, LEWIS HENSLEY, JOHN HENSLEY, PATSEY HENSLEY the children of my wife PHEBEY MCKINNEY gives unto them the following: to JEAN HENSLEY one negro wench named Mary to PATSY HENSLEY two negros Alsey and Edmund. All my household furniture that may remain after my and my present wifes deaths and when all my just debts are paid then to be divided equally between JEAN HENSLEY and PATSY HENSLEY. Unto LEWIS HENSLEY and JOHN HENSLEY all that part of my land that layeth below the dividing lines with the Ridge Path, WILLIAM HOLT, DANIEL SMITH, and all of my stock. I give unto MARK MCKINNEY and THOMAS MCKINNEY the upper tract of my land joining JOHN WALLER when they arrived at 21 years. I give unto my daughter MARY VAUGHAN one shilling. Wit: ABEL WILLIS, THOMAS WILLIS, JOHN WALLER. Signed: KINNEY (X) MCKINNEY. Proved: 26 July 1802.

Pages 388-389. 28 Aug. 1802. Deed of Trust. WILLIAM C. REA to JOHN ROWLAND, JR. REA is indebted to GEORGE HAIRSTON in the amount of Seventy five pounds, secures with all his cattle, furniture, kitchen utensils, guns etc. Wit: THOMAS WILLIAMS, JR., WILLIAM DILLION, JR., SAMUEL STAPLES. Signed: WILLIAM C. REA, JOHN ROWLAND, JR. Proved: 30 Aug. 1802.

Pages 389-390. 14 July 1802. Deed of Trust. BARNABA WELLS to SAMUEL CALLAND of Pittsylvania County - debt Seventy pounds four shillings four pence, the amount of three bonds. Secures with: 100 acres of land whereon he now lives and bought of HENRY CLARK, deeded by Gen. JOSEPH MARTIN, as deed will more fully appear. Due 25 Dec. 1805. Wit: JOHN CALLAND, WILLIAM CALLAND, HARTWELL ALLEN. Signed: BARNABA WELLS. Proved: 30 Aug. 1802.

Pages 390-391. 25 Feb. 1802. Deed of Trust. NATHAN

HARRIS of Patrick County to THOMAS JARVIS of Henry County - debt Twelve pounds four pence secures with a horse, cattle and other personal property. Wit: CHARLES HIBBERT, ELIZABETH (X) JARVIS, NANCY (X) JARVIS. Signed: NATHAN HARRIS. Proved: 27 Sept. 1802.

Pages 391-393. 7 Feb. 1802. WILLIAM FRENCH of Henry County to AUGUSTINE THOMAS of Patrick County to secure debts. (1) To PETER SCALES of Patrick County in the amount of $261.36, which PETER SCALES paid JOHN REDD to discharge WILLIAM FRENCH'S land and store dealings with him the said JOHN REDD. (2) $338.64 which this day hath WILLIAM FRENCH received from PETER SCALES by way of a loan. Makes a total of $600.00. Secures eith: land in Henry County on both sides of Horsepasture Creek, it being the tract whereon WILLIAM FRENCH now lives, 400 acres more or less. Debt due 25 Dec. next. Wit: JOSEPH SCALES, RICHARD MILLS, WILLIAM HUTCHESON. Signed: WILLIAM FRENCH, AUGUSTINE THOMAS. Proved: 27 Feb. 1802.

Page 393. No date. Received of WILLIAM FRENCH One hundred eighty four pounds siteen shillings and nine pence in full discharge of the within mentioned sum of $600.00 and interest. I hereby release the said WILLIAM FRENCH from the above claim. 1 Jan. 1803. Wit: WALLER REDD, THOMAS (X) CHANDLER. Signed: AUGUSTINE THOMAS, PETER SCALES.

Page 394. No date. Justices of Campbell County, Virginia. WILLIAM HEATH conveyed 100 acres to JOHN FRENCH of Henry County and JOHN FRENCH conveyed said land to WILLIAM SHARP of Dinwiddie County, town of Petersburg. SALLY B. HEATH, the wife of WILLIAM HEATH, releases her right of dower to the above. Proved: 25 Oct. 1802.

Page 395. 25 Oct. 1802. WILLIAM CUNNINGHAM and POLLY CUNNINGHAM his wife of Pittsylvania County to WILLIAM BARNTON of Henry County for Twenty six pouns sells land in Henry County on the waters of the Rocky fork of Sandy River, 100 acres it being the land formerly owned by JOHN MITCHELL and BENJAMIN MITCHELL his son and CRAIN. Wit: JOSEPH THOMAS, WILLIAM (X) CRUM, MEREDITH ROBINSON. Signed: WILLIAM CUNNINGHAM. Proved: 25 Oct. 1802.

Page 396. 26 Apr. 1802. Bill of Sale. LUKE ADAMS of Henry County to RANDOLPH ADAMS of the same for the sum of Eighty two pounds nine pence sells: 1 mare, 3 colts, 15 hogs, 1 trunk, 1 chest, 2 featherbeds and furniture, 3 potts, 2 dishes, 9 plates, 1 set knives and forks, 2 tables, 5 head cattle, 2 saddles, 1 iron kettle, 2 basons, 2 tubs, 1 pale, 3 piggins and a parcel of tobacco about 2500#, 1 flat iron. Wit: GEORGE WALLER, JR., WILLIAM WALLER, JOHN SALMON, JR. Signed: LUKE ADAMS. Proved: 25 Oct.1802.

Page 396. 6 Sept. 1802. Power of Attorney. JAMES HUNT of Henry County appoints EDWARD NUNNELY to sell and convey land in Hallifax County on the heads of the Childry and Runway Creeks. Wit: JAMES LYELL, JAMES JOHNSTON, THOMAS DICKERSON. Signed: JAMES HUNT. Proved: 25 Oct. 1802.

Page 397. No date. DAVID HARBOUR of Partick County to THOMAS HARBOUR of Henry County for the sum of $1.00 conveys all right and title he has to a certain tract of land in Henry County on the head branches of Fall Creek and Marrowbone Creek, by survey 239 acres, joins DAVID WITT. Wit: BENJAMIN (X) MOORE, THOMAS JAMESON, SR., DAVID MOORE. Signed: DAVID HARBOUR. Proved: 29 Nov. 1802.

Page 398. 24 Nov. 1802. ADRIN ANGLIN and SARAH ANGLIN his wife of Henry County to ELISHA WILLIAMS of Charlotte County for Fourty three pounds ten shillings sells land on Grassey fork of Leatherwood Creek, 400 acres, joins GEORGE HAIRSTON, NICHOLAS AIKEN, JOSEPH GRAVELY and JOSEPH GRAVELY, JR. Signed: ADRIN ANGLIN, SARAH ANGLIN. Proved: 29 Nov. 1802.

Pages 399-400. 29 Nov. 1802. GEORGE HAIRSTON of Henry County to THOMAS WILSON, JR. of the same for Fifty pounds sells 297 acres on Turkey Cock Creek joins GEORGE GILLEY and WILSON'S own land. No wit. Signed: GEORGE HAIRSTON. Proved: 29 Nov.1802.

Pages 400-401. 29 Nov. 1802. SAMUEL ELLIOTT of Henry County to GEORGE HAIRSTON of the same for One hundred twenty pounds sells all that mesuage, plantation and tract of land on the branches of Muster Branch of Leatherwood Creek 200 acres by patent joins GEORGE RUNNOLD and WILLIAM BARNARD. Signed: SAMUEL ELLIOTT. Proved: 29 Nov. 1802. . . .POLLEY ELLIOTT, wife of SAMUEL ELLIOTT releases her right of dower.

Pages 401-402. 9 Nov. 1802. ROBERT PEDIGO, SENR. and PHEBE PEDIGO his wife of Henry County to HENRY HEFFLEFINGER of the same for Twenty five pounds seventeen shillings sells land on the waters of Talbert Creek, 43 1/8 acres. Wit: JOSEPH

ALEXANDER, JOHN ALEXANDER, THOMAS DIX. Signed: ROBERT PEDIGO, SR. Proved: 29 Nov. 1802. . . .PHEBE PEDIGO released dower rights.

Pages 402-403. 27 Dec. 1802. INGRAM ALEXANDER of Henry County to JAMES DYER of the same for One hundred forty four pounds three shillings sells land on the waters of Leatherwood Creek, by survey 120 1/8 acre joins SAMUEL SUTHERLAND. Signed: INGRAM ALEXANDER. Proved: 27 Dec. 1802.

Pages 403-404. 27 Dec. 1802. THOMAS ALEXANDER of Henry County to JOHN ALEXANDER of the same for Two hundred pounds three shillings sells land on the waters of Smith River, it being part of the Grey order contains 157 acres by survey, joins JOSEPH MARTIN where Grays order line crosses Graves Road to THOMAS GRAVES. Signed: THOMAS ALEXANDER. Proved: 27 Dec. 1802.

Pages 404-405. 27 Dec. 1802. Bond of GEORGE HAIRSTON who is appointed Sherif 29 Aug. 1801 and shall collect, account for and pay revenue tax to the Treasurer of the Commonwealth for the year 1802. Bondsman: JOHN ALEXANDER. Proved: 27 Dec. 1802.

Page 405. No date. JOHN KING, SENR. of Rockingham County, North Carolina paid by his son-in-law HENRY MCKINNEY of Rockingham County, North Carolina for all what is coming to me from my father-in-law SAMUEL LANIER, deceased. Wit: GARROT WILLIAMS, EPHRAIM WILLIAMS, DAVID WILLIAMS. Signed: JOHN KING, SENR. Proved: 27 Dec. 1802.

Pages 405-407. 5 Oct. 1802. Deed of Trust. THOMAS H. WATSON to JOHN FRENCH. To make secure and safe JOHN TRAVIS the following judgments. (1) Nineteen pounds nineteen shillings. (2) Thirteen pounds four shillings ten pence, a total of Thirty seven pounds eleven shillings 1 pence includes judgment cost and Sherif commission with legal interest from 24th Aug. last which WILLIAM SHARP Assignee of JOHN FRENCH recovered. The said JOHN TRAVIS security (of J. H. WATSON) on two bonds. To JOHN FRENCH all that portion of the undivided tract that JOHN WATSON died seized of contains 1280 acres on both sides of Horsepasture Creek, the portion that will come to WATSON will be 420 acres. To be sold after 1st Jan. next or as much as will satisfy the debt. Wit: HENRY LYNE, JOHN COX, FLEMING COX. Signed: THOMAS H. WATSON. Proved: 27 Dec. 1802.

Pages 407-408. 12 Jan. 1803. JOHN KING and MARY KING his wife of Henry County to FRANCIS DEGRAFFINREID for a certain sum sells 100 acres on the south waters of Leatherwood Creek, joins Col. GEORGE HAIRSTON, WILLIAM SIMSON, WILLIAM ROBERTS, Capt. NORTH- CUT and Capt. SAMUEL MARSHALL. Wit: WILLIAM DEGRAFFEN- REID, JOHN DEGRAFFENREID, FRANCIS NORTHCUTT. Signed: JOHN KING, MARY KING. Proved: 31 Jan. 1803.

Pages 408-409. No date. MARTEL LESUEUR appoints JOHN LESUEUR of Charlotte County my attor- ney to recover all monies due me and recover all per- sonal estate that is or may be my right. Wit: JOHN ROWLAND, JR., WASHINGTON ROWLAND. Signed: MARTEL LESUEUR. Proved: 31 Jan. 1803.

Pages 409-410. 31 Jan. 1803. THOMAS H. WATSON to JOHN COX, trustee for CARR WALLER. WATSON is indebted to WALLER in the amount of $51.00 from 10 Nov. last, secures with his portion of his father's estate (land) his portion to be 420 acres. Debt due 1 March next. Signed: THOMAS H. WATSON. Proved: 31 Jan. 1803.

Pages 410-411. 28 Feb. 1803. JOHN JONES of Henry County to THOMAS JONES of the same for One hundred fifty pounds sells land on the waters of Leatherwood Creek 141 acres joins LOMAX & Company and crosses a fork of Suck Egg. Signed: JOHN JONES. Proved: 28 Feb. 1803. . . .DOLLEY JONES, wife of JOHN JONES, releases her right of dower.

Pages 411-413. 1 Dec. 1802. Deed of Trust. WILLIAM FRENCH to STANWIX HORD, GEORGE WALLER, JR. and WILLIAM WALLER, Trustees for JOHN REDD. WILLIAM FRENCH hat executed to JOHN REDD bonds for Two hundred fourteen pounds sixteen shillings nine pence payable 1 Sept. next secures with: land on Horsepas- ture Creek where he now lives 300 acres more or less. Wit: WALLER REDD, JOHN COX, JOHN STAPLES. Signed: WILLIAM FRENCH. Proved: 28 Feb. 1803.

Pages 413-414. 25 Feb. 1803. GEORGE WALLER, JR. to JOHN WALLER all of Henry County for Sixty pounds sells land on the south side of Smith River a tract of 182 acres joins COLE and SALMONS. No wit. Signed: GEORGE WALLER, JR. Proved: 3 Mar. 1803.

Pages 414-415. 26 Mar. 1803. JUNOR MEREDITH of Henry County to ELIJAH MEREDITH of the same for Fifty pound sells 100 acres more or less on both sides of Big Reedy Creek joins STEPHEN KING and JOHN PYRTLE. Wit: STEPHEN KING, JESSE MAUPIN, JOSEPH (X) MEREDITH. Signed: JUNOR (X) MEREDITH. Proved: 28 Mar. 1803.

Pages 415-416. 28 Mar. 1803. HENRY LYNE of Henry County to THOMAS STARLING of the same for love and affection deeds all that tract on both sides of Ramseys Creek by estimate 550 acres, Buck Branch and joins the land where HENRY LYNE lives. No wit. Signed: HENRY LYNE. Proved: 28 Mar. 1803.

Pages 416-417. No date. DANIEL SMITH for the love and goodwill he has towards his three sons JAMES SMITH, PETER SMITH and JOHN SMITH deeds land on Butrum Town Creek whereon the said SMITH now lives contains by new and part of the old survey 372 acres. Wit: JEREMIAH TURNER, JAMES RANDALS, LEWIS ROSS. Signed: DANIEL SMITH. Proved: 28 Mar. 1803.

Pages 417-418. 5 Nov. 1794. PATRICK HENRY of Charlotte County to MARTHA FONTAINE of Henry County for the natural love and affection he has for his daughter and in consideration of the said MARTHA FONTAINE paying off and discharging all debts due and owing from the estate of EDWARD HENRY, deceased, grant all land in Henry County whereof the said EDWARD HENRY died seized of, the said EDWARD HENRY being the son of PATRICK HENRY and dying intestate without a wife or child. The land hereby conveyed became vested by Law to PATRICK HENRY. Wit: N. W. DANDRIDGE, JR., PATRICK H. FONTAINE, BYRD BROWN. Signed: PATRICK HENRY. Proved: 28 May 1798 & 13 Dec. 1803.

Pages 418-419. 28 Mar. 1803. MARTHA FONTAINE of Henry County to JOSEPH HOPSON of the same for the sum of Seven hundred two pounds sells land on the south side of Leatherwood Creek, by estimate to be 936 acres more or less joins FONTAINE and HENRY. Wit: NATHANIEL W. DANDRIDGE, HUGH NIESLER, WILLIAM HALE. Signed: MARTHA FONTAINE. Proved: 28 Mar. 1803.

Page 420. 25 Nov. 1796. EDWARD ADAMS appoints JONADAB WADE attorney to make REUBEN WADE a right of indenture of, in and to a parcel of land in Henry County formerly belonging to JOHN WILBOURN, deceased. (ADAMS brought a suit in Henry County against the heirs of the said WILBOURN, deceased). Wit: PETER LEAKE, JOEL WITT. Signed: EDWARD ADAMS.

Proved: 28 Mar. 1803.

Pages 420-421. 25 Mar. 1803. JONADAB WADE, attorney for EDWARD ADAMS to REUBEN WADE for the sum of Seventy four pounds sells land on Marrowbone Creek 100 acres more or less joins GEORGE HAIRSTON, THOMAS STOVALL, deceased and ALEXANDER MOORE. Wit: JOHN CHRISTIAN, JOHN MULLINS, WILLIAM MORRIS, PETER LEAKE. Signed: JONADAB WADE. Proved: 28 Mar. 1803.

Page 421. 8 Mar. 1803. Bill of Sale. ANN STANLEY sells to REUBEN WADE five negroes: Phill, Harry, Phillis, Stephen and Luce for the sum $100.00 together with his obligation for my ample support during my lifetime. Wit: JOHN MULLINS, WILLIAM MORRIS. Signed: ANN (X) STANLEY. Proved: 28 Mar. 1803.

Page 422. 5 Jan. 1803. Lease. ANDREW DONALD of Bedford County to ARCHIBALD MORRIS and GEORGE MORRIS of Henry County to let and to farm for 7 years all that cleared land on Horsepasture Creek which was leased to and occupied by ARCHIBALD MORRIS last year. Now to ARCHIBALD MORRIS and GEORGE MORRIS with priveledge of clearing not more than 30,000 tobacco hills each year, not to clear the lowland outside the fence, will not cut timber fit for rails or boards, will put plants and future clearings under a sound rail fence 5 ft. high and divide into 4 or more fields by similar fences also agree to sow on the land the fall previous to expiration of the lease 21½ bu. of rye and allow DONALD to sow the same amount of grain on the land at the usual time. Likewise to deliver at the expiration of the lease 7 bu. wheat, 87½ bu. oats, 84 ft. corn tops, 1 cock of blades, 21 hogs 1 yr. old, 21 pigs 3 mos. old and 4 sows 4 yrs. old. To REUBEN WADE while employed in repairing the house with provisions and to move the shingles in place. Also to pay unto ANDREW DONALD or assignee an annual rent of 5,250# net of Lynchburg crop inspected tobacco prized in hogsheads weighing at least 1200 # each and to be paid 1 January of each year. MORRIS agrees that he will not cultivate any of the ground 2 sucessive years in Indian Corn. Wit: REUBEN WADE, THOMAS S. HILL, FARRAR MORRIS. Signed: ANDREW DONALD, ARCHIBALD MORRIS, GEORGE MORRIS. Proved: 28 Mar. 1803.

Page 423. 25 Mar. 1803. PETER LEAKE of Henry County to JOHN CHRISTIAN of the same for Sixty pounds sells 68½ acres joins JOHN WALLER and JORDON. Wit: JOHN WALLER, WILLIAM WALLER. Signed: PETER LEAKE.

Proved: 28 Mar. 1803.

Page 424. 25 Feb. 1803. JOSEPH MARTIN, SENR. to AMBROSE EDWARDS both of Henry County for the sum of Two hundred two pounds sells by estimate 362 acres on the branches of Leatherwood, joins the Leatherwood Road. No wit. Signed: JOSEPH MARTIN. Proved: 28 Mar. 1803.

Page 425. No date. JOSEPH MARTIN of Henry County to ARCHELAUS HUGHES of the same for Sixty eight pounds sells by survey 300 acres, joins the Road above the Mill. No wit. Signed: JOSEPH MARTIN. Proved: 28 May 1803.

Page 426. No date. Inquisition ordered and taken 15 March 1803 to summon and empower a Jury at the plantation of ARIS VAUGHAN on Reed Creek to ascertain damages that VAUGHAN would sustain by a road going through his land. Jury: JOHN JAMISON, CARR WALLER, JOHN CAHILL, STEPHEN KING, JOHN HOMES, JUNOR MEREDITH, JAMES HOWARD, WILLIAM HEARD, SHADRACK DENT, WILLIAM WARREN, ISHAM NANCE, JAMES MURPHEY declare damages would be Thirteen pounds ten shillings. Proved: 28 Mar. 1803.

Page 427. 25 April 1803. WILLIAM MILLS and ELIZABETH MILLS his wife to JOSHUA HOPPER sells for the sum of $300.00 100 acres more or less on the waters of Matrimony Creek joins ELIJAH SAMS. No wit. Signed: WILLIAM MILLS, ELIZABETH MILLS. Proved: 25 Apr. 1803.

Page 428. 25 Apr. 1803. JOHN COX of Henry County to JOSEPH COX of the same for the love and affection he bears unto his son deeds that divident, tract or parcel of land on the waters of Ramseys Creek by estimate 50 acres more or less, joins Mountain Road, Col. HENRY LYNE and is the upper part of the tract where JOHN COX now lives. No wit. Signed: JOHN COX. Proved: 25 Apr. 1803.

Pages 429-430. 23 Apr. 1803. SAMUEL MARSHALL, WILLIAM TOOMBS and JOHN WILLS to DENNIS LARK all of Henry County for the sum of One hundred pounds sells three tracts 1) SAMUEL MARSHALL conveys 7 acres 2) WILLIAM TOOMBS conveys 89 acres and 3) JOHN WILLS 4 acres. Wit: GEORGE WALLER, JR., MARKHAM LOVELL. Signed: SAMUEL MARSHALL, WILLIAM (X) TOOMBS, JOHN WILLS. Proved: 25 Apr. 1803.

Pages 430-431. 27 Jan. 1803. BRICE MARTIN of Henry County to WILLIAM MARTIN of the same for the sum of Thirty seven pounds sells by estimate 50 acres on the waters of Grassy Creek joins GREEN BOULDIN and JOHN SALMON. No wit. Signed: BRICE MARTIN. Proved: 25 Apr. 1803.

Pages 431-432. 18 Apr. 1803. THOMAS JAMISON and ANN JAMISON his wife of Henry County to ABRAHAM MAYSE of the same for the sum of Fifty two pounds ten shillings sells 100 acres more or less on the south branches of Marrowbone Creek joins GEORGE HAIRSTON, WILLIAM JENKINS and GOODWIN MAYSE, the land now in the possession of ABRAHAM MAYSE. Wit: DAVID (X) MAYSE, ISAAC (X) MAYSE, THOMAS HARBOUR. Signed: THOMAS JAMISON, ANN JAMISON. Proved: 25 Apr. 1803.

Pages 432-433. 25 Apr. 1803. WILLIAM STEPHENS, SENR. of Henry County to WILLIAM STEPHENS, JR. of the same for One hundred pounds sells land on the east side of Home Creek by estimate 166 acres joins lines of JOHN STEPHENS and NATHANIEL DURHAM. No wit. Signed: WILLIAM STEPHENS, SR. Proved: 25 Apr. 1803.

Pages 433-434. No date. JOHN SALMON for the natural love and affection he bears his son JOHN SALMON, JR., reserving for myself and my wife ELIZABETH SALMON during our natural life the same rights and priveledges as we now enjoy deed the lands hereafter described, also my son JOHN SALMON, JR. will pay unto my grandson OBADIAH SALMON, son of THADEUS SALMON, deceased, Thirty three and one third dollars when he arrives at 21 years of age. Should OBADIAH SALMON die before then the sum to be divided between my grandsons GEORGE SALMON and JOHN SALMON sons of THADEUS SALMON. The land is 200 acres more or less joins GEORGE WALLER, JOHN WALLER and HENRY LYNE, presently LEWIS FRANKLIN and HENRY LYNE'S Mill seat. No wit. Signed: JOHN SALMON. Proved: 25 Apr. 1803.

Pages 434-435. 23 Apr. 1803. JAMES REA, SENR. of Henry County to JOHN REA for the sum of One hundred pounds sells by estimate 100 acres (part of 400 acres purchased of ROBERTSON) joins P. GARLAND. No wit. Signed: JAMES REA, SENR. Proved: 25 Apr. 1803.

Pages 435-436. 18 Apr. 1803. JAMES DYER of Henry County to JOSEPH MULLINS of the same for Thirty four pounds sells by survey 66 acres on the waters of Leatherwood Creek it being the tract purchased of JONATHAN STONE, joins JESSE DELOZEAR, NICHOLAS AKIN. Wit: BARNA WELLS, MEREDITH PEARSON, SAMUEL SUTHERLAND. Signed: JAMES DYER. Proved: 25 Apr. 1803.

Pages 436-437. 12 Mar. 1803. FREDERICK HUTCHENS of Stokes County, North Carolina to THOMAS CHILDRESS of Henry County for $100.00 sells 67 acres on the South Mayo River joins JOHN DILLARD, HENRY FEE and BALLINGER WADE. Wit: JESSE ATKISSON, SENR., JESSE ATKISSON, JR. Signed: FREDERICK (X) HUTCHENS. Proved: 25 Apr. 1803.

Pages 437-438. 25 Apr. 1803. GEORGE F. HARRIS of Henry County to WILLIAM HARRIS of the same for Twenty five pounds sells 91 acres on the waters of Cascade Creek...lines: WILLIAM STEPHENS, Meeting House Branch, JOHN HAMMOND, NATHANIEL DURHAM. No wit. Signed: GEORGE F. HARRIS. Proved: 25 Apr. 1803.

Page 438. 23 Apr. 1803. GEORGE F. HARRIS of Pittsylvania County to AARON F. HARRIS for the sum of One hundred pounds sells land (no acreage) on the head branches of Fall Creek joins BARNET, DICKERSON and CLAY. No wit. Signed: GEORGE F. HARRIS. Proved: 25 Apr. 1803.

Page 439. 9 Apr. 1803. AMBROSE WHITE and SALLY WHITE his wife of Stokes County, North Carolina to THOMAS CHILDRESS of Henry County for $65.00 sells 75 acres on the south fork of the Mayo River joins HENRY FRANCE, now in the possession of THOMAS CHILDRESS. Wit: WILLIAM DODSON, SOLOMAN ATKISSON, FRANCIS BUNDREN. Signed: AMBROSE (X) WHITE. Proved: 25 Apr. 1803.

Page 440. 25 Apr. 1803. FRANCIS GILLEY and MARY GILLEY his wife to DUDLEY STEPHENS for the sum of Thirty pounds sells land on the waters of Leatherwood Creek, the tract contains 674 acres by survey but they are selling only 300 acres to DUDLEY STEPHENS. Wit: JAMES BARNS, AUG. HEWLETT, CRASSEY KEY. Signed: FRANCIS GILLEY, MARY GILLEY. Proved: 25 Apr. 1803.

Page 441. 26 Mar. 1803. JOHN STONE of Henry County to BARTLET WADE of the same for the sum of One Hundred pounds sells 100 acres more or less on Rock Run Creek joins Davis Branch, JAMES BAKER, ISHAM CRADOCK, HENRY SUMPTER (now GEORGE HAIRSTON). Wit:

JESSE CARTER, JAMES BAKER, SENR., JAMES BAKER, JR., JAMES SMITH. Signed: JOHN STONE. Proved: 25 Apr. 1803.

Page 442. 23 Apr. 1803. BALLENGER WADE of Henry County to PEARCE WADE of the same gives and grants by estimate 250 acres more or less joining JESSE WITT, MCCRAW and RANDOLPH & Company. No wit. Signed: BALLENGER WADE. Proved: 25 Apr. 1803.

Pages 442-443. 23 Apr. 1803. GEORGE TAYLOR of Henry County to JOHN TAYLOR of the same does hereby give and grant by estimate 50 acres on the North Mayo River joins JAMES TAYLOR. Wit: BALLENGER WADE, WILLIAM FEE, JOSIAH TAYLOR. Signed: GEORGE TAYLOR. Proved: 25 Apr. 1803.

Pages 443-444. 20 Apr. 1803. PRESLEY SIMPSON of Henry County to ADRION ANGLIN of the same for the sum of Thirty three pounds sells 100 acres more or less on the branches of Fishing Fork of Leatherwood Creek joins SAMUEL ANGLIN, Gen. MARTIN, JORDON and THOMASSON. No wit. Signed: PRESLEY (X) SIMPSON. Proved: 25 Apr. 1803.

Page 444. 6 Nov. 1798. JAMES CLAYBROOK of Henry County to DAVID ALEXANDER of the same sells 154 acres on the draughts of Toeclout Creek joins WILLIAM JAMES. (No value stated.) Wit: JAMES FITZ-GERALD, ROBERT STRONG, ELISHA ALEXANDER. Signed: JAMES CLAYBROOK. Proved: 29 Apr. 1799 & 26 Apr. 1803.

Pages 445-446. 30 May 1803. WILLIAM BAYSE of Henry County to THOMAS WILKINS of the same for the sum of Ninety pounds sells land on the waters of Cascade Creek being 178 acres joins Gibsons branch, GEORGE F. HARRIS and JOSEPH AMBROSE. No wit. Signed: WILLIAM (X) BAYSE. Proved: 30 May 1803.

Page 446. 30 May 1803. THOMAS WILKINS of Henry County to THOMAS FOSTER of the same for the sum of One hundred pounds sells 86 acres exclusive of 52 acres heretofore conveyed on the waters of Leatherwood Creek. No wit. Signed: THOMAS (X) WILKINS. Proved: 30 May 1803.

Pages 447-448. 30 May 1803. ROBERT PEDIGO of Henry County to Col. GEORGE HAIRSTON of the same for the sum of $470.00 paid to HENRY LYNE for WILLIAM GARDNER for land the said ROBERT PEDIGO purchased of WILLIAM GARDNER at the head of the Smith

River, also Twenty five pounds to HENRY PEDIGO and
Sixteen pounds to ROBERT PEDIGO, SENR., likewise
Twelve pounds to JOHN DAVIS, the tract on Camp Branch
and Rock Run of Leatherwood Creek joins lines of
JAMES HOWARD, REUBEN NANCE, Conway's old spring branch,
LOMAX & Company and EPHRIAM GORDER, the tract is 900
acres. No wit. Signed: ROBERT PEDIGO. Proved: 30
May 1803.

Pages 448-449. 17 Jan. 1803. DAVID MEADE RANDOLPH
of the city of Richmond the surviving
partner of BENJAMIN HARRISON, deceased and DAVID M.
RANDOLPH to JOSEPH MARTIN for the sum of Four hundred
Eighty pounds to the said DAVID MEADE RANDOLPH and
CARTER B. HARRISON executor of BENJAMIN HARRISON, JR.
conveyed land in Henry County 1,038 acres more or less
it being the remainder of the last tract conveyed in
a Deed of Indenture bearing the date 15 Feb. 1793
from THOMAS LOMAX and other to BENJAMIN HARRISON
received in General Court of the Commonwealth of
Virginia and is 1,338 acres, deed will give boundries.
3,000 acres to ROBERT STOCKTON which leaves a balance
of 1,038 acres to JOSEPH MARTIN. Wit: GEORGE WALLER,
JR., CHARLES FOSTER, BENJAMIN COOK, JOHN FULKERSON,
GREENSVILLE PENN, BENJAMIN JONES. Signed: DAVID M.
RANDOLPH and for BENJAMIN HARRISON. Proved: 27 June
1803.

Pages 449-450. 27 Dec. 1802. HENRY L. WATSON to
JOHN FRENCH, his portion of the land
on Horsepasture Creek (1200 acres his father JOHN
WATSON died seized of and whereon his widow and relict now lives)..he secures a debt to CHARLES FODRELL
of Nine pounds nine pence with interest, with his
portion of the land that will come to him. Debt due
27 April ensuing. Wit: THOMAS H. WATSON, WILLIAM
FRENCH, HENRY CLARK. Signed: HENRY L. WATSON, JOHN
FRENCH. Proved: 27 June 1803.

Pages 450-451. No date. JOHN JONES and DOROTHY JONES
his wife of Henry County to JOHN
GRIGGS, SENR. for the sum of One hundred thirty pounds
sells 204 acres on both sides of the south fork of
Sandy River it being land granted to NICHOLAS DANIEL
1 March 1781. Wit: D. LANIER, JOHN MINTER, JAMES
GRIGGS. Signed: JOHN JONES, DOROTHY JONES.

Pages 451-452. 5 Jan. 1803. Legatees of INGRAM NUNN,
deceased have settled with SANFORD
REAMEY and have received a negro woman and child named
Biddy and Ned in full as legatees of INGRAM NUNN, de-

ceased. Wit: THOMAS EAST. Signed: WATERS NUNN, WILLIAM J. PACE, THOMAS NUNN, WILLIAM NUNN, LANGSTON PACE, INGRAM ALEXANDER. Proved: 27 June 1803.

Page 452. 1 June 1803. Bond of GEORGE HAIRSTON. The Coroner, HENRY LYNE hath in his hands of the Estate of JOHN KING one negro boy named Reuben as mentioned in an order of sail (sic) in favour of GEORGE HAIRSTON of Sixty four pounds nineteen shillings and ten pence. GEORGE HAIRSTON will indemnify the said Cornonor HENRY LYNE against all claims that might occur of his selling the said negro to satisfy GEORGE HAIRSTON'S order of sail (sic). Wit: HENRY CLARK, THOMAS GRATSY. Signed: GEORGE HAIRSTON. Proved: 27 June 1803.

Pages 452-453. 27 Aug. 1802. PHILLIP RYAN, SENR. of Henry County to PHILLIP RYAN, JR. of the same for the sum of Two hundred and fifty pounds sells a tract of land on the waters of Leatherwood Creek 200 acres more or less, including all land PHILLIP RYAN purchased of ROBERT STOCKTON with all houses, fences, etc. joins lines of GEORGE HAIRSTON. Wit: ABIJAH HUGHES, JOSEPH ALEXANDER, THOMAS DIX. Signed: PHILIP RYAN. Proved: 27 June 1803. . . .The said PHILLIP RYAN and OBEDIENCE RYAN his wife, to have the said land without molestation whatsoever during their lives and PHILLIP RYAN, JR. is not to settle anyone else on the said land.

Pages 453-454. 30 May 1803. WILLIAM DEGRAFFENRIED to ARCHIBALD PARKERSON of Henry County for Fifty pounds sells 203 acres on the branches of the fishing fork and Grassy fork of Leatherwood Creek joins RICHARDSON, AIKEN, SIMPSON and PROCTOR. Wit: WILLIAM ROBERTS, BAZEL BURCH, JOSHUA PROCKTOR. Signed: WILLIAM DEGRAFFENRIED. Proved: 29 Aug. 1803.

Pages 454-455. 29 Aug. 1803. GEORGE REYNOLDS of Pittsylvania County to RICHARD REYNOLDS of Henry County for the sum of Fifty pounds sells land on the head of the Bold Branch of Leatherwood Creek 469 acres joins WILLIAM BARNARD. Wit: EDWARD HARRIS, PERMANAS WILLIAMS, BENNETT WILLIAMS. Signed: GEORGE REYNOLDS. Proved: 29 Aug. 1803.

Pages 455-456. 9 Aug. 1803. THOMAS WILKINS of Henry County to JACOB SMITH of the same for Forty pounds sells 75 acres more or less on the waters of Cascade Creek joins AARON WILSON. No wit. Signed: THOMAS (X) WILKINS. Proved: 29 Aug. 1803.

Pages 456-457.   14 May 1803.   SAMUEL CALLAND of Pittsylvania County to THOMAS LINTHICUM of the same for One hundred fifty three pounds a tract of land in Henry County on Turkey Cock Creek 175 acres, joins JOHN CUNNINGHAM, EDWARD SMITH'S old line. Wit: THOMAS GRATSY, HARTWILL ALLEN. Signed: SAMUEL CALLAND. Proved: 27 June 1803 & 29 Aug. 1803.

Pages 457-458.   11 Aug. 1803.   JOSHUA PROCTOR and CHARITY PROCTOR his wife to THOMAS DIX of Henry County and DAVID PANNILL of Pittsylvania County. JOSHUA PROCTOR is indebted to DAVID PANNILL by judgment in Henry County Curt (by a bond given BAZZEL BURCH for Fifteen pounds nineteen shillings and six pence dated 10th of this month with interest). Secures with land on the Middle fork of Leatherwood Creek by estimate 222 acres where PROCTOR now lives which land was deeded by SAMUEL JOHNSON to JOSHUA PROCTOR. This is due 25 December next. Wit: JOSEPH MARTIN, A. HUGHES, WILLIAM DESHAZO. Signed: JOSHUA (X) PROCTOR. Proved: 29 Aug. 1803.

Pages 458-459.   27 Oct. 1800.   BLIZARD MAGRUDER of Henry County to THOMAS EGGLETON of the same for Thirty Dollars by estimate 30 acres that joins the land of MICHAEL WATSON. Wit: ELEAS (X) THOMASON, PRESLEY (X) SIMPSON, SHADRACK MOORE. Signed: BLIZARD MAGRUDER. Proved: 23 Feb. 1801 certified 29 Aug. 1803.

Pages 459-460.   No date.   JOHN EAST for the love and affection he bears unto his son WILLIAM EAST deeds him one negro slave called Starling. Wit: JOHN PACE, JR., THOMAS (X) EAST, LEWIS LAMPKIN. Signed: JOHN (X) EAST.

Pages 460-461.   25 Jan. 1803.   ISABELLA KEY to WILLIAM HEWLETT Trustee for WILLIAM MITCHELL, executor of GEORGE KEY, deceased. She in indebted as follows: 1) note signed by ISABELLA KEY to FRANCIS COX 7 Jan. 1800 for Twenty four pounds seven shillings. 2) note for twelve pounds. 3) 1 hogshead of tobacco lent by WILLIAM MITCHELL $60.00. Secured with that part of the land which ISABELLA KEY possesses of GEORGE KEY, deceased and laid off as her dower, 1 negro man Manec, 1 woman Feby, 2 horses, 8 head cattle. Wit: THOMAS CHOWNING, AUGUSTON HEWLETT, L. MITCHELL. Signed: ISABELLA (X) KEY. Proved: 29 Aug. 1803.

Pages 461-462.   16 May 1803.   WILLIAM HORD of Hawkins County, Tennessee to GEORGE HAIRSTON of Henry County for the sum of Two hundred fity pounds sells land on the waters of Little Beaver Creek, 589 acres joins lines of GEORGE HAIRSTON to JAMES ANTHONY'S corner of a lot conveyed to Henry County. Wit: JOHN REDD, STANWIX HORD, MICHAEL HICKEY. Signed: WILLIAM HORD. Proved: 29 Aug. 1803. . . .Memorandum: GEORGE HAIRSTON is to give up any timber as shall be sufficient to improve 1 acre of land whereon ROBERT WILLIAMSON Store now stands to HENRY KOGER, was deeded to the said KOGER by WILLIAM HORD. Also any pine timber JOSEPH ANTHONY may want for his own use westward of an old path where WILLIAM POSEY lived and in the road making from Beaver Creek to Henry Courthouse. Signed: GEORGE HAIRSTON.

Page 463. 25 July 1803. Bond of WILLIAM HEARD who is to serve Henry County as Constable for a two year term. Bondsmen: JOHN CAHILL and JESSE HEARD.

Pages 463-464. 25 July 1803. Bond of WILLIAM MOORE who is appointed to serve as Constable for two years, bondsmen: GEORGE WALLER, JR. and JOHN COX.

Page 464. 25 July 1803. Bond of JOHN SALMON, JR. who is to serve as Constable for two years, bondsmen: JOHN SALMON, SENR., and JOHN COX.

Page 465. 25 July 1803. Bond of JOHN SMITH who is to serve as Constable for two years, bondsmen: JOHN CREASEY and ROBERT SMITH.

Page 466. 25 July 1803. Bond of WILLIAM L. COX who is to serve as Constable for two years, bondsmen: GEORGE HAIRSTON and DUDLEY (X) STEPHENS.

Pages 466-467. 25 July 1803. Bond of JAMES DYER who is to serve as Constable for two years, bondsmen: GEORGE HAIRSTON and GEORGE DYER.

Pages 467-468. 26 Sept. 1803. RICHARD REYNOLDS of Henry County to SAMUEL HIGGS of the same for the sum of Twenty one pounds sells 100 acres more or less on the waters of the Bold Branch of Leatherwood Creek. No wit. Signed: RICHARD REYNOLDS. Proved: 26 Sept. 1803.

Pages 468-469. 26 Sept. 1803. RICHARD REYNOLDS of Henry County to JAMES CLARK of the same for the sum of Thirty pounds sells and conveys 200 acres on the waters of Bold Branch of Leatherwood

Creek. No wit. Signed: RICHARD REYNOLDS. Proved: 26 Sept. 1803.

Pages 469-470. 19 Aug. 1803. JOSEPH GRAVELY and HEALING GRAVELY his wife of Henry County to ABRAM WILLIAMS of Pittsylvania County for the sum of Sixty seven pounds sells 100 acres on the branches of fishing fork of Leatherwood Creek joins lines of Col. G. HAIRSTON, Genl. JOSEPH MARTIN, SAMUEL ANGLIN, MICHAEL AKIN, on Grassy fork of Leatherwood Creek and ELISHA WILLIAMS line. Wit: ELISHA WILLIAMS, JOHN DAVIS, JOHN CONNAWAY. Signed: JOSEPH (X) GRAVELY. Proved: 26 Sept. 1803.

Pages 470-471. 6 Aug. 1803. Bill of Sale. PETER PERKINS to THOMAS BOULDIN & Company for the sum of One hundred fifty pounds sells two negros Charles 26 years of age and Bob 12 years of age. Wit: JOHN COX, ARCHD. (X) PHERIS (FARRIS??). Signed: PETER PERKINS. Proved: 26 Sept. 1803. . . . Memo: Be it remembered that if PETER PERKINS does pay THOMAS BOULDIN and Company Sixty nine pounds three shillings and five pence in space of 18 months with interest also agreed if PETER PERKINS delivers to THOMAS BOULDIN & Co. in the month of March next at Lynchburg a quantity of good merchantable bacon in the amount of One hundred thirty eight pounds, six shillings and ten pence then the Bill of Sale is void. Signed: THOMAS BOULDIN & CO.

Page 471. 26 Sept. 1803. Bond of MANION (MANNING) HILL, a Baptist Minister, is granted license to perform the rites of Matrimony. His security is JACOB FARRIS. Proved: 26 Sept. 1803.

Pages 471-472. 27 Sept. 1801. KINNEY MCKINNEY and PHEBE MCKINNEY his wife of Henry County to THOMAS BOULDIN for the sum of Fifty pounds sells by estimate 50 acres on the waters of Grassey Creek it being the tract that ARCHIBALD ROBERTSON conveyed to STEPHEN RENNO, joins lines of JOHN SIMMONS, JOHN HARDMAN. Wit: EDM. WALLER, THOMAS GRAVES, SIR JAMES BOULDING, GREEN BOULDIN. Signed: KINNEY MCKINNEY. Proved: Certified 30 Nov. 1801 & 26 Sept. 1803.

Page 473. 26 Sept. 1803. AMIE PEREGOY of Henry County to HENRY HEFFLEFINGER of the same for the sum of Eighteen pounds sells 40 acres more or less on the waters of Ralph's Branch, joins SAMUEL WATSON'S spring branch and RANDOLPH & Company. No wit.

Signed: AMIE (X) PEREGOY. Proved: 26 Sept. 1803.

Pages 474-475. 10 Mar. 1795. HENRY HARRIS of Henry County to WILLIAM WARREN of the same for the sum of One hundred fifty pounds sells 333 acres on Ready Creek joins HENRY LYNE. Wit: HENRY LYNE, JOHN JAMESON, JOHN WATSON. Signed: HENRY HARRIS. Certified Aug. 1794; Proved: 26 Sept. 1803.

Page 475. No date. Power of Attorney. HENRY LYNE appoints WARDEN POPE, Esq. of Jefferson County, Kentucky to convey to RICHARD REYNOLDS of Jefferson County, Kentucky 2/3 of a tract on the waters of Harrods Creek and the other 1/3 unto ABRAHAM HITE, Esq. of the same. The tract contains 500 acres and was patented in my name. Signed: HENRY LYNE. Proved: 31 Oct. 1803. . . .N.B. Some years ago I gave Power of Attorney to ABRAHAM HITE to convey the land in my behalf - hereby revoke that Power of Attorney. Signed: HENRY LYNE.

Pages 476-477. 10 Aug. 1803. Deed of Trust. MEREDITH PEARSON and RHODA PEARSON his wife of Henry County to THOMAS DIX Trustee for DAVID PANNILL of Pittsylvania County. Debt is Eleven pounds eight shillings due 1 March next. Places in trust: land on the waters of Leatherwood Creek 100 acres that was willed RHODA PEARSON then RHODA DELOSIER by her father EDWARD DELOZIER and is the place where MEREDITH PEARSON and his wife live. Wit: HENRY AIRSTRIP, ROBERT SMITH, COLLEN STEART. Signed: MEREDITH (X) PEARSON, RHODA (X) PEARSON, THOMAS DIX, DAVID PANNILL. Witnesses to the signature of RHODA PEARSON: BARNA WELLS, TABITHIA (X) MULLINS, SALLEY (X) MULLINS. Proved: 29 Aug. 1803.

Page 477. 1 Oct. 1803. JOHN HOLMNS of Henry County to JOSEPH ANTHONY of the same for the sum of $500.00 sells 100 acres more or less joins STOKES and HAIRSTON. Wit: WILLIAM BARTON, JR., JOSEPH ANTHONY, JR., JOHN (X) MASTERS. Signed: JOHN (X) HOLMNS. Proved: 31 Oct. 1803. . . .FRANCES HOLMNS wife of JOHN HOLMNS releases her right of dower.

Page 478. 28 Nov. 1803. WILLIAM MITCHELL of Henry County to GEORGE HAIRSTON of the same for the sum of Thirty pounds sells 70 acres more or less on the north side of Smith River joins THOMAS CHOWNING and Middle Creek. No wit. Signed: WILLIAM MITCHELL. Proved: 28 Nov. 1803.

Page 479. 8 Nov. 1803. WILLIAM MITCHELL of Henry County to GEORGE HAIRSTON of the same for the sum of Four hundred pounds sells a parcel of land on the south side of Smith River, which lands conveyed by CHARLES GILLEY, an heir of FRANCIS GILLEY, by survey 250 acres more or less on Turkey Cock Creek. No wit. Signed: WILLIAM MITCHELL. Proved: 28 Nov. 1803.

Page 480. 28 Nov. 1803. JOHN PARSLEY and HANNAH PARSLEY his wife of Henry County to GEORGE HAIRSTON of the same for the sum of One hundred pounds sells 300 acres more or less on the waters of Beaver Creek and Crabtree Branch, joins STEPHEN CARTER. No wit. Signed: JOHN PARSLEY. Proved: 28 Nov. 1803. . . HANNAH PARSLEY releases her right of dower.

Page 481. 24 Sept. 1803. Deed of Trust. WILLIAM SANDS indebted to GEORGE HAIRSTON, bond dated 24 Sept. 1803 in the amount of Nineteen pounds due the 3 Jan. next. Puts in trust to JOHN ROWLAND, JR. 1 mare and colt, 3 beds and furniture, 1 pr. cards, 1 trunk, 1 looking glass, 1 cradle and kitchen utensils. Wit: THOMAS EAST, GILBERT ROWLAND. Signed: WILLIAM SANDS, JOHN ROWLAND, JR. Proved: 28 Nov. 1803.

Pages 482-483. 24 Sept. 1803. NELSON POWELL JONES of Asnin (Anson?) County, North Carolina to CHARLES JONES of Grayson County, Virginia for the sum of One hundred pounds sells land in Henry County on the waters of Leatherwood Creek 315 acres joins DANIEL MCBRIDE, GRIFFIN GRIFFITY, Lomax & Co. Wit: MOIRTEL LANIER, W. JONES, EDWARD (X) COOK. Signed: NELSON POWELL JONES. Proved: 28 Nov. 1803 and certified by the Clerk of Grayson County, Virginia.

Pages 483-484. 20 Oct. 1803. Deed of Trust. REES HUGHES to JOSEPH ALEXANDER and THOMAS DIX & Company, HUGHES has 2 bonds due to THOMAS DIX & Co. (1) dated 8 Aug. 1801 amount of Ł19 sh, 8 p. (2) Ł10, 5 sh, 6 p. due the 28 Oct. 1806..places in trust to JOHN ALEXANDER land on the waters of Middle Creek 150 acres. Wit: CHARLES ROYSTER, HENRY AIRSROP, EDWARD ROYSTER, A. HUGHES. Signed: REES HUGHES, THOMAS DIX & CO., JOHN ALEXANDER.

Page 485. 28 Nov. 1803. Bond of ALEXANDER HUNTER who is appointed Sheriff dated 1 Oct. last and to collect taxes, etc. Signed: ALEXANDER HUNTER, GEORGE HAIRSTON. Proved: 28 Nov. 1803.

Pages 485-486. 27 Feb. 1804. Bond of JOSEPH MARTIN who is appointed Sheriff. Bondsman: GEORGE HAIRSTON. Proved: 27 Feb. 1804.

Page 486. Duplicate of 485.

Page 487. Duplicate of 485.

Page 488. 27 Dec. 1803. JOHN PELFREY and ELIZABETH PELFREY his wife of Henry County to JOHN STONE of the same for the sum of Two hundred pounds sells 267 acres on Smith River joins GEORGE HAIRSTON and PHILPOTT. Wit: JOHN PHILPOTT, SAMUEL PHILPOTT, EDWARD PHILPOTT, SAMUEL PHILPOTT. Signed: JOHN (X) PERLREY, ELIZABETH (X) PELFREY. Proved: 31 Jan. 1804.

Page 489. 31 Jan. 1804. Bond of GEORGE HAIRSTON who is appointed Coronor, his bondsman JOHN COX. Proved: 31 Jan. 1804.

Page 490. 13 Sept. 1803. I, JOSHUA HICKEY do assign unto LARKIN TURNER all my right and title for land lying on Gray's fork of Town Creek for value received. Wit: JOHN BARROTT, JOHN TURNER, WILLIAM TURNER, MICHAEL HICKEY. Signed: JOSHUA HICKEY.

Pages 490-491. Feb. 1804. GOODWIN MAYSE of Henry County to MICHAEL THOMAS of Rockingham County, North Carolina for the sum of $100.00 land on Matrimony Creek that joins JESSE MURPHY to a hickory bush in the North Carolina line. Wit: JOHN ROWLAND, JR. Signed: GOODWIN (X) MAYSE. Proved: 27 Feb. 1804.

Pages 491-492. 16 Feb. 1804. Bond of JOSEPH MARTIN, Sheriff who is to collect all levies, fines for Henry County. His bondsman is GEORGE HAIRSTON. Proved: 27 Feb. 1804.

Pages 492-493. No date. WILLIAM HEARD, SENR. for the love and affection to his son JESSE HURD after my decease and my wife MARGARET, to him my manor plantation whereon I now live with land adjacent 230 acres on both sides of Read Creek joins GEORGE HAIRSTON, ARISTEPHUS VAUGHAN, will all horses and stock and four negros girl Anne, girl Judith boy Kitt and by Jerry and all household furniture of every sort. Wit: JAMES LETCHER, JOHN (X) GARNER, ELIMELOCK GARROT. Signed: WILLIAM HEARD. Proved: 20 Feb. 1804.

Pages 493-494. 29 Nov. 1803. DAVID ALEXANDER and

UNITY ALEXANDER his wife of Henry County to JOHN PRATT for the sum of One hundred pounds by survey 152 acres on Toeclout Creek joins WILLIAM JAMISON. Wit: JOHN (X) RICE, ARON (X) ANOY, ROBERT (X) ROSS. Signed: DAVID (X) ALEXANDER. Proved: 26 Mar. 1804.

Page 495. 22 Dec. 1803. LEONARD CHEATHAM sells to his son LEONARD CHEATHAM, JR. for Sixty pounds four negros Ceaser, Betty and her two children Squire and Sarah. Wit: JOHN DILLARD, JAMES DILLARD. Signed: LEONARD CHEATHAM. Proved: 26 Mar. 1804.

Pages 495-496. 1 Feb. 1804. EUSEBOUS STONE, JR. of Henry County to ISSAH MAYNARD for Fifty five pounds land on the north side of Smith River 50 acres more or less. No wit. Signed: EEUSBUS STONE. Proved: 26 Mar. 1804.

Pages 496-497. 26 Mar. 1804. GEORGE WASHINGTON SPENCER and PATSY SPENCER his wife of the state of Tennessee to WILLIAM HILL for the sum of $1,000.00 sells 236 acres on Horsepasture Creek that joins HILL, GREG. DURHAM, JOHN SMITH and JAMES SHELTON, it being the tract that SPENCER received as the dividend of his father's estate. Signed: GEORGE WASHINGTON SPENCER. Proved: 26 Mar. 1804.

Page 497. 26 Mar. 1803. HENRY LYNE of Henry County to LEWIS FRANKLIN of the same for the sum of Forty five pounds sells 100 acres more or less that joins GEORGE WALLER, JOHN COX and HORD. No wit. Signed: HENRY LYNE. Proved: 26 Mar. 1804.

Page 498. 26 March 1804. Dimension for building a prison (that is to say). To be built of hewed logs 12 inches square, a double body to be dovetailed, floor to be laid white oak logs, 16 ft. by 18 ft., eight logs high, the floor then 8 logs high, roof of good chestnut shingles 21 inches long, well weatherboarded with planks 1½ inch thick put on with 6 inch spikes and 16 spikes to each plank. Both rooms sealed with 1½ inch planks, each room to have a double door, 2 outside doors to be plated over with sheet iron outside, and inside to be drove full of 10d nails not over an inch apart. The inside doors to have a whole left 6 inches square and bound with plate iron. Doors to have 3 large hinges to extend across each with large hooks and outside locks. Each room a window 1 foot square with double grates, bars of iron 3 inches by 1 inch. A common iron stove in the Debtors room with pipes to convey smoke out. The roof is to be painted red, the body white. There is to be a necessary hole in each room well plated with iron on the inside. The steps are to be out of Oak. . . .Henry Court - March 1804. JOHN SAMLON, JOHN COX or GEORGE HAIRSTON or any two of them to let to the lowest bidder the building. A stock and pillory are to be furnished with the prison. REUBEN WADE bids for the jail $996. Stock and Pillory $14 for a total of $1010. Signed: JOHN SALMON.

Page 499. 26 Mar. 1804. Bond of REUBEN WADE, the lowest bidder to build for the use of Henry County a Jail, stocks and pillory for $1,010.00, his securities are JOSEPH ANTHONY and WILLIAM F. MILLS. Wit: JOHN SALMON, JOHN COX, GEORGE HAIRSTON. Proved: 20 Mar. 1804.

Page 500. 18 Feb. 1804. LARKIN TURNER and MARY TURNER his wife of Franklin County to WILLIAM TURNER of Henry County for the sum of Fifty two pounds sells 33 acres on Butrum Town Creek begins at LARKIN TURNER'S still house branch to JEREMIAH TURNER'S line. Wit: PETER SMITH, JOSIAH TURNER, JOHN TURNER. Signed: LARKIN TURNER, MARY (X) TURNER. . . .MARY TURNER releases her right of dower to the above.

Page 501. 30 Apr. 1804. JOSEPH MARTIN of Henry County to ROBERT PEDIGO of the same for the sum of Five shillings sells and conveys 130 acres more or less being part of a tract PEDIGO sold to GRIFFITH GRIFFIN and CHARLES JONES on the branches of Leatherwood Creek. No wit. Signed: JOSEPH MARTIN. Proved: 30 Apr. 1804.

Page 502. 25 Dec. 1801. WILLIAM HAYS to WILLIAM SMITH both of Henry County for the sum of One hundred pounds sells 75 acres on the waters of Mayo River joins PHILIP ANGLIN. Wit: DRURY SMITH, JOSEPH ODELL, GEORGE TAYLOR. Signed: WILLIAM HAYS. Proved: 30 Apr. 1804.

Page 503. 8 Jan. 1804. ROBERT GARLAND of Lunenburg County to PETER GARLAND of Henry County for the sum of Five hundred fifty pounds fifteen shillings sells by estimate 500 and -- acres that joins JAMES REA, ABNER REA, THOMAS ALEXANDER (now JOHN ALEXANDER), JOHN ROWLAND, REUBEN PAYNE and GILMORE'S order. Refer to deed from PETER GARLAND to ROBERT GARLAND in Henry County. Also it being the residue of a tract PETER GARLAND purchased of PETER HAIRSTON and sold to ROBERT GARLAND. Wit; JOHN M. ALEXANDER,

POLLY ALEXANDER, LEONARD MURRAY. Signed: ROBERT GARLAND. Proved: 30 Apr. 1804.

Page 504. 28 Apr. 1804. GOODWIN MAYSE of Henry County to WILLIAM OAKLEY of the same for the sum of Thirty five pounds sells 50 acres on Long Branch of Marrowbone Creek joins THOMAS JAMISON. No wit. Signed: GOODWIN MAYSE. Proved: 30 Apr. 1804.

Pages 504-505. 30 Apr. 1804. JOSEPH MARTIN, SR. to JOSEPH GRAVELY, JR. both of Henry County for the sum of One hundred fifty five pounds sells 195 acres on the branches of the south fork of Leatherwood Creek, joins lines of JAMES HOWARD, GEORGE HAIRSTON, a field formerly called Mathews. Signed: JOSEPH MARTIN. Proved: 30 Apr. 1804. . . .Memo: JOSEPH MARTIN agrees that if any lines do not agree whatever loses GRAVELY might have MARTIN will make up out of the land that he possesses adjoining.

Pages 506-507. 3 Mar. 1804. JOSEPH MARTIN and SUSANNAH MARTIN his wife to WILLIAM HEREFORD for the sum of One thousand four hundred and fifty pounds sells the following tracts on Smith River (1) 1827 acres on the north side of Smith River joins BOULDIN and a branch of Mulberry Creek, to a white oak near the Courthouse Road, Turkey Pen branch, Rug Creek, Hammocks Branch, (2) on the south side of Smith River 28 3/4 acres joins THOMAS GRAVES line. Wit: THOMAS DIX, JAMES ALEXANDER, B. MARTIN. Signed: JOSEPH MARTIN, SUSANNAH MARTIN. Proved: 1 May 1804.

Pages 507-508. No date. SUSANNAH MARTIN, wife of JOSEPH MARTIN, releases her right of dower to the above.

Page 508. No date. Bond of WILLIAM S. COX is to serve as Constable, his bondsman GEORGE HAIRSTON. Proved: 1 May 1804.

Page 509. 16 May 1804. JEREMIAH STONE of Henry County to JAMES BAKER for the sum of One hundred twenty pounds sells one negro woman Jeany and one boy Nathan and one horse. Wit: JOHN COX, TUNSTALL COX, JOHN COX, JR. Signed: JEREMIAH STONE. Proved: 28 May 1804.

Page 509. No date. HENRY MCKINNEY of Rockingham County, North Carolina appoints HARBERT KING of Patrick County, Virginia his attorney to attend the sale of one negro boy named Reuben, which was executed by GILBERT ROWLAND, Deputy Sherif of Henry County to satisfy Clerks Ticket which was due from JOHN KING, SNR. of Rockingham, North Carolina. Wit: GEORGE W. KING, DAVID KING, THOMAS MAYS, WILLIAM R. SMITH. Signed: HENRY (X) MCKINNEY. Proved: 28 May 1804.

Page 510. March Court 1804. Henry County. Ordered that THOMAS BOULDIN, JR., JOHN WALLER, ARCHIBALD FARRIS and JAMES LARIMORE are to view, mark and lay off the most convenient way for a road from FARRIS' to intersect the road leading from Col. LYNE'S and report. . . .Report: They have marked a new road to made leaving the old road at the first fork to turn right then left at BURWELL BASSETTS.

Page 510-511. 26 Dec. 1803. JAMES WILSON of Henry County to GEORGE HAIRSTON of the same for the sum of Eighty pounds sells land on Leatherwood Creek joins the lines of DAVID WEATHERFORD, the Bold branch and LOMAX & Company (25 acres has been lately deeded by the heirs of DAVID WEATHERFORD to JAMES WILSON). This transaction being 100 acres. Signed: JAMES WILSON. Proved: 25 June 1804.

Pages 511-512. No date. Mortgage. WILLIAM HEREFORD to JOSEPH MARTIN, four bonds for a total of $1,798.00 dated 1 March 1804 and payable: (1) $449.50 due 1 Mar. 1805. (2) $449.50 due 1 Mar. 1806. (3) $449.50 due 1 Mar. 1807. (4) $449.50 due 1 Mar. 1808. Security 855 3/4 acres that WILLIAM HEREFORD purchased of JOSEPH MARTIN. Wit: THOMAS DIX, B. MARTIN, JAMES ALEXANDER. Signed: WILLIAM HEREFORD, JOSEPH MARTIN. Proved: 5 Mar. 1804.

Pages 513-514. 15 Jan. 1804. DUDLEY STEPHENS of Henry County to JAMES LYELL of the same for the sum of Fifty pounds sells 237 acres on Leatherwood Creek, joins INGRAM ALEXANDER. No wit or Signature given. Proved: 30 July 1804.

Page 514. 7 Feb. 1804. WILLIAM NUNN makes over and releases to SANDFORD RAMEY SENR. all his claim to two negros Lewis and Cloe conveyed by WATERS DUNN, SENR. of Georgia as a Deed of Gift 7 Feb. 1802 and recorded at Columbia County, Georgia 27 Feb. 1802. Wit: P. GARLAND, C. G. LLEWELLEN. Signed: WILLIAM NUNN. Proved: 30 July 1804.

Page 515. 11 Aug. 1804. WILLIAM TOOMBS and SUSAN TOOMBS his wife of Henry County to WILLIAM

NIXSON of the same for the sum of Sixty five pounds sells 266 acres, it being the same more or less on the branches of the south fork of Leatherwood Creek joins JOSEPH GRAVELY, GENERAL MARTIN, CHARLES JONES, the Ridge Path and WILLIAM SIMPSON. Wit: JAMES HOWARD, WILLIAM SIMPSON, JAMES CASSEY. Signed: WILLIAM (X) TOOMBS, SUSAN (X) TOOMBS. Proved: 27 Aug. 1804.

Page 516. 1789. HENRY FRANCE of Henry County to JOHN FENDAL CARR of Rockingham County, North Carolina for the sum of Fifty pounds sells 100 acres on Crooked Creek on both sides of the South Mayo River, it being part of a tract granted by patent to JOHN SIMS dated 1 Mar. 1781. Wit: AUGUSTINE THOMAS, MANN- ING HILL, FREDERICK FULKERSON, JOHN DILLARD. Signed: HENRY FRANCE. Proved: 29 June 1789 & 27 Aug. 1804.

Page 517. 27 Aug. 1804. GEORGE HAIRSTON of Henry County to THOMAS EAST of the same for the sum of Twenty five pounds sells 50 acres on Drag Creek, a branch of Smith River joins JOHN KELLEY. No wit. Signed: GEORGE HAIRSTON. Proved: 27 Aug. 1804.

Pages 518-519. 4 Aug. 1804. DANIEL REAMY and MARY REAMY his wife of Henry County to GEORGE HAIRSTON of the same for the sum of $387.00 sells 250 acres on the Muster Branch of Leatherwood Creek joins LOMAX & Company and JOHN CREASEY'S lines. Wit: GILBERT ROWLAND, WILLIAM STOKES, GEORGE CLARK. Signed: DANIEL REAMY. Proved: 27 Aug. 1804.

Pages 519-520. 16 Dec. 1802. JAMES COGHLIN of Rock- ingham County, North Carolina to ISHAM BROWN of Dinwiddie County, Va. for the sum of $500.00 sells land in Henry County, Va. on the shores of Drag Creek and Stuarts Creek, part of a tract given by JACOB CAYTON to WILLIAM CAYTON being 297 acres. Wit: EDWARD PEGRAM, JR., ROBERT WILLIAMS, JOHN JONES. Signed: JAMES COGHLIN. Proved: 29 Oct. 1804. . . . Town of Petersburg, 15 Jan. 1803. Before me, GEORGE PEGRAM, Mayor, came JAMES COGHLIN and acknowledged the within instrument to be his act and deed.

Pages 521-522. 6 Oct. 1804. WILLIAM BARKSDALE of Henry County to SARAH BARKSDALE for the sum of Three hundred sixty pounds sells all that divident tract on the north side of Smith River being part of a tract whereon SARAH BARKSDALE now lives and the land given by JOHN BARKSDALE to WILLIAM BARKSDALE being by estimate 150 acres, joins THOMAS NUNN and the Old wagon road. Wit: JOHN COX, TUNSTALL COX, CHARLES

HIBBERT, BARTLET WADE, THOMAS H. WATSON. Signed: WILLIAM BARKSDALE. Proved: 29 Oct. 1804.

Pages 522-523. 1804. JOHN P. PYRTLE and MARY PYRTLE his wife of Henry County to TABITHIA BRADBERRY for the sum of $100.00 sell land on the south side of Reedy Creek by estimate 33 acres. No wit. Signed: JOHN P. PYRTLE. Proved: 29 Oct. 1804.

Pages 523-524. 2 Sept. 1804. LANGSTON PACE of Henry County to THOMAS NUNN of the same for the sum of $200.00 sells 50 acres that joins Col. HAIRSTON, DANIEL RAMEY and SANDFORD RAMEY. Signed: LANGSTON PACE. Proved: 29 Oct. 1804.

Pages 523-524. 16 Mar. 1804. BLIZARD MAGRUDER of Henry County to THOMAS EGGLETON of the same for the sum of $30.00 sells 30 acres on the branches of the fishing fork of Leatherwood Creek. Wit: PRESLEY (X) SIMPSON, WILLIAM SHACKLEFORD, GEORGE EGLETON. Signed: BLIZARD MAGRUDER. Proved: 30 July 1804.

Page 525. 29 Oct. 1804. JOHN HAMMONS of Henry County to THOMAS JONES of the same for the sum of One hundred sixty pounds sells 200 acres more or less. Lines FREDERICK RICKELS, The Meeting House Fork of Cascade Creek, Home Creek. No wit. Signed: JOHN HAMMONS. . . .WELTHY HAMMONS, wife of JOHN HAMMONS, releases her right of dower.

Page 526. 19 May 1804. SAMUEL ANGLIN of Henry County to THOMAS WILLIAMS, ANGILICHE WILLIAMS, SUSANNA W. WILLIAMS and TABITHIA WILLIAMS of Henry County for the sum of Fifty pounds sells 100 acres more or less on the branches of fishing fork of Leatherwood Creek. Lines joins Gen. JOSEPH MARTIN, ABRAM WILLIAMS, MICHAEL AKINS and PRESLEY SIMPSON. Wit: MEREDITH PERSON, ELIZABETH WILLIAMS. Signed: SAMUEL ANGLIN. Proved: 29 Oct. 1804. . . .CATEY ANGLIN, wife of SAMUEL ANGLIN, releases her right of dower.

Pages 527-528. 14 Sept. 1804. Deed of Trust. THOMAS H. WATSON to WILLIAM F. MILLS Trustee for ROBERT ALLEN, debt in the amount of $154.00 due the 20th Dec. 1804. Secures with his portion of an undivided tract (1280 acres) of his late father's (JOHN WATSON) in Patrick and Henry Counties on both sides of Horsepasture Creek (his portion to be 420 acres.) Wit: ROBERT TAYLOR, JAMES M. SLEATOR, JOHN KING, JR., JOHN COX, SENR., DAVID MULLINS, TUNSTALL

COX. Signed: THOMAS H. WATSON, WILLIAM F. MILLS. Proved: 29 Oct. 1804.

Pages 528-529. 29 Jan. 1803. DAVID WILLS of Franklin County to JOHN CAHILL of the County of Henry for the sum of One hundred pounds sells 200 acres on Glady fork of Reed Creek joins TOWNLING and BURCHITT. Wit: PHILLIP MOLLING, JOSEPH TOWNLIN, WILLIAM WARRANT. Signed: DAVID WILLIS. Proved: 26 Sept. 1803 & 29 Oct. 1804.

Pages 529-530. 19 Oct. 1804. JOHN BAILEY of Henry County to GEORGE WALLER, JR. Trustee of JAMES BAKER, amount due 25 Dec. next, the amount is Twelve pounds eighteen shillings, secures with a horse called Chickasaw. Signed: JOHN BAILEY, GEORGE WALLER, JR. Proved: 29 Oct. 1804.

Pages 530-531. Bill of Sale. No date. JOHN ADKINS of Patrick County to JOHN REDD, one gray mare, 12 yrs. old blind, formerly the property of FREDERICK ECHOLS, cattle, 1 bay mare, hogs. Wit: WALLER REDD, IGNATIOUS SIMMS. Signed: JOHN (X) ADKINS. Proved: 29 Oct. 1806.

Pages 531-532. 13 Mar. 1804. Deed of Trust. JOSEPH PHIFER of Henry County to GEORGE WALLER, JR. and WALLER REDD Trustees for JOHN REDD, debt Sixty eight pounds nine shilling 2 pence, secures with: two tracts on Rock Run Creek whereon he now lives one tract 120 acres the other 100 acres being part of a tract granted JOHN DILLEN by patent 20 Feb. 1794, joins JOHN BARKSDALE, Ironworks Rd. and JO. DILLEN. Wit: JEREMIAH ROBERTS, EPHRIAM WILSON, ANN STARLING. Signed: JOSEPH (X) PHIFER, GEORGE WALLER, JR., WALLER REDD. Proved: 29 Oct. 1804.

Pages 533-534. 2 Dec. 1802. JOHN COOK and BILLY HUTCHERSON of Franklin County to WILLIAM DEGRAFFENREID for the sum of Fifty pounds sells land in Henry County 203 acres on the waters of Leatherwood Creek joins ELIJAH RICHARDSON. Wit: JOHN KING, JR., JOHN REDD, JOHN DEGRAFFENREID. Signed: JOHN COOK, BILLY HUTCHERSON, Proved: 29 Oct. 1804.

Page 534. 7 Sept. 1804. Bond of GEORGE HAIRSTON who is to build a bridge across Marrowbone Creek near his Marrowbone Store, his security WASHINGTON ROWLAND. Wit: GILBERT ROWLAND. Signed: GEORGE HAIRSTON. Proved: 29 Oct. 1804.

Pages 535-536. 29 Oct. 1804. JOHN ROWLAND, SR. of Henry County to BALDWIN ROWLAND, JR. for the sum of Two hundred pounds sells 100 acres that joins BRICE MARTIN, JOHN ALEXANDER, PETER GARLAND, REUBEN PAYNE and to the Main Road from ROWLAND'S ford. Signed: JOHN ROWLAND. Proved: 29 Oct. 1804.

Pages 536-537. 29 Oct. 1804. JOHN HAMMONDS of Henry County to GEORGE HAIRSTON of the same for the sum of Three hundred pounds sells 321 acres more or less on the waters of Leatherwood Creek and Smith River, joins WILLIAM ROBERTSON. Also 60 acres of DAVID WEATHERFORD including the Mill (see deed) 84 acres purchased of WILLIAM DUNN, 82 acres by grant. To include all land JOHN HAMMONDS owns on Leatherwood Creek. Signed: JOHN HAMMONDS. Proved: 29 Oct. 1804.

. . . .WELTHY HAMMONDS, wife of JOHN HAMMONDS releases her right of dower.

Pages 537-538. 26 Nov. 1804. Bond of JOSEPH MARTIN who is appointed Sheriff of Henry County, GEORGE HAIRSTON Bondsman. Proved: 26 Nov.1804.

Page 538. No date. JOSEPH MARTIN is to collect all levies and taxes. Proved: 26 Nov. 1804.

Page 539. No date. Bond of JOSEPH MARTIN who as Sheriff, is to collect the revenue tax for 1804. Proved: 26 Nov. 1804.

Pages 539-540. 27 Sept. 1804. FREDERICK UHLES and his wife PHEBEY UHLES to CARR WALLER for the sum of Two hundred fifty five pounds sells 200 acres on Leatherwood Creek it being the same UHLES purchased of JOSEPH MARTIN. Wit: BARNA WELLS, GEORGE B. HOPSON, JOS. MARTIN, B. MARTIN. Signed: FREDERICK UHLES, PHEBEY (X) UHLES. Proved: 26 Nov. 1804.

Pages 541-542. 3 May 1803. DANIEL REAMEY of Henry County to GEORGE HAIRSTON of the same for Two hundred pounds sells all that plantation and land on Muster Branch of Leatherwood Creek 230 acres by patent granted GEORGE REYNOLDS 15 July 1780 and part of a grant to MURRELL, lines of FRANCIS COX, JOHN ALEXANDER, JOHN GIBSON. Wit: WASHINGTON ROWLAND, RAMOUTH (X) REAMY, SUSANA (X) PACE. Signed: DANIEL REAMEY. Proved: 26 Nov. 1804.

Pages 542-543. 12 Jan. 1804. Deed of Trust. REUBEN WADE to JOHN MULLINS, Trustee for

ROBERT ALLEN, debt Sixty seven pounds, due 25 Dec. 1804. secures with land whereon he now lives on Marrowbone Creek 100 acres more or less. Wit: J. LARIMORE, NANCY LARIMORE, THOMAS BOULDIN, son of THOMAS. Signed: REUBEN WADE, JOHN MULLINS. Proved: 26 Nov. 1804.

Pages 543-544. 26 Nov. 1804. CHARLES T. PHILPOTT of Henry County to GEORGE HAIRSTON of the same for the sum of Two hundred pounds sells 500 acres more or less on Beaver Creek, begins at the mouth of the Long Branch, joins land of ZACKERIAH PHILPOTT. Signed: CHARLES T. PHILPOTT. Proved: 26 Nov. 1804.

Pages 544-545. 31 Dec. 1804. THOMAS JONES of Henry County to AMBROSE EDWARDS of the same for the sum of One hundred seventy five pounds sells 141 acres on Leatherwood Creek joins LOMAX & Company. Signed: THOMAS JONES. Proved: 31 Dec. 1804. . . . ELIZABETH JONES, wife of THOMAS JONES, releases her right of dower.

Pages 545-547. 1 Dec. 1804. SAMUEL D. SOUTHERLAND and JUDITH SOUTHERLAND, his wife of Henry County to BARNY WELLS for the sum of Fifty pounds sells 30 acres on Leatherwood Creek joins JAMES DYER. Wit: JOHN RAMEY, A. HUGHES, JAMES DYER, FRANCIS NORTHCUTT. Signed: SAMUEL D. SOUTHERLAND, JUDITH SOUTHERLAND. Proved: 28 Jan. 1805. . . .JUDITY SOUTHERLAND, wife of SAMUEL D. SOUTHERLAND, releases her right of dower.

Pages 547-548. 27 Aug. 1804. JOSIAH TAYLOR of Henry County to THOMAS CHILDRESS of the same for the sum of Sixty pounds sells 50 acres on the south side of the south fork of the Mayo River at the mouth of a branch below the plantation of FREDERICK HUTCHINSON and the County Line. Signed: JOSIAH TAYLOR. Proved: 28 Jan. 1805.

Pages 548-549. 4 Aug. 1804. JAMES METHVIN and NIECEY METHVIN his wife to WILLIAM NIXSON for the sum of Ten pounds sells 50 acres, it being part of a tract formerly belonging to DANIEL MCBRIDE on the branches of the south fork of Leatherwood Creek joins JOSEPH GRAVELY, GEN. JOSEPH MARTIN. Wit: CHARLES AGEE, LEWIS AGEE, ISAM LAWSON. Signed: JAMES (X) METHVIN, NIECEY (X) METHVIN. Proved: 28 Jan. 1805.

Pages 549-560. 21 Dec. 1804. EDMUND WINSTON and GEORGE DABNEY WINSTON next acting executors of PATRICK HENRY, deceased and DORTHEA WINSTON lately DORTHEA HENRY, widow and executrix of PATRICK HENRY to CHARLES ROYSTER. PATRICK HENRY in his lifetime sold to CHARLES ROYESTER 1,200 acres for the sum of One thousand pounds which was fully paid but a conveyance was not executed to the said CHARLES ROYSTER. DORTHEA HENRY was empowered to make a conveyance for all the land sold, by the will of PATRICK HENRY. But she having intermarried with EDMUND WINSTON, it is doubted whether the conveyance by her alone would be sufficient. Therefore, EDMUND WINSTON and GEORGE DABNEY WINSTON grant the said tract to CHARLES ROYSTER..it begins on Stony Hill a ford of Leatherwood Creek, Henry's Old Mill. Wit: JOHN TRAHORN, ABRAHAM KEELING, JOHN REYNOLDS. Signed: EDMUND WINSTON, GEORGE D. WINSTON, DORTHEA WINSTON. Proved: 28 Jan. 1805.

Page 561. 30 Nov. 1804. Bill of Sale. JOHN VERELL of Dinwiddie County, Virginia to JAMES OAKES of Henry County for the sum of One hundred Twenty pounds sells one negro boy Dilly. Wit: PETER RIGGS, JAMES HOPPER, ELIAS NORMAN. Signed: JOHN VERELL. Proved: 30 Jan. 1805.

Pages 561-562. 25 Feb. 1805. THOMAS CHILDRESS and his wife BETSY CHILDRESS to GEORGE MARTIN of Amerst County for and in consideration of a tract of land in Amerherst County to sell and convey to GEORGE MARTIN three tracts in Henry County on both sides of the South Mayo River contains 327 acres. One - 202 acres on the north side of Mayo River joins WILLIAM HAYS line, JOHN DILLARD, BALLENGER WADE and HENRY FEE. (2) 75 acres on the south side of the river up to a long rock, HENRY FRANCE, the Carolina line, then east. (3) 50 acres joins the river, the Carolina line and Dodson. This land is now in the possession of GEORGE MARTIN. Signed: THOMAS CHILDRESS. Proved: 25 Feb. 1805.

Page 562. 2 Feb. 1805. ABNER STULTS and NANCY STULTS his wife to DANIEL SHACKLEFORD all of Henry County, for the sum of Sixty pounds sells by estimate 75 acres on the head branches of the south fork of Leatherwood Creek. Wit: JOHN CONNAWAY, JOHN WILLS, WILLIAM (X) SIMPSON. Signed: ABNER STULTS, NANCY (X) STULTS. Proved: 25 Feb. 1805.

Pages 563-565. 25 Feb. 1805. ABNER STULTS and NANCY STULTS of Henry County to THOMAS TAYLOR for the sum of Sixty four pounds ten shillings sells 128 acres...joins JOHN KING, SENR., DENNIS LARKS, the same land that was granted ABNER STULTS. Signed: ABNER STULTS, NANCY (X) STULTS. Proved: 25 Feb. 1805.

Pages 565-566. 25 Feb. 1805. MOSES WILSON of Henry County to STEPHEN TURNER of the same for the sum of Eighty six pounds sells 164 acres on Home Creek joins LOMAX & Company. No wit. Signed: MOSES WILSON. Proved: 25 Feb. 1805.

Pages 567-568. 23 Feb. 1805. ELIZABETH LANE, DUTTON LANE, THOMAS NICHOLS, MOLLY LANE to WILLIAM NORMAN for the sum of Three hundred sixty pounds sells 200 acres on Smith River, one of the lines is "Ingin Rige Ridge" being the dividing line between WILLIAM, THOMAS and JAMES EDWARDS. The LANE'S are legatees of DUTTON LANE, deceased. Wit: JAMES OAKES, JAMES HOPPER, WILLIAM PULLAM. Signed: ELIZABETH (X) LANE, DUTTON LANE, THOMAS NICHOLS, MOLLY (X) LANE. Proved: 25 Feb. 1805.

Pages 568-569. 18 Aug. 1804. BLIZARD MAGRUDER of Henry County to JESSE WITT of the same for the sum of $45.00 sells 41 acres that joins JESSE WITT. Wit: JOHN WALLER, WILLIAM DURHAM, REUBIN LONG. Signed: BLIZARD MAGRUDER. Proved: 28 Jan. 1805.

Pages 569-570. 26 Mar. 1804. Deed of Trust. ARCHIBLAD PEREGUSON to WILLIAM DEGRAFFINREID debt in the amount of Thirty five pounds due the 20th of June ensuing...secures with land on Leatherwood Creek, it being the land that DEGRAFFINREID sold to PEREGUSON, 203 acres. Wit: B. MARTIN, A. HUGHES, JOHN COOK. Signed: ARCHIBLAD PEREGUSON. Proved: 29 Oct. 1804.

Page 571. 2 Feb. 1805. SPENCER GROGAN of Henry County to TINSLEY VERNON of Rockingham County, North Carolina for the sum of $175.00 sells by estimate 200 acres on the south side of Smith River that joins JOHN GROGAN. Wit: TAYLOR LINDSAY, HENRY SCALES. Signed: SPENCER (X) GROGAN.

Page 572. April 1801. Bond of GEORGE HAIRSTON who is to build a bridge across Leatherwood Creek. Proved: 25 Feb. 1805.

Pages 572-573. 4 Dec. 1804. SAMUEL SOUTHERLAND and JUDITH SOUTHERLAND his wife of Henry County to JAMES DYER of the same for the sum of One hundred fifteen pounds sells 70 acres on Leatherwood

Creek joins DYER and BARNA WELLS. Wit: BARNA WELLS, FRANCIS NORTHCUTT, A. HUGHES, JOHN CONNAWAY. Signed: SAMUEL SOUTHERLAND. Proved: 25 Mar. 1805.

Page 574. 25 March 1805. JUDITH SOUTHERLAND releases her right of dower to the above deed.

Pages 575-576. 25 May 1804. JAMES COOK, ELIZABETH COOK, POLLY COOK and NANCY COOK to CHARLES JONES for the sum of One hundred pounds sells 117 acres on Horsepasture Creek that joins THOMAS JARVIS and another tract that was patened to JAMES EAST 10 Apr. 1781 joins THOMAS JARVIS, WILLIAM WOOLARD being a total acreage of 310 acres. Wit: WILLIAM F. MILLS, JOHN (X) TRAVIS, THOMAS (X) JARVIS, JOHN BAILEY. Signed: JAMES COOK, ELIZABETH (X) COOK, POLLY COOK, NANCY COOK. Proved: 25 Mar. 1805.

Pages 576-577. 22 Mar. 1805. MARTHA FONTAINE of Henry County to THOMAS DIX & Company for the sum of Four hund. forty nine pounds and eighteen shillings sells 119 acres by survey on Leatherwood Creek joins SAMUEL HESTER, THOMAS BARTON and Camp Branch. Wit: ROBERT ALEXANDER, NATHANIEL W. DANDRIDGE, JOSEPH BOULDIN, JR. Signed: MARTHA FONTAINE. Proved: 25 Mar. 1805.

Pages 578-579. 5 Mar. 1805. BENJAMIN WEATHERFORD, DAVID WEATHERFORD, ELY BRYANT and THOMAS WHITWORTH heirs of DAVID WEATHERFORD, deceased to JONATHAN STONE for one stud horse and $500.00 sell by survey 349 acres on the waters of Leatherwood Creek, joins JAMES WILSON, IVEY HILL, LOMAX & Company. Wit: THOMAS BARTON, GEORGE GILLEY, JAMES (X) WILSON, INGRAM ALEXANDER. Signed: BENJAMIN WEATHERFORD, DAVID WEATHERFORD, ELY (X) BRYANT, THOMAS (X) WITHWORTH. Proved: 25 Mar. 1805.

Pages 579-580. 23 Mar. 1805. ROBERT SMITH of Henry County to JONATHAN STONE of the same for the sum of $120.00 sells 112 acres by survey on the branches of Fall Creek and Bold Branch of Leatherwood Creek joins THOMAS BARTON. Wit: JOSEPH BOULDIN, JR., THOMAS BARTON, PETER GEARHART, GEORGE GILLEY. Signed: ROBERT SMITH. Proved: 25 Mar. 1805.

Pages 580-581. 25 Mar. 1805. THOMAS BOULDIN of Henry County to POLLY BOULDIN of the same for the sum of Ninety pounds sells by estimate 310 acres on the water courses of Marrowbone Creek, joins JOHN WEAVER, Ore Bank and MAGRUDER. No wit. Signed:

THOMAS BOULDIN. Proved: 25 Mar. 1805.

Pages 581-582. 18 Mar. 1805. ADAM STULTS and MARY (MOLLY) STULTS his wife of Henry County to FRANCIS NORTHCUTT for the sum of Fifty seven pounds sells 100 acres on the headwaters of Leatherwood Creek joins WILLIAM BROWN. Wit: SAMUEL MARSHALL, BENJAMIN MARSHALL, JOHN HILL. Signed: ADAM (X) STULTS, MARY (X) STULTS. Proved: 25 Mar. 1805.

Page 583. 18 Mar. 1805. ROBERT SMITH of Henry County to THOMAS BARTON of the same for the sum of Twenty five pounds sells 112 acres on the big bold branch of Leatherwood Creek. Wit: ABNER REY, JONATHAN STONE, WILLIAM BARTON, JR. Signed: ROBERT SMITH. Proved: 25 Mar. 1805.

Page 584. 6 Nov. 1804. ELIZABETH WILKINS wife of THOMAS WILKINS releases her right of dower to a deed to THOMAS FOSTER for 138 acres. Proved: 25 Mar. 1805.

Pages 584-585. 23 Mar. 1805. JOHN PHILPOTT of Henry County to JOHN DILLEN of the same for the sum of $5.00 sells 15 acres on Town Creek joins REDD. No wit. Signed: JOHN PHILPOTT. Proved: 25 Mar. 1805.

Pages 585-586. 29 Sept. 1804. Deed of Trust. WILLIAM FRENCH to BARTLETT WADE Trustee for JAMES BAKER, in the amount of One hundred fifty pounds due 25 December next, secures with 400 acres of land purchased of HENRY LYNE, as the deed will more fully show, recorded in Henry County. Wit: TUNSTALL COX, WARREN COX, CHARLES HIBBERT. Signed: WILLIAM FRENCH, BARTLETT WADE. Proved: 29 Oct. 1805.

Page 587. No date. ROBERT STOCKTON of Benon (?) County, Kentucky is hereunto moving and appoints his friend RICHARD STOCKTON of Franklin County, Virginia to receive any sums of money due him and sell all of his lands in Henry, Franklin and Patrick County. Wit: JOHN COX, JOSEPH COX. Signed: ROBERT STOCKTON. Proved: 25 Mar. 1805.

Pages 588-589. 13 Feb. 1805. Deed of Trust. ELIJAH MEREDITH to GEORGE WALLER, JR. and JOHN COX, SENR. Trustees for JOHN REDD, debt in the amount of Thirty pounds two shillings eleven pence.. secures with 100 acres more or less on Reed Creek that joins STEPHEN KING and JOHN PYRTLE. Wit: JEREMIAH

ROBERTS, JAMES (X) FIFER, FLEMING THOMASSON. Signed: ELIJAH MEREDITH, GEORGE WALLER, JR., JOHN COX, JR. Proved: 25 Mar. 1805.

Pages 590-591. 29 Apr. 1805. CARR WALLER of Henry County to GEORGE HAIRSTON of the same for the sum of One hundred thirty five pounds seventeen shillings sells 104½ acres by survey on both sides of Little Beaver Creek joins AGNES WADE, JOSEPH ANTHONY and STOKES. No wit. Signed: CARR WALLER. Proved: 29 Apr. 1805.

Pages 591-592. 29 Apr. 1805. GEORGE HAIRSTON of Henry County to GEORGE DYER of the same for the sum of Three hundred fifty pounds sells by survey, 300 acres on the waters of Leatherwood Creek, joins JOSEPH MARTIN and DYER. No wit. Signed: GEORGE HAIRSTON. Proved: 29 Apr. 1805.

Pages 592-593. 29 Apr. 1805. GEORGE HAIRSTON of Henry County to ROBERT HAIRSTON of the same for the sum of $1,000.00 sells 688 acres more or less (488 acres was deeded from DANIEL RAMEY and 200 acres from SAMUEL ELLIOTT) see these deeds for further description, on the Muster Branch of Leatherwood Creek. Signed: GEORGE HAIRSTON. Proved: 29 Apr. 1805.

Pages 594-594. 14 Jan. 1805. Deed of Trust. JOSEPH EAST to GEORGE HAIRSTON and GILBERT ROWLAND..debt a bond dated 14 Jan. 1805 in the amount of Eighty one pounds five shillings and one and three-fourths pence due the 25th December next..secures with 500 hds. of tobacco, 50# cotton, 1 horse, cattle, household furniture and kitchen utensils. Wit: ROBERT ANDERSON, WILLIAM EAST. Signed: JOSEPH (X) EAST. Proved: 29 Apr. 1805.

Pages 595-596. 29 Apr. 1805. WILLIAM MILLS of Henry County to THOMAS OAKLEY of the same for the sum of Ninety pounds sells 100 acres on Matrimony Creek joins HOPPER & SAMES. Signed: WILLIAM MILLS. Proved: 29 Apr. 1805.

Pages 596-597. 23 Apr. 1805. WILLIAM MILLS of Henry County to JOHN OAKLEY of the same for the sum of $56.00 sells 56 3/4 acres on the waters of Matrimony Creek. No wit. Signed: WILLIAM MILLS. Proved: 29 Apr. 1805.

Page 597. No date. Inquist taken on a Public Road leading from Smith River, leading by JOHN

ROWLAND'S Store, near the said Store on the 30 Mar. 1805, GEORGE HAIRSTON Coroner of Henry County came to view the body of the late HUGH ONEAL then and there lying dead. Jury: JOHN ALEXANDER, THOMAS GRAVES, JOHN QUARLES, SANDFORD RAMEY, THOMAS HILL, ROBERT ANDERSON, GREEN BOULDIN, JOSEPH BOULDIN, JOHN PACE, WILLIAM FRANCIS, ABNER REA and JOHN REA. The said HUGH ONEAL was found to have no wounds on his body and appeared to be intoxicated with spirits and died in a natural way. Proved: 29 Apr. 1805.

Page 598. 29 Apr. 1805. WILLIAM FENCH of Henry County to JOHN GARDNER of the same for the sum of $1,000.00 sells by estimate 80 acres on Horsepasture Creek, with the water grist mill, on Hutt's Branch, Old Mill Road. Signed: WILLIAM FRENCH. Proved: 29 Apr. 1805 & 30 Dec. 1805.

Page ?. 30 Dec. 1805. JOHN REDD relinquishes all claim that he might have to this property.

Pages 599-600. 5 Dec. 1804. DUDLEY STEPHENS to SARY LYLE for the sum of Thirty pounds sells 30 acres by estimate on the Bold Branch of Leatherwood Creek and Haw Branch. Wit: THOMAS BARTON, HENRY AISTROP, THOMAS DIX, TERRY HUGHES. Signed: DUDLEY (X) STEPHENS. Proved: 29 Apr. 1805.

Pages 600-601. 4 Feb. 1805. FRANCES BUNCH of Henry County to TERRY HUGHES and WILLIAM RAMEY of the same for the sum of $100.00 sells by estimate 100 acres on the waters of the Mayo River joins BLIZARD MAGRUDER, JAMES LARIMORE and is part of a tract purchased by FRANCES BUNCH and her son BENJAMIN BUNCH of WILLIAM KELLUM, the balance of the tract was sold by BENJAMIN BUNCH to JAMES LARIMORE. Wit: SAMUEL WILLIAMS, OZBURN WILLIAMS, ALEXANDER MOORE. Signed: FRANCES (X) BUNCH. Proved: 29 Apr. 1805.

Pages 601-602. 30 Nov. 1804. DUDLEY STEPHENS of Henry County to COLLEN STEWARD (STUART-spelled both ways) for the sum of Ninety pounds sell 200 acres by estimate on the Bold Branch of Leatherwood Creek that joins JAMES LYLES and the Haw Branch. Wit: THOMAS DIX, MICAJAH HUGHES, REUBEN ALEXANDER. Signed: DUDLEY (X) STEPHENS, NANCY (X) STEPHENS. Proved: 29 Apr. 1805.

Page 602. 30 Jan. 1805. DUTTON LANE of Henry County to WINNEY ROCK for the sum of Forty five pounds sells and conveys a parcel of land containing

65 acres joins Morgan's Road, Stewart's Creek, LANNY COX..see the deed of JACOB CAYTON to DUTTON LANE for more details. Wit: ARCHIBALD MURPHY, NATHANIEL MURPHY, RICHARD GILLEY. Signed: DUTTON LANE. Proved: 29 Apr. 1805.

Page 603. 22 Apr. 1805. FLEMING THOMASON and JOSEPH THOMASON to WILLIAM SHACKLEFORD all of Henry County for the sum of Twenty seven pounds sells 100 acres more or less on the branches of fishing fork of Leatherwood Creek. Signed: FLEMING THOMASON, JOSEPH THOMASON. Proved: 29 Apr. 1805.

Page 604. 30 Apr. 1805. DAVID MAYS of Henry County to DAVID EPPERSON of the same for the sum of Thirty pounds sells 50 acres that begins at EPPERSON'S gate to the Long Branch and joins GEORGE HAIRSTON. Signed: DAVID (X) MAYS. Proved: 29 Apr. 1805.

Pages 604-605. 27 Feb. 1805. BETSY CHILDRESS wife of THOMAS CHILDRESS releases her right of dower to a deed to GEORGE MARTIN for 327 acres.

Pages 605-606. 2 Nov. 1804. THOMAS WILKINS and ELIZABETH WILKINS his wife of Henry County to THOMAS JONES of the same for the sum of Seventy pounds sells and conveys 108 acres more or less on the waters of Cascade Creeks, joins GEORGE F. HARRIS, JACOB SMITH and GIBSON'S spring branch. Wit: JOHN SMITH, ROBERT SMITH, JOHN ROWLAND, WILLIAM CHAPMAN. Signed: THOMAS (X) WILKINS, ELIZABETH (X) WILKINS, SARY (X) BAYS. Proved: 29 Apr. 1805 by the oaths of THOMAS WILKINS, ELIZABETH WILKINS and SARY BAYS.

Pages 606-607. 1 Oct. 1804. JOHN REDD of Henry County to WALLER REDD of the same for the sum of $200.00 sells 150 acres on the fork of Ready Creek, joins BURCHETTS Mill. Signed: JOHN REDD. Proved: 29 Apr. 1805.

Pages 607-608. 10 Apr. 1805. JACOB CAYTON of Henry County to HENRY COX of the same for the sum of Fifty dollars sells 60 acres more or less.. joins Morgan's Road. Wit: REUBIN PAYNE, SPENCER (X) GROGAN, BENJAMIN (X) SMITH. Signed: JACOB (X) CAYTON, MARGARET (X) CAYTON.

Page 608. 29 Apr. 1805. Deed of Trust. WILLIAM F. MILLS to ROBERT ALLEN. THOMAS H. WATSON by his deed 14 Sept. 1804 conveyed to WILLIAM F. MILLS his proportion part of his father's land (JOHN WATSON-1280 acres) in Patrick and Henry County, his portion being 420 acres. WILLIAM F. MILLS should after the 20 Dec. 1804 sell as much as needed to satisfy ROBERT ALLEN'S $150.00 and costs, the amount of the debt. ALLEN was the highest bidder at $154.00 for 390 acres, and was struck off for him. Signed: WILLIAM F. MILLS. Proved: 29 Apr. 1805.

Pages 609-610. 17 Oct. <u>1798</u>. RICHARD OAKLEY of Henry County to GEORGE HAIRSTON of the same for the sum of Fifty pounds sells 434 acres on Matrimony Creek joins SAMS Mill, the Bold Branch. Wit: THOMAS GRAVES, ABRAM PENN, BALDWIN ROWLAND. Signed: RICHARD (X) OAKLEY. Proved: 29 Apr. 1805.

Pages 610-611. 29 Apr. 1805. GENERAL JOSEPH MARTIN of Henry County to JOSEPH GRAVELY, JR. of the same for the sum of One hundred Fifty pounds sells 187 acres lately surveyed by THOMAS BARTON on the branches of Leatherwood Creek. Lines of JAMES HOWARD and GEORGE HAIRSTON. Signed: JOSEPH MARTIN. Proved: 29 Apr. 1805.

Page 612. 27 Mar. 1805. JOHN PHILLIPS of Stokes County, North Carolina to JOHN DILLEN of Henry County for the sum of Thirty pounds sells by estimate 30 acres on Hickey's Mill Creek. Wit: JOHN COX, JOHN FRENCH, CHARLES HIBBERT. Signed: JOHN (X) PHILLIPS. Proved: 29 Apr. 1805.

Page 613. 12 Jan. 1805. Deed of Trust. JESSE SIMPSON to GRIFFITH GRIFFIN debt Sixteen pounds twelve shillings and two pence secures with: 3 featherbeds and furniture, 1 cow, 1 yearling, pewter, earthen ware, household furniture. Due on/before 25 Dec. next. Wit: JOHN CONNAWAY, WILLIAM BAYLES. Signed: <u>GRIFFIN GRIFFITH</u>, JESSE SIMPSON.

Pages 613-614. 28 Nov. 1803. JAMES SMITH of Surry County, North Carolina to GEORGE HAIRSTON of Henry County for the sum of $100.00 sells 300 acres more or less on Middle Creek and Smith River..nevertheless, subject to the dower of GEORGE KEY'S widow as already laid off by Law. Wit: F. MITCHELL, WILLIAM HEWLETT, ELIZABETH (X) HEWLETT. Signed: JAMES SMITH. Proved: 29 Apr. 1805.

Pages 614-615. 11 June 1804. BLIZARD MAGRUDER of Henry County to ARCHIBALD FARRIS of the same for the sum of Forty pounds sells 170 acres more or less on the Main Road and across Jennings Creek joins DAVID MULLINS. Wit: DAVID MULLINS, AARON MILLS, JAMES HOPPER, JOHN CHRISTIAN. Signed: BLIZARD MAGRUDER. Proved: 29 Apr. 1805.

Page 616. 25 June 1804. JOHN GROGAN of Henry County to CHARLES COX of the same for the sum of $400.00 sells 150 acres on Stewarts Creek on Smith River to the bend before the falls. Wit: MASON KELLY, THOMAS KELLY, SPENCER GROGAN. Signed: JOHN GROGAN, NANCY GROGAN. Proved: 29 Oct. 1804. . . .NANCY GROGAN, wife of JOHN GROGAN releases her right of dower.

Pages 616-617. 2 Feb. 1805. THOMAS COX of Henry County to JOHN PRICE of the same for the sum of Forty pounds sells by estimate 80 acres.. on a branch..old lines. Wit: ARCHIBALD MURPHEY, THOMAS KELLY, CORNELIUS CAYTON. Signed: THOMAS COX, LUCY (X) COX. Proved: 29 Apr. 1805. . . .LUCY COX, wife of THOMAS COX releases her right of dower.

Pages 617-618. 2 Feb. 1805. CHARLES COX of Henry County to JOHN PRICE of the same for the sum of Forty pounds sells by estimate 80 acres on Turkey Pen Branch joins THOMAS COX. Signed: CHARLES COX, FRANCES COX. Proved: 29 Apr. 1805. . . .FRANCES COX, wife of CHARLES COX releases her right of dower.

Page 618-619. 17 May 1805. Inquist at JOSEPH GOODWIN'S. GEORGE HAIRSTON, Coroner for Henry County to view the body of LITTLEBERRY MORGAN late of Henry County, then and there lying dead. Jurors: WILLIAM HEWLETT, WILLIAM (X) DILLIAN, PHILLIP CONNOR, JOHN KELLY, THOMAS CHOWNING, CHATTEN CHOWNING, DAVID BURGESS, WILLIAM S. COX, THOMAS (X) WILSON, SENR., RICE HUGHES, MASON, KELLY and JAMES OAKES...Do say that ELIZABETH BROSHEARS of this County, spinister on the 26th of May with a gun (value $1200) then and there charged the gun with powder and leadin bullet then and there held in both her hands casually and by misfortune and against the will of ELIZABETH BROSHEARS discharged and shot in him the LITTLEBERRY MORGAN in his belly one mortal wound of which he instantly died. Proved: 27 May 1805.

Pages 619-620. 4 June 1805. ELIZABETH MASTERS (one of the legatees of JOHN MASTERS deceased) to JACOB MASTERS (another legatee) for the sum of Twenty pounds all her part of the land laid off to her of her father's estate by estimate 42 acres on the waters of Mulberry Creek joins ADLER AGEE. Wit:

HENRY CLARK, JAMES MASTERS, SALLY (X) MASTERS. Signed: ELIZABETH MASTERS. Proved: 24 June 1805.

Pages 620-621. 7 July 1805. MASON KELLY of Henry County to JOHN PRICE of the same for the sum of One hundred pounds sells 300 acres more or less on the south side of Smith River, Drag Creek, lines of JOHN KELLY and JACOB CAYTON. Signed: MASON KELLY. Proved: 29 July 1805.

Page 621. 29 July 1805. GEORGE WALLER, SENR. for the natural love and affection he bears GEORGE WALLER, JR. and WILLIAM WALLER gives them land in the county of Roan, state of Tennessee by patent 1,000 acres more or less on the Clinch River and known by the name of Pappaw Ford, Bluff Mountain. Signed: GEORGE WALLER, SENR. Proved: 29 July 1805.

Page 622. 15 May 1803. SAMUEL ROSE attorney for WILLIAM CABELL and PATRICK ROSE executors, and for CAROLINE ROSE widow of HUGH ROSE, deceased (agreeable to a power of attorney executed Amherst County 1802) to SAMUEL HILL and JOHN B. TRENT in consideration of $1.00 sell land in Henry County commonly called Poison Fields, joins Col. HENRY LYNE and Capt. JOHN SALMON it being 1,968 acres. Wit: SAMUEL IRVIN, NATHANIEL OFFUTT, WILSON DAVENPORT. Signed: SAMUEL ROSE. Proved in a court held for Amherst County 20 June 1803. Proved Henry County 29 July 1805 and recorded.

Page 623. 1 Dec. 1804. PRESLEY SIMPSON and his wife PATTY SIMPSON to ADREN ANGLIN for the sum of Eighty three pounds sells 200 acres more or less on the branches of the fishing fork of Leatherwood Creek, joins Gen. J. MARTIN, MICHAEL AKIN, ELIJAH RICHARDSON, ARCHELUS PURGASON, Col. HAIRSTON and Blue Knob. Signed: PRESLEY (X) SIMPSON, PATTY (X) SIMPSON. Proved: 25 Feb. 1805. . . .PATTY SIMPSON, wife of PRESLEY SIMPSON releases her right to dower to the above deed.

Page 624. 26 June 1805. GREGORY DURHAM of Henry County to WILLIAM HILL of the same for $130.00 sells land on the waters of Horsepasture Creek 26 acres joins WILLIAM SHELTON, JAMES SHELTON. Wit: JOHN STAPLES, WILLIAM SHELTON, JAMES ALEXANDER. Signed: GREGORY DURHAM. Proved: 29 July 1805.

Page 625. 29 July 1805. Bond of JOHN DILLARD who is appointed Coroner for Henry County, bondsmen JOHN REDD, WILLIAM HILL and BALLENGER WADE.

Pages 625-626. 25 June 1805. THOMAS BOULDIN of Henry County to THOMAS BOULDIN, JR. of the same for the sum of Five pounds sells 278 acres on Marrowbone Creek and Grassy Creek joins JOHN WEAVER. Wit: JOHN WEAVER, POLLY BOULDIN, MARTHA M. BOULDIN. Signed: THOMAS BOULDIN. Proved: 29 July 1805.

Pages 626-627. 20 June 1805. THOMAS BOULDIN to WILLIAM BOULDIN for the sum of Forty shillings sells by survey 623 acres more or less joins GREEN BOULDIN, POLLY BOULDIN and CRUTCHER. Wit: JOHN WEAVER, POLLY BOULDIN, MARTHA M. BOULDIN. Signed: THOMAS BOULDIN. Proved: 29 July 1805.

Page 628. 29 July 1805. Bond of WILLIAM MOORE who is appointed Constable. Bondsmen: JOHN REA, JOHN COX. Proved: 30 July 1805.

Page 628. 29 July 1805. WILLIAM HEARD is appointed Constable, bondsmen are JOHN REDD and LARKIN TURNER. Proved: 30 July 1805.

Page 629. 30 July 1805. JOHN SMITH appointed Constable. Bondsmen JOHN PACE and JOHN REANY. Proved: 30 July 1805.

Pages 629-630. 1 Jan. 1805. Deed of Trust. SACKVILLE BREWER, JR. of Patrick County indebted to GEORGE HAIRSTON in the amount of 15 barrels of corn, balance of the rent for the plantation whereon he now lives which rent is due for the year 1804. Due 15 Feb. next, secure with 1 horse, corn at $4.00 bbl., also an account at the Marrowbone and Hardin Hairston Store. A negro in trust, but to be used by SACKVILLE BREWER. Wit: JOSEPH ANTHONY, JR. Signed: SACKVILLE BREWER, JR. Proved: 26 Aug. 1805.

Pages 630-631. 23 Aug. 1805. ELIZABETH MASTERS, SENR., JAMES MASTERS, THOMAS MASTERS, JACOB MASTERS, ELIZABETH MASTERS, JR., ADLER AGEE and his wife JOYCE, JOHN EDINS and his wife MARY to HENRY HEFFLEFINGER for the sum of Twenty six pounds sell 3 acres on Mulberry Creek. Wit: CHARLES AGEE, LEWIS AGEE, BENJAMIN SMITH. Signed: ELIZABETH MASTERS, SR., JAMES MASTERS, THOMAS MASTERS, JACOB MASTERS, ELIZABETH MASTERS, JR., ADLER AGEE, JOYCE AGEE, JOHN EDINS, MARY EDINS. Proved: 26 Aug. 1805.

Pages 632-633. 30 Sept. 1805. JESSE MURPHY of Henry County to GEORGE HAIRSTON of the same for the sum of Sixty pounds sells 115 acres on the

branches of Matrimony Creek. Signed: JESSE (X)
MURPHY. Proved: 30 Sept. 1805. . . .PEGGY MURPHY,
sife of JESSE MURPHY release her right of dower.

Pages 633-634. 30 Sept. 1805. WILLIAM NIXON (NIXSON)
of Henry County to JAMES MASTERS of
the same for the sum of Thirty eight pounds sells
51¼ acres by survey on the waters of the south fork
of Leatherwood Creek, joins JOSEPH GRAVELY. Signed:
WILLIAM (X) NIXSON. Proved: 30 Sept. 1805.

Pages 634-635. 16 Mar. 1805. LANGSTON PACE and MILLEY
PACE his wife of Henry County to SAN-
FORD REAMEY for the sum of Fifty pounds sell 50 acres
it being part of a tract purchased of my father in
1798, also the land where I now live joins DANIEL
REAMEY, THOMAS NUNN and Col. HAIRSTON. Wit: JOHN PACE,
WILLIAM PACE, JOHN ALEXANDER. Signed: LANGSTON PACE.
Proved: 26 Aug. 1805. . . .MILLEY PACE, wife of LANGS-
TON PACE releases her right of dower.

Pages 635-636. 25 Apr. 1804. MARTHA FONTAINE of
Henry County to WILLIAM COX of the same
for Five shillings sells 50 acres on the waters of
Smith River, joins JOHN PACE. Wit: MICAJAH (X) COX.
Signed: MARTHA FONTAINE. Proved: 10 Sept. 1805.

Pages 636-637. 23 Sept. 1805. THOMAS STUART (STEWART)
of Henry County to JOSEPH MARTIN of the
same for the sum of Eighty three pounds five shillings
sells 111 acres on the waters of Leatherwood Creek.
Wit: JOHN DEGRAFFENRIED, JOSEPH MARTIN, JR., THOMAS
MARTIN. Signed: THOMAS STEWART. Proved: 30 Sept.1805.

Pages 637-638. 8 Oct. 1805. JOHN COX, JR. and his
wife JEAN COX to JOHN COX, SENR. for
the sum of One hundred pounds sells by estimate 100
acres on the branches of Rock Run Creek, joins Baker's
Path and Goings Wagon Road, JOHN WATSON'S School path,
Bull Mountain Road. Wit: TUNSTALL COX JOSEPH COX,
CHARLES HIBBERT. Signed: JOHN COX, JR., JEAN (X) COX.

Page 639. 1805. WILLIAM S. COX to DAVIS BURGESS of
Henry County for the sum of Seventy pounds
sells 150 acres more or less on Smith River, joins
MARTHA FONTAINE. Signed: WILLIAM S. COX, MARY (X)
COX. Proved: 30 Sept. 1805.

Pages 640-641. 14 Apr. 1805. Deed of Trust. THOMAS
MOORE to WALLER REDD and THOMAS STARL-
ING Trustees for JOHN REDD, amount Thirty five pounds

three shillings 1 pence with interest due 25 Dec. 1805, secures with negro woman Rachel 22 years old. Wit: JOHN P. PYRTLE, CHARLES (X) HARDY, BERRY (X) DILLEN. Signed: THOMAS MOORE, WALLER REDD, THOMAS STARLING. Proved: 30 Sept. 1805.

Pages 641-643. 26 Aug. 1805. SAMUEL HUNTER and PEYTON HUNTER acting executors of ALEXANDER HUNTER, deceased to MARTHA HUNTER widow and executrix of ALEXANDER HUNTER, ALEXANDER HUNTER died seized of several tracts of land on both sides of Smith River and the waters thereof and on the Carolina Road by estimate 1,535 acres and by his last will and testament date -- Nov. 1803, gave to MARTHA HUNTER 1/3 part of the estate during her natural life. The executors to sell at 12 months credit the residue of the said land and agreeable to this, did sell the residue on 15 February last by estimate 1,026 2/3 acres at which sale MARTHA HUNTER became the purchaser for Four hundred five pounds. The land was conveyed to ALEXANDER HUNTER by GEORGE HAIRSTON, EDMOND LYNE, MARY HICKY and others by deeds and by grants from the Registers Office in Richmond. Wit: ROBERT ROWLAND, THOMAS C. BOULDIN, BENJAMIN HARRISON, THOMAS WASH, JUNER MERADY, ALEXANDER HUNTER. Signed: SAMUEL HUNTER, PEYTON HUNTER. Proved: 30 Sept. 1805. . . .Received of MARTHA HUNTER the sum of Four hundred five pounds the date aforesaid.

Page 643. 12 Mar. 1805. EDITH RICE & JOHN A. VERDEL of Patrick County for the sum of $120.00 to WILLIAM HILL of Henry County a negro boy named William 14 years of age. Wit: WILLIAM SPENCER, THOMAS HILL, GEORGE SWITZLER. Signed: EDITH RICE, JOHN A. VERDEL. Proved: 30 Sept. 1805.

Page 644. 3 Jan. 1805. BLIZARD MAGRUDER of Henry County to PETER LEAK of the same for the sum of $60.00 sells 50 acres more or less on the waters of Sionas?? Creek joins Capt. JOHN WALLER, JOHN B. TRENT (formerly ROSE) and JOHN CHRISTIAN. Wit: JAMES ALEXANDER, JAMES STAPLES, JAMES STAPLES, JR., EDWARD STAPLES. Signed: BLIZARD MAGRUDER. Proved: 30 Aug. 1805.

Pages 644-646. 30 Sept. 1805. WILLIAM STOKES of Henry County to GEORGE HAIRSTON of the same for the sum of Three hundred pounds sells 232 acres on Beaver Creek joins JOSEPH ANTHONY, ISHAM NANCE, HENRY CLARK, JACOB FARRIS and CARR WALLER. Signed: WILLIAM STOKES. Proved: 30 Sept. 1805.

ISBELL STOKES, wife of WILLIAM STOKES releases her right of dower.

Page 646. 29 Sept. 1805. RICHARD GILLEY of Henry County to HENRY DILLENDER of the same for the sum of Fifty pounds sells and conveys 130 acres on the north side of Turkey Cock Creek (refer to the original deed for more details). Wit: WILLIAM S. COX, MICAJAH (X) COX, JOHN FARRIS. Signed: RICHARD (X) GILLEY. Proved: 30 Sept. 1805.

Pages 646-647. 1 Oct. 1805. REUBEN WADE of Henry County to JOHN SMITH of the same for the sum of One hundred forty pounds sells 100 acres more or less on the waters of Marrowbone Creek joins ALEXANDER MOORE, THOMAS STOVALL. Wit: SACKVILLE BREWER, JR., GEORGE MORRIS, WILLIAM SMITH. Signed: REUBEN WADE. Proved: 28 Oct. 1805. . . .LUCY WADE, wife of REUBEN WADE, releases her right of dower.

Pages 647-648. 8 Oct. 1805. JOHN STEPHENS and MILLEA STEPHENS his wife of Henry County to THOMAS HARRIS of Pittsylvania County for the sum of Thirty three pounds sells 100 acres on the waters of Home Creek, joins WILSON, SMITH. Wit: SANDFORD JONES, THOMAS JONES, BENJAMIN JONES, SAMUEL SHUMATE. Signed: JOHN (X) STEPHENS, MILLEA (X) STEPHENS. Proved: 28 Oct. 1805.

Pages 648-649. 28 Oct. 1805. BALDWIN ROWLAND of Henry County to JOHN ROWLAND of the same for the sum of Two hundred pounds sells 100 acres more or less that joins REUBEN PAYNE, PETER GARLAND, JOHN ALEXANDER, BRICE MARTIN and Rowlands Ford. Signed: BALDWIN ROWLAND. Proved: 28 Oct. 1805.

Page 649. 28 Oct. 1805. SANDFORD RAMEY appoints SANDFORD CONNELLY of Fluvannah County, Virginia to act in a certain tract of land surveyed for me and in my name in the county of Mason, state of Kentucky whereon now lives the Widow RAMEY. I empower my attorney to rent, lease or sell the said land. Signed: SANDFORD RAMEY. Proved: 28 Oct. 1805.

Page 650. 9 Oct. 1805. LUCY ALEXANDER wife of JOHN ALEXANDER releases her right of dower to a deed made to DANIEL RAMEY. Proved: 28 Oct. 1805.

Pages 650-651. 20 Nov. 1805. JACOB FARRIS for the love and affection he bears unto his daughter FRANKEY MARTIN wife of WILLIAM MARTIN of the state of Tennessee gives unto her five negros Jane, James, Major, Sally, and Aimy. Wit: JOSEPH ANTHONY, JOSIAH FARRIS, JAMES DILLEN, JOHN NORTON. Signed: JACOB FARRIS. Proved: 25 Nov. 1805.

Pages 651-652. 11 July 1805. BLIZARD MAGRUDER of Henry County to PETER PERKINS for the sum of $100.00 sells 100 acres on the north waters of Fall Creek joins ANGLINS line. Wit: BRETT STOVALL, JESSE ATKISSON, ISIAH ATKISSON, JOHN DILLARD, TERRY HUGHES. Signed: BLIZARD MAGRUDER. Proved: 25 Nov. 1805.

Pages 652-653. 1 Nov. 1805. JOHN ALEXANDER to JOSEPH ALEXANDER for the sum of $1,000.00 sells 157 acres by survey on the waters of Smith River it being part of Grey's Order. Joins Gen. JOSEPH MARTIN now WILLIAM HEREFORD, THOMAS GRAVES. Wit: JOHN PACE, BALLINGER WADE, BRETT STOVALL, NATHANIEL W. DANDRIDGE. Signed: JOHN ALEXANDER. Proved: 25 Nov. 1805.

Page 653. 1 Nov. 1805. JOHN ALEXANDER to JOSEPH ALEXANDER for the sum of $151.00 sells land on the waters of Little Marrowbone Creek and Grassy Creek. Wit: JOHN PACE, BALLINGER WADE, BRETT STOVALL, NATHANIEL W. DANDRIDGE. Signed: JOHN ALEXANDER. Proved: 25 Nov. 1805.

Page 654. 25 Nov. 1805. Bond of JAMES DYER appointed Constable his bondsmen BENJAMIN DYER and REUBEN NANCE.

Pages 654-655. 26 Aug. 1805. JACOB MASTERS of Henry County to WILLIAM HALE of the same for the sum of Twenty nine pounds sells 42 acres more or less on Mulberry Creek. Wit: JOSEPH MARTIN, A. HUGHS, BRICE EDWARDS. Signed: JACOB (X) MASTERS. Proved: 30 Dec. 1805.

Page 655. 6 Sept. 1805. Inquist at a place called the Narrowson Smith River to view the body of JAMES SMITH blacksmith. Jury JOHN COX, WILLIAM STOKES, JOHN S. WOODSON, JAMES BAKER, JAMES MURPHY, FRANCIS MURPHY, BARTLETT WADE, ISOM NANCE, GEORGE WALLER, WILLIAM DRAPER, WILLIAM FRENCH, JOSEPH PHIFER. The said JAMES SMITH drowned by accident in the Smith River. Proved: 30 Dec. 1805.

Page 656. 17 Oct. 1805. THOMAS RICHARDSON of Henry County to GEORGE DYER of the same for the sum of Twenty five pounds sells 50 acres by estimate on a branch of Leatherwood Creek called the fishing fork on both sides, joins LOMAX & Company and NICHOLAS AIKEN, patented to PETER PERKINS. Wit: ELIAS (X) THOMASSON, ARNAL (X) THOMASSON, JAMES DYER. Signed: THOMAS RICHARDSON. Proved: 30 Dec. 1805.

Pages 656-657. 26 Sept. 1805. EDWARD COCKRAN of Franklin County to ELIJAH PEDIGO of Henry County for the sum of $100.00 sells 165 acres more or less on the south branch of Stuarts Creek joins JACOB CARTER, the county line. Wit: JOHN HALL, JOHN HALL, JR., NATHAN HALL, JR., JAMES INGRUM. Signed: EDWARD COCKRAN (X). Proved: 30 Dec. 1805.

Page 657. 14 Nov. 1804. Bond of JOSEPH MARTIN who is appointed Sheriff of Henry County and is to collect revenue tax for the year 1805. Proved: 30 Dec. 1805.

Pages 657-658. 28 Dec. 1805. NICHOLAS AIKEN and his wife JANEY AIKEN to MICHAEL AIKEN for the sum of Fifty pounds sells 33 1/3 acre on the branch of fishing fork of Leatherwood Creek being part of a tract NICHOLAS AIKEN purchased of WILLIAM LOVELL, joins THOMAS AIKEN, JOHN ROBERTS, JOHN DAVIS, JOSEPH GRAVELY, ELISHA WILLIAMS and SAMUEL WATSON. Signed: NICHOLAS AIKEN. Proved: 30 Dec. 1805. . . .JEAN AIKEN, wife of NICHOLAS AIKEN releases her right of dower.

Pages 658-659. 28 Dec. 1805. NICHOLAS AIKEN and his wife JANEY AIKEN to THOMAS AIKEN for the sum of Forty pounds sells 33 1/3 acre on the fishing fork of Leatherwood Creek, being part of a tract purchased of WILLIAM LOVELL. Signed: NICHOLAS AIKEN. Proved: 30 Dec. 1805. . . .JEAN AIKEN releases her right of dower.

Pages 659-660. 28 Dec. 1805. NICHOLAS AIKEN and his wife JANEY AIKEN to JOHN ROBERTS for the sum of Forty pounds sells 33 1/3 acre part of a tract purchased of JOSEPH GRAVELY and part of WILLIAM LOVELL, on a branch of fishing fork of Leatherwood Creek. Signed: NICHOLAS AIKEN. Proved: 30 Dec. 1805. . . . .JEAN AIKEN releases her right of dower.

INDEX

COMPILED BY

ELLA EVADNA LEE SHEFFIELD

TEXAS CITY, TEXAS 77590

____ANOY, Aron 124
ABINGTON, Bowles 17; John 17
ACUFF, Cain 13, 46, 48; Esther 46; John 13, 46; William 13, 48
ADAMS, ____103; Absalom 24, 37; E. 13; Edward 12, 26, 110, 111; Jacob 32, L. 85, Luke 88, 106, 107; Randolph 6, 106; Richard 54; Thomas, Jr. 1, 6; Thomas R.G. 56; Thomas R.L. 6
ADKINS, John 130
AGEE, Adler 141, 143; Charles 92, 132, 143; Jacob 92; Joyce 143; Lewis 132, 143
AIKEN, ____117; Janey 148; Jean 148; Nicholas 94, 107, 148; Thomas 148
AIRSROP, Henry 122
AIRSTRIP, Henry 121
AISTROP, Henry 138
AKIN, Michael 85, 93, 120, 129, 142; Nicholas 35, 53, 114
ALEXANDER, David 115, 123, 124; Elisha 115; Ingram 1, 81, 87, 108, 117, 127; James 93, 126, 127, 142, 145; John 1, 8, 9, 12, 26, 35, 44, 75, 81, 82, 85, 88, 92, 93, 94, 97, 108, 122, 125, 131, 138, 144, 146, 147; John M. 21, 125; Joseph 94, 107, 108, 117, 122, 147; Lucy 12, 146; Polly 126; Reuben 138; Robert 135; Samuel 71; T. 50; Thomas 3, 79, 86, 92, 101, 108, 125; Unity 124; William 1, 9, 81
ALLEN, Hartwell 105; Hartwill 118; Pines 104, 105; Robert 78, 129, 132, 139, 140; Samuel 30
AMBROSE, Joseph 51, 81, 115
ANDERSON, David 18, 19, 90; James 36; John 13; Robert 12, 66, 88, 137, 138
ANGLIN, ____4, 147; Adren 142; Adrin 107; Adrion 115; Adron 92; Caleb 92; Catey 129, Philip 3, 14, 36, 85, 125; Samuel 93, 115, 120, 129; Sarah 107
ANTHONY, James 119; Joseph 13, 18, 20, 35, 60, 74, 77, 80, ' 83, 95, 101, 119, 121, 125, 137, 145, 147; Joseph, Jr. 121, 143; M. 6; Samuel 85
ARNOLD, Elisha 70; Nancy 101, 102
ARTHUR, Thomas 40
ATKISSON, Isiah 147; Jesse 26, 42, 70, 75, 147; Jesse, Jr. 26, 42, 114; Jesse, Sr. 114; Mary 26; Ruth 42; Soloman 114; Stephen 4, 42
AUSTIN, Stephen 97

BADEN, William 97
BAILES, Bailey 68; Elijah 68; Jesse 68; Nancy 68; William, Jr. 68; William, Sr. 69
BAILEY, ____72; John 104, 130, 135; Joseph 102, 103; Patty 102, 103
BAKER, ____17; Caleb 21, Daniel 97; David 89; James 3, 24, 30, 41, 65, 88, 97, 114,

James, Continued: 126, 130, 136, 147; James, Jr. 115, James, Sr. 115; Thomas 97
BALLENGER, A. 19; Achillis 39, 70; Milley 38
BALLINGER, Archellus 28; Milley 28
BARKSDALE, John 3, 8, 24, 41, 67, 89, 93, 128, 130; Sally 93; Sarah 128; William 30, 89, 90, 93, 128, 129
BARNARD, ____97; William 82, 107, 117
BARNET, ____114
BARNS, James 114
BARNTON, William 106
BARRET, Robert 54
BARRINGTON, Joseph 84, 104
BARROTT, John 123
BARTLETT, William 18
BARTON, Thomas 12, 50, 81, 82, 92, 94, 101, 135, 136, 138, 140; William, Jr. 121, 136
BASSETT, Burrel 41; Burwell 127; Margaret 78; Nathaniel 46, 65, 78
BAUGHAN, Mary 57
BAYLES, Bailey 69, 70; Elijah 8, 69, 70; Jesse 70; Nancy 69, 70; Sally 70; William 39, 69, 140; William, Jr. 70; William, Sr. 28, 70
BAYS, Sary 139
BAYSE, William 51, 115
BEDFORD, Thomas 58
BEEK, John 65
BENNETT, Casson, 31; William 31
BERKELEY, William 69
BERNARD, Thornton 92, 93, 94; Walter 5; William 92, 94, 96
BIBB, Richard 19
BIRD, ____98; Milley 75; Samuel 18
BISWELL, John, Jr. 18; John, Sr. 18
BITTING, Anthony 22, 27, 28, 45, 61
BLEVINS, Dillian 36; James 15, 57; 57; William, Senr. 36
BOHANNON, James 94
BOLING, ____44; James 32; Thomas 37
BOLLING, Christopher 2, 15, 57; Green 16; Thomas 14, 16, 34
BOLT, John 77
BOOTH, John 76
BORSHEARS, Robert 29
BOTTOM, Joel 42; John 42; Rowland 42
BOULDIN, ____39, 89; Green 16, 33, 34, 39, 62, 75, 88, 112, 138, 143; James 42, 43, 52, 64, 120; Joseph 52, 80,83,90,91 93, 96, 138; Joseph, Jr. 135, Martha 75, 96, 97; Martha M. 143; Polly 135, 143; Thomas 16, 33, 39, 41, 42, 43, 62, 63, 70, 75, 96, 97, 120, 132, 135, 136, 143; Thomas, Jr. 39, 127, 143; Thomas, Sr. 41, 62, 75; Thomas C. 76, 145; William 33, 39, 42, 43, 72, 143;
BOULDING, James 95
BOWLES, John M. 90
BOYD, Harrison 52, 80
BRADBERRY, Tabithia 129

BRADFIELD, James 92
BRANCH, Davis 24, 30
BRANS, James 91
BRASHARES, Nanny 102, 103; Robert 15
BRASHER, James 29; Phillip 29
BRAXTON, T. 54; William Fitzhugh 54
BREATHET, ____28
BRETHART, Elizabeth 6, 74; William 6, 51, 73, 74, 86
BRETHETT, Elizabeth 7, 9, 10; William 7, 8, 9
BREWER, Sackville 143; Sackville, Jr. 143, 146; William 46
BRISCO, Dr. John 9
BRITTAIN, George 50, 51; Judith 51
BROSHEARS, Elizabeth 141; Patty 102; Philip 29, 102
BROWN, ____2, 71; Byrd 110; Isham 128; John 75; Marget 4; Peggy 70; Ruffin 39; Stark 8; William 4, 8, 14, 39, 40, 44, 70, 71, 74, 94, 102, 136; William, Jr. 59; William, Sr. 59
BRYANT, Ely 135
BRYDIE, Alexander 91
BUNCH, Anna 33; Benjamin 33, 60, 138; David 33, 104; Fanny 40; Frances 138; Francis 33; Marthy 33; Martin 33, Mary 60;
BUNDREN, Francis 114
BURCH, Bazel 117, 118; Garrot 8; Janet 86; Jarard 74; Jarrot 73; John 14, 18, 69; John, Jr. 14; John, Sr. 14
BURCHETT, ____139; John 85
BURCHITT, ____130
BURGESS, David 141, 144; Davis 37; Jo. 75; John 2, 37; Katherine Elizabeth 35
BURNET, Thomas 92
BURNETT, ____39; Charles 15, 21, 38, 98; William 24, 25
BURNIT, Charles 8; O. 65
BURNLY, ____5; John 5; Zackeriah 5
BURNS, Charles 38
BURRIS, William 90
BUSH, Thomas 1

CABALL, William 102
CAHILL, John 8, 29, 112, 119
CALL, ____38; John 5, 20; William 38
CALLAHAM, John 95
CALLAND, John 14, 105; Samuel 32, 105, 117; William 105
CALLAY, ____78
CALLIM, Spencer 60
CAMERON, Uriah 83
CAMPBELL, ____36, 45; Thomas 80
CARLIN, Daniel 69
CARR, Ann 24; John Fendal 128; Joseph 24, 37; Samuel 88
CARROLL, Charles 71
CARTER, Jacob 148; Jesse 45, 115
CARTSON, William 30
CASON, Edward 11, 19, 20; Lucy 11, 19
CASSEY, James 128
CATON, Cornelius 39; Jacob 38, 39, 95

CATRON, Jacob 15
CAYTON, Cornelius 38, 99, 141; Jacob 46, 81, 87, 88, 95, 128, 139, 142; Margaret 139; Roday 99; William 27, 88, 128
CHANDLER, Charity 24, 25; Jesse 2, 97; Joseph 6; Robert 1; Thomas 24, 25, 106
CHAPMAN, Thomas 20, 88, 100; William 139
CHATTERS, J. 88
CHEATHAM, Leonard 124; Leonard, Jr. 124
CHEWNING, Thomas 50
CHILDRESS, Betsy 133, 139; Thomas 114, 132, 133, 139
CHITWOOD, Joel 40
CHOWNING, Chatten 141; Thomas 29, 32, 33, 49, 50, 66, 69, 118, 121, 141
CHRISTIAN, John 111, 141, 145; William 49
CHYSHER, Daniel 13
CLARK, Ann 22; George 128; George R. 31; Henry, 14, 22, 25, 45, 60, 61, 75, 83, 85, 95, 105, 116, 117, 142, 145; James 119; John 18; Jonathan 83; Joseph 50; Timan 31, 38
CLAY, ____114; Thomas 16
CLAYBROCK, ____30
CLAYBROOK, James 30, 31, 115; Jesse 31
CLIFFT, Joseph 23
CLIFT, Joseph 97; Sarah 97
CLINTON, Henry 99
CLOYS, Thomas 23
COCKRAM, ____95; Edward 57, 148; Mary 57
COGHLIN, James 128
COLE, ____109; Mrs. ____17; Sally 16, 17; Samuel 88; W.K. 38, 41; Walter King 1, 6, 7, 9, 16, 35, 88, 103
COLLIER, ____71; John 10, 13, 15
CONNAWAY, John 120, 133, 135, 140
CONNELLY, Sanford 146
CONNOR, Philip 33, 43, 51, 75, 141
CONWAY, John 13, 20, 35, 38, 85
COOK, Benjamin 91, 116; Edward 122; Elizabeth 135; Harmon 15; James 91, 135; John 130, 134; M. 15; Margaret 13; Nancy 135; Polly 135; William 13
COOKE, ____94
COOLEY, Jacob 13, 35, 57; Nancy 35
COOLLEY, Jacob 32
COOPER, ____28; Elizabeth 50; Joseph 7; Rachel 64; Sarah 8; Thomas 8, 12, 50, 51, 61, 100; Thomas, Sr. 29
COPLAND, ____36, 56, 71; Peter 97
CORN, Jesse 53, 54, 66
CORNWELL, Richard 6
COUTTS, Patrick 54; William 54
COVINGTON, Edmund 24, 25; Nancy 24, 25
COX, ____42, 87; Charles 10, 19, 30, 31, 57, 68, 80, 141; Charles, Jr. 68; Charles, Sr. 68; Ellender 68; Fleming 108; Frances 141; Francis 21, 24, 25, 30, 39, 75, 78, 81, 95, 96, 97, 98, 118, 131; Henry 139; Hannah 97; Jean 97; John 11, 12, 15, 18, 19, 23, 24, 30, 32, 34, 35, 41, 58, 67, 68, 74, 76, 84, 85, 97, 108, 109, 112,

John, continued: 119, 120, 123, 124, 125, 126, 128, 136, 140, 143, 144, 147; John, Jr. 27, 34, 68, 126, 137, 144; John, Sr. 129, 136, 144; John Coates 88; Joseph 67, 112, 136, 144; Laney 11, 139; Lucy 141; Margaret 10; Mary 30, 44; Micajah 144, 146; Robert 63, 67; Russell 46; Thomas 47, 68, 96, 97, 141; Tunstall 11, 27, 31, 45, 58, 63, 65, 68, 74, 76, 126, 128, 129, 130, 136, 144; Warren 136; William 4, 144; William L. 119; William S. 34, 47, 126, 141, 144, 146
CRADOCK, Isham 24, 30, 65, 114
CRAIN, ____106; William 30
CRANE, Rebecca 54; Rebeckan 16; William 16, 54
CREASEY, John 75, 81, 92, 93, 94, 100, 119, 128; Obedience 81
CROUCH, Jesse 15; John 9, 81
CRUM, Margaret 84; William 54, 84, 104, 106
CRUTCHER, ____143; Charles 32; Samuel 32
CRUTCHFIELD, Samuel 45
CUMTON, Banar 42
CUNNINGHAM, Frankey 40; Henry Barsdale 53; James 74; John 19, 32, 118; Joseph 16; Polly 106; Sarah 19; William 78, 106
CURSEY, John 65

DAINES, Jacob 50, 77; Mary 67; Nancy 50
DAINS, Jacob 16, 55, 56, 67; Nancy 55
DALTON, Martin 32
DANCE, Thomas 59
DANDRIDGE, A. B. 58; Archibald B. 53; N. W. 22, 38, 110; Nathaniel 90; Nathaniel W. 31, 47, 48, 53, 91, 93, 96, 103, 110, 135, 147; Nathaniel W. Jr. 43, 48, 49, 50, 58; William 75
DANES, R. A. 90
DANIEL, ____45; Edward 11, 69, 75, 79; Nicholas 116
DAVENPORT, Wilson 142
DAVIS, ____65; Charles 8, 92; Elizabeth 61; John 32, 36, 38, 61, 86, 116, 120, 148
DEAN, Jacob 77
DEATHERAGE, Bird 73
DEEN, Jacob 22
DEGRAFFINREID, Francis 109; John 109, 130, 144; William 109, 117, 130, 134
DEJARNATT, Daniel 32
DELOSIER, Rhoda 121
DELOSURE, Edward 7
DELOTHER, Jesse 13
DELOZAR, Jesse D. 17
DELOZEAR, Edw. 57; Jesse 114
DELOZER, Jesse 51, 94
DELOZIER, Edward 121
DELOZORS, ____73
DEMEY, Joel 77; William 77
DEMPSEY, John 36, 75
DENT, ____45; Shadrick 7, 22, 61, 62, 74, 75, 83, 92, 112
DESHAZO, William 61, 76, 86, 101, 118
DICKENSON, Thomas, Jr. 21
DICKERSON, ____94, 114; Charles 15, 57; Robert 57; Thomas 18, 34, 107; Thomas, Jr. 74; Thomas, Sr. 7, 15

DICKINSON, Griffith 20; Thomas 79; Thomas, Jr. 21
DILLARD, James 101, 124; John 11, 12, 17, 21, 34, 42, 43, 55, 64, 70, 76, 78, 80, 85, 94, 96, 97, 114, 124, 128, 133, 142, 147; Sarah 42, 43
DILLEN, ____72; Benjamin 24, 104; Carter 95, 96; Hannah 96; Henry 63, 68, 95, 105; John 130; William 37, 72, 95
DILLENGER, Henry 146; Jacob 43, 48; Rhody 48
DILLIAN, William 72, 75, 141
DILLINGHAM, Joshua 26
DILLION, Henry 45; John 24; Joseph 30; Sarah 24; Susanah 30
DILLON, Berry 145; James 147; John 3, 18, 27, 130, 136, 140; Sally 27; William 32, 55; William, Jr. 105
DIX, Thomas 94, 108, 117, 121, 122, 127, 135, 138
DODSON, William 114
DONALD, Andrew 111; James 97; Richard 22; Robert 53
DONELSON, ____83; Elizabeth 78, 53; Stockley 69
DORNELL, Nicholas 30
DORR, Alexander 84
DOUGLAS, James 48
DOWDIE, John 35, 73, 86; Mary 86
DRAPER, William 27, 41, 67, 147
DUNCAN, Charles 98; John 29;
DUNCIN, John 29; Milly 29
DUNKIN, John 29; Milly 29
DUNN, Hezekiah 76; Mary 75; Waters 27; Waters, Sr. 127; William 63, 74, 75, 76, 89, 131
DUNSON, Jeremiah 30
DURHAM, Gregory 58, 64, 84, 124, 142; Nathaniel 113, 114; William 134
DUVALL, Samuel 55, 61; William 35, 54
DYER, ____135; Benjamin 147; George 119, 137, 147; James 94, 108, 113, 114, 119, 132, 134, 147, 148

EARLY, John 7
EASLEY, Miller 13
EAST, James 15, 31, 135; John 1, 118; Joseph 137; Thomas 6, 37, 41, 46, 49, 50, 85, 117, 118, 122, 128; William 118, 137
ECHOLS, Frederick 77, 78
ECKHOLS, Frederick 76, 80, 130
ECTON, James 18
EDINS, John 143; Mary 143
EDWARDS, Ambrose 112, 132; Brice 147; Edmund 11, 83; Isham 43, 44, 57; James 11, 19, 43, 44, 134; James, Jr. 81; James, Sr. 81; Judith 11; Lucey 81; Mary 11; Sellman 39; Thomas 11, 19, 134; William 19, 134
EGGLETON, George 129; Thomas 51, 118, 129
ELLIOTT, George 10; Polley 107; Samuel 1, 2, 8, 24, 25, 75, 77, 81, 98, 107, 137
EPPERSON, ____139; David 79, 86
EVENS, James 33

FARDING, Charles 47
FARGUSON, Millicent 76; Robert 76
FARIS, Jacob 28
FARRIS, Archibald 12, 40, 46, 47, 56, 69, 72, 75, 90, 120, 127, 140; Charles 7, 23, 37;

FARRIS, continued: Charles, Jr. 37; Charles, Sr. 1, 7, 37; Jacob 120, 145, 146, 147; John 68, 146; Josiah 147; Thomas 23
FEE, Henry 133; John 81, 82, 83, 84; Parthena 84; William 81, 82, 83, 115
FENNIS, Thomas 54
FERRIS, Jacob 13, 20; Josiah 20
FIELDS, ____38
FIFER, James 137; Joseph 67
FINCH, ____6; Charles 6; Polly 98; Robert 98; Susannah 98
FINE, Thomas 40
FISHER, James 37; Jonathan 37
FITZGERALD, James 115
FITZHUGH, William 71
FITZPATRICK, Thomas 20, 38
FLETCHER, John 35
FLOWERS, Thomas 30, 70
FODRELL, Charles 116
FOLEY, Luke 103
FONTAINE, ____34, 44; Charles 91; John 10, 19, 21, 52, 53, 58, 67, 91; Martha 10, 19, 21, 23, 25, 31, 43, 47, 49, 90, 91, 96, 110, 135, 144; P. H. 21, 43, 47, 58, 88, 90, 96, 103; Patrick H. 110; Patrick Henry 10, 19, 25, 69; William 52
FOODRILL, Charles 84
FORD, Andrew 32; Daniel 9
FORSSIE, ____5; John 5
FOSTER, Charles 116; Thomas 86, 115, 136
FRANCE, Henry 55, 114, 128, 133
FRANCIS, William 32, 79, 138
FRANCISCO, Peter 41
FRANKLIN, Lewis 41, 113, 124
FRASHER, George 103
FRENCH, John 68, 76, 91, 98, 106, 108, 116, 140; Sidney 98; William 15, 17, 69, 104, 105, 106, 109, 116, 136, 138, 147
FULKERSON, Frederick 128; John 116
FUQUA, Joseph 28

GARDNER, ____48; John 138; William 67, 68, 70, 115
GARLAND, ____5, 76, 86; P. 3, 69, 88, 113, 127; Peter 40, 79, 82, 86, 89, 125, 131, 146; Robert 125, 126; T. P. 94
GARNER, John 123
GARROT, Elimelock 123
GEARHEART, Peter 93, 94, 135
GIBSON ____139; John 131
GILLEY, Charles 122; Francis 10, 29, 114, 122, Francis, Jr. 43; George 10, 27, 33, 37, 38, 107, 135; Mary 10, 114; Richard 10, 139, 146
GILLIAM, William 12, 13
GILMORE, ____125; George 41
GOING, John 30, 65, 66
GOLDSBY, Daniel 4
GOODE, ____80; John 64
GOODWIN, Joseph 10, 11, 19, 20, 43, 87, 141
GOOLDSBY, ____4
GORD, ____80
GORDER, Ephriam 116
GOVER, John 18
GRATSY, Thomas 117, 118; William 104
GRAVELY, ____71, 93; Ellender 39; Healin 85; Healing 120; Jabez 32, 39; John 14; Joseph 10, 22, 53, 107, 120;

Joseph, continued:128, 132, 144, 148; Joseph, Jr. 85, 107; 126, 140; Peggey 14
GRAVES, ____79; John 74; Thomas 20, 36, 37, 48, 49, 55, 66, 74, 99, 108, 138, 140, 147; William 74
GRAY, ____45
GRIFFIN, ____61; Griffith 125, 140
GRIFFITH, Griffin 51, 53, 81, 122, 140
GRIGGS, ____44, 71; James 116; John 10, 35, 80, 104; John, Jr. 10; John, Sr. 104, 116
GRIGS, John 33; Mical 33
GROGAN, Henry 43, 44, 68; John 30, 38, 43, 44, 57, 80, 95, 134, 141; Mary 80; Nancy 141; Spencer 95, 134, 139, 141
GROGEN, Brice 68; Henry 68; Lettice 54
GROGINS, ____39
GUFFEE, Henry 30

HAILE, ____76
HAILEY, ____64, 65; Barneba 8; John 8, 14, 89; Rhody 8
HAIRSTON, ____5, 93, 121, 129, 142, 144; Elizabeth 41, 63, 64, 101, 102, G. 120; G. 120; George 1-9, 12, 15-17, 20-30, 32, 33, 36-39, 41, 44-46, 48, 50-53, 55, 57, 58, 61-68, 71-77, 79, 80, 82-86, 88-90, 93, 95, 96, 98, 100-102, 104, 105, 107-109, 111, 113-115, 117-119, 121-123, 125-128, 130-132, 134, 137-141, 143-145; George, Jr. 101; Hardin 99, 101; Peter 1, 79, 125; Robert 73, 75, 86, 137; Ruth 86
HALE, John 54; William 110, 147
HALEY, Barnaba 8; Barny 40; Edward 48; James 71; John 14, 40, 82; Martha 82; Rody 8
HALL, ____4; John 148; John, Jr. 148; Nathan 4; Nathan, Jr. 148
HAMMON, ____63; John 81
HAMMOND, John 33, 42, 43, 74, 76, 114, 129, 131
HAMMONS, Welthy 129
HAMONS, John 101
HAMPTON, James 30; Labon 40, 42
HANCOCK, Bennet 80; George 5
HANIER, John H. 95
HANKINS, ____39; Daniel 23, 97; William 80, 97
HANNAH,William 81
HARBOUR, ____4; David 47, 107; Mary 47; Thomas 55, 107, 113; W. 28
HARDEMAN, Constt. 69
HARDEN, M. 66; Mark 49
HARDMAN, John 6, 9, 33, 37; Thomas 65; Uriah 9, 33
HARDWAY, ____39; Stanfield 80
HARDY, Charles 145
HARMER, ____4, 41; John 8
HAROU, John 54
HARRIS, Aaron F. 114; Bennet 68; David 22; Edward 117; Franky 68, 70; G. F. 51; George F. 81, 114, 115, 139; George G. 22; George Fuller 35, 81; Henry 25, 21; John 30, 73, 94; Nathan 105,106; Peter 67; Thomas 146; William 114
HARRISON, Benjamin 35, 36, 53, 66,69,88,91,103,116,145; Benjamin, Jr. 38, 51-53, 103, 116 Carter B. 116; Elizabeth 103; John 84; Sally 35, 36, 38, 103

HART, Caleb 18; Patrick 91
HATCHER, Archibald 55, 69, 72; Hubbard 97, 101
HAY, William 54
HAYES, William 33; William, Jr. 55; William, Sr. 55
HAYS, Sally 80; William 125; 133; William, Jr. 80; William, Sr. 80, 81
HEARD, James 92; Jesse 119; John 26; William 8, 37, 50, 63, 65, 85, 112, 119, 143; William, Senr. 123
HEATH, Sally B. 106; Sally Bet 31, 45, 68; William 31, 45, 63, 68, 91, 104, 106, 123
HEDSPETH, Robert 29
HEFFLEFINGER, Henry 100, 107, 120, 143; John 9, 12, 44, 45; Mary 44, 45
HENDERSON, ____5; James 86; John 5; Thomas 67
HENDREN, James 8;
HENRY, ____63, 110; Mrs. ____50; Dorthea 52, 58, 133; Edward 19, 25, 31, 52, 110; P. 49; Patrick 10, 12, 25, 31, 44, 48, 52, 58, 67, 96, 110, 133
HENSLEY, Jane 57; Jean 105; John 105; Lewis 58, 105; Patsey 105
HEREFORD, William 126, 127, 147
HERNDON, Richardson 56, 72, 76, 90
HESTER, Samuel 50, 135
HEWLETT, Aug. 114; Augustine 118; Elizabeth 140; John Watkins 71; William 71, 118, 140, 141
HEWLITT, William 32, 57;
HIBBERT, Charles 106, 128, 129, 136, 140, 144
HICKEY, Joshua 123; Mary 76; Michael 119, 123
HICKKEY, Mary 76, 77
HICKS, ____75, 104; James 39; John 39; Judith 39
HICKY, Mary 145
HIGGS, Samuel 119
HILL, ____124; George 87; John 136; Manion 120; Manning 120, 128; Samuel 142; Thomas 94, 138, 145; Thomas S. 111; William 44, 75, 78, 94, 124, 142, 145
HITE, Abraham 121
HOBART, Elizabeth 17; Harrison 17; Jean 17; John 17; Saberah 17
HOBSON, ____52; Joseph 52, 67, 75
HODGE, ____50; Moses 22
HOFF, Thomas 30
HOLLANDSWORTH, Isaac 89
HOLMNS, Frances 121; John 112, 121
HOLT, William 2, 59, 60, 70, 105
HOOKER, ____74; Robert 29; Samuel 29
HOPPER, ____137; James 133, 134, 141; Joshua 112
HOPSON, ____67; George B. 131; John 94, 95; Joseph 58, 81, 110
HORD, ____17, 58, 124; John 58, 59, 61, 77; Mordecai 3, 48, 49, 58, 61; Ruth 58, 59, 61, 77; S. 31; Stanwix 89, 90, 93, 119; William 31, 59, 61, 118, 119
HOWARD, James 9, 28, 68, 75, 82, 83, 95, 101, 112, 116, 126, 140
HUGHES, ____122; A. 118, 122, 132, 134, 135, 147; Alijah 5, 117; Arch, 7; Archelaus 21,

HUGHES, Archelaus, Continued: 112; Fred 55; Micajah, 100, 138; Rees 101, 122; Rice 141; Rus 49; Samuel 5, 32; Terry 138, 147
HUNT, ___ 39; James 79, 80, 107
HUNTER, ___ 17; Alexander 7, 34, 43, 58, 59, 61, 76, 77, 122, 145; John W. 5; Martha 145; Peyton 145; Robert H. 77; Samuel 145; Titus 54, 92; William 64, 65
HURD, Jesse 123; Margaret 123
HURT, Littleberry 92
HUTCHENS, Frederick 55, 99, 114; John 99; John, Senr. 99; Molly 99
HUTCHERSON, Billy 130; William 106
HUTCHINSON, Frederick 132

INGRAM, Elizabeth 40; John 40
INGRUM, James 148
INNES, James 77, 78; James, J. 78
IRVIN, Samuel 142

JABY, Edward 104
JACKSON, Thomas 65
JAMERSON, John 44
JAMES, William 115
JAMESON, Thomas 63; Thomas, Sr. 107
JAMISON, Ann 113; John 112; John, Sr. 16; Thomas 3, 6, 28, 49, 75, 77, 113, 126; William 124
JARVIS, Elizabeth 106; Nancy 106; Thomas 91, 106, 135
JENKINS, William 113
JENNINGS, Jacob 19, 23; Mary 67; Samuel 78; Samuel H. 58; Samuel K. 63, 64
JETT, Thomas 35, 44, 52, 58, 66, 67, 75, 81, 82, 100
JINKINS, Francis 28; Joseph 14; Nancy 28
JOHNSON, ___ 39; Betsy 8; James 5, 19, 52, 67; Joseph Ray 5; Mary 36; Nancy 11; Samuel 1, 5, 7, 8, 19, 118; William 36, 77
JOHNSTON, Betty 8; James 14, 32, 39, 107; Samuel 71, 73
JONES, Ambrose 7, 14, 16, 79; Armstead 21; Bartlet 101, Benjamin 3, 14, 56, 75, 100, 101, 116, 146; Charles 6, 61, 76, 122, 125, 128, 135; Dolley 109; Dorothy 116; Edward 13; Elizabeth 132; Henry 3, 24, 50, 56, 81, 100; John 23, 30, 109, 116, 128; Joseph 23, 30, 50, 51, 54, 78, 104; Lewis 50; Nelson Powell 122; Pamela 62; Sandford 146; Susannah 24; Thomas 62, 109, 129, 132, 139, 146; W. 122; William 16, 79
JORDON, ___ 84, 111, 115; Samuel 102
JOSEPH, William 38, 95
JOYCE, Elizabeth 73; Robert 56, 73

KARR, Joseph 24
KEATON, Jacob 46
KEELING, Abraham 133
KELLEY, Caty 31; John 43, 95, 128; Mason 29, 31, 95, 141; Thomas 31, 141
KELLUM, William 60, 138
KELLY, ___ 39; Caty 31; John 50, 141, 142; Mason 141, 142
KETCHAM, William 27

KEY, Creassy 114; George 82, 96, 118, 140; Isabella 103, 118; Martin 26, 48
KINDRICK, John 30
KING, ___ 71; Asa 17; David 126; George 39, 76, 89; George W. 126; Harbert 126; John 1, 39, 40, 61, 63, 70, 76, 82, 109, 117; John, Jr. 82, 129, 130; John, Sr. 108, 126, 134; Joseph 93; Mary 109; Stephen 110, 112, 136; Thomas 61; Walter 26; William 5
KLEMAN, ___ 72
KOGER, Henry 65, 119

LACKEY, Adam 30; John 30
LAMPKIN, Lewis 118
LAND, Dutton 68
LANE, Dutton 10, 29, 31, 81, 87, 134, 138, 139; Dutton, Jr. 31, 95; Elizabeth 134; Molly 134; Samuel 29
LANIER, ___ 94; Benjamin 45, 51, 66; D. 16, 97, 116; David 7, 8, 11, 12, 21, 28, 34-36, 44, 45, 49, 51, 53, 66, 72, 73, 75, 80, 90, 98; Elizabeth 28, 44, 48; James 73; John 8; John H. 44, 72, 73; John M. 103; Major 36; Mary 7, 8, 12, 36, 44, 90; Moirtel 122; Nancy 28; Samuel 20, 23, 108; Washington 4, 23, 37, 40, 48
LANSFORD, Henry 11, 50; Isham 49, 66;
LARIMORE, J. 132; James 56, 127, 138; Nancy 132; Thomas J. W. 96
LARK, Dennis 112; Peter 89
LARKS, Dennis 134
LARRANCE, ___ 87; Henry 69; William 69, 87
LARRIMORE, James 60, 69
LASEURE, Polly 90
LAURANCE, Henry 14, 100; William 14, 100
LAUTON, Robert 5, 6
LAWLESS, ___ 45; Augustine 24; Austin 2; Jesse 15, 34
LAWRANCE, Henry 5; William 5
LAWRENCE, Henry 4, 8, 39
LAWSON, Isam 132
LAYNE, Dutton 15
LEAK, Hannah 34; John 88; Joseah 76; Josiah 97, 104, 105; Peter 34, 43, 55, 64, 69, 84, 89, 110, 145
LEAKE, Peter 47, 111
LEE, Stephen 46
LESUEUR, John 109; Martel 90, 109; Polly 90
LETCHER, James 123
LEWIS, Benjamin 54
LILTRELL, John 18
LINDSAY, Daniel 73; Elizabeth 73; Jacob 36, 54, 69, 73, 89; James 54, 56, 73; Reuben 73; Taylor 134; William 22, 34, 49, 52, 54, 60, 67
LINTHICUM, Thomas 118
LLEWELLEN, C. G. 127
LOCKHEART, Elizabeth 11; Thomas 11
LOMAX, ___ 53, 59, 61, 73, 74, 80, 83, 85-87, 91, 95, 99, 101, 109, 116, 122, 127, 128, 132, 134, 148; Thomas 116
LONG, Reuben 134
LOVELL, Daniel 53; Markham 3, 16, 27, 44, 112; Mary 71; William 51, 71, 148
LOZEAR, Jesse D. 17
LUMPKIN, John 76

LYELL, Ann 37, 62; James 107, 127; John 59; Jonathan 62; Joseph 37, 62; Richard 62
LYLES, James 138
LYNE, ___ 127; Edmond 84, 145; Edmund 7; Henry 3, 12, 15, 17, 24, 30, 31, 35, 39, 40, 49, 58, 67, 70, 81, 84, 101, 102, 108, 110, 112, 113, 115, 117, 121, 124, 136, 142
LYON, James 4, 5, 21, 22
LYSEL, Ann 59; Joseph 59

MABRY, Joseph 22, 56
MAGRUDER, ___ 44, 89, 102, 104, 135; Blizzard 27, 46, 71, 72, 76, 84, 85, 118, 129, 134, 138, 140, 141, 145, 147; Christian 27, 71
MAINER, Richard Tucker 36
MAMESON, John 36
MANKINS, James 12, 13; John 13
MANNING, John 61; Suckey 61
MANOER, Jearry 36
MARR, ___ 46; John 10, 11, 19, 20, 34, 49, 58, 65, 66, 85; S. 49; Susannah 11, 49, 65, 66; W. M. 65
MARSHALL, ___ 89; Benjamin 136; Samuel 70, 104, 109, 112, 136; T. 50; Thomas 22
MARTIN, ___ 44, 115; B. 39, 92, 126, 127, 131, 134 Brice 3, 14, 16, 41, 44, 79, 88, 97, 113, 131, 146; Brice, Jr. 75, 83; Frankey 146; General 128; George 133, 139; Hugh 45; J. 142; Joseph 2-4, 7, 14, 17, 20, 37, 42-44, 53-55, 66, 69, 80, 83-85, 87, 90, 91, 93, 96, 99, 101, 105, 108, 112, 116, 118, 120, 123, 125-127, 129, 131, 132, 140, 144, 147, 148; Joseph, Jr. 144; Joseph, Sr. 87, 112, 126; Susannah 99, 126; Thomas 144; William 113, 146
MASON, Nathan 80; Peter 74
MASTEN, James 14, Sally 83
MASTERS, Elizabeth 141, 142; Elizabeth, Jr. 143; Elizabeth, Sr. 143; Jacob 141, 143, 147; Jo. 52; John 121, 141; Sally 142; Thomas 143
MASTIN, James 31, 83
MATHES, Thomas 42
MATHEWS, John 7; Thomas 42
MAUPIN, Jesse 110
MAY, Caleb 11; Charity 35; James 11, 15; John 3, 13, 35, 83
MAYNARD, Issah 124
MAYNOR, Richard 77
MAYS, David 86, 87, 139; Jesse 86; Legan 75; Little B. 3; Milley 86; Thomas 127
MAYSE, Abraham 113; Abram 45; David 46, 63, 69, 79, 113; Goodwin 79, 113, 123, 126; Henry 6, 46; Isaac 113; Ligin 63; Sherwood 63
McALEXANDER, John 1
McBRIDE, ___ 51; Daniel 8, 13, 61, 64, 122, 132
McCRAW, ___ 115; Jacob 3; James 65; John C. 65
McCULLOCK, ___ 48; Alexander 85, 89, 90, 100; Lydia 89, 90
McDANIEL, Auirilla 93; Michael 93, 100
McGROODER, ___ 59
McGRUDER, Blizzard 39, 56
McKEAND, John 54
McKEANS, ___ 6
McKINNEY, Henry 108, 126, 127; Kinney 105; Mark 105; Pheba

McKINNEY, Phebe, continued: 105; Thomas 105; Willingham 39
McKINSEY, Kinney 57, 58, 60, 70; Phebe 57, 60, 105; Phereby 70
McKINSLEY, Mary 57
McROBERTS, Thomas B. 20
McWILLIAMS, James 26
MELVIN, James 13
MERADY, Juner 145
MEREDITH, Bradley 85; Elijah 109, 136, 137; James 44, 59; Joseph 110; Junor 8, 62, 64, 109, 110, 112
METHVIN, James 132; Niecey 132
MICHAUX, Jacob 49, 54, 56, 73
MILLER, William 77
MILLS, Aaron 77, 141; Charles 70; Elizabeth 66, 112; Richard 106; William 41, 46, 50, 66, 112, 137; William F. 72, 90, 95, 96, 125, 129, 130, 135, 139, 140
MINTER, John 13, 33, 39, 47, 73, 79, 116
MITCHELL, Benjamin 16, 78, 106; Elizabeth 61; F. 140; John 54, 70, 78, 106; L. 118; Richard 61; Robert 35; Samuel 35; Thomas 5; William 29, 32, 33, 49, 66, 69, 70, 82, 85, 88, 96, 118, 121, 122; William M. 38
MOLLING, Phillip 130
MONTGOMERY, A. 74
MOODE, John 37
MOORE, Alexander 60, 70, 79, 97, 111, 138, 146; Andrew 68, 69; Benjamin 107; David 107; Peggy 68, 70; Shadrack 118; Thomas 144, 145; William 12, 51, 55, 56, 66, 85, 119, 143
MORGAN, ____ 39, 46; Anney 11; Littleberry 141
MORRIS, ____ 87; Archibald 111; Farrar III; George 111, 146; Henry 59, 90; Henry, Sr. 60, 72, 23, 90; Joseph 58, 64, 84; Samuel, Jr. 34; Samuel C. 43, 84, 90; William 111
MORTON, ____ 21; Elizabeth 32; James 21, 32, 34, 60; Joseph 32, 59, 62
MOTLEY, William 33
MULLINS, David 56, 66, 69, 90, 97, 129, 141; John 111, 131, 132; Joseph 113; Salley 121, Tabithia 121; William 85;
MURCHIE, John 53
MURPHEY, Archibald 141; James 7, 97; James, Sr. 97
MURPHY, Archibald 10, 29, 43, 139; Clement 44; Elizabeth 22, 96; Francis 97, 147; James 96, 112, 147; James Jr. 96; James Sr. 22, 96; Jesse 41, 75, 123, 143, 144; Nathaniel 139; Peggy 144
MURRAY, Leonard 126

NANCE, Bird 21, 38; Isham 112, 145; Isom 147; John 14, 21, 40, 46, 76; Mary 21, 38, 76, 98; Molly 76; Nancy 15; Reuben 13, 15, 20, 36, 38, 48, 85, 88, 89, 90, 94
NASH, Marvel 49
NEELEY, William 6
NELSON, Thomas 27
NEWMAN, Daniel 36
NICHOLDS, John 99
NICHOLS, Thomas 134
NICKELIEN, George 54
NIESLER, Hugh 10
NIXON, ____ 76; John 38, 98, 99; Joseph 76; William 144

NIXSON, William 127, 128, 132, 144
NORMAN, Betsy 11; Elias 133; William 11, 27, 31, 49, 68, 95, 134
NORRIS, John 16, 25, 36, 44, 56; Nathan 16, 36, 44, 59; Zebulon 56, 59
NORTHCUTT, ____ 91; Capt. ____ 109; Francis 51, 71, 91, 102, 109, 132, 135, 136
NORTON, ____ 94; John 6, 52, 147
NUNN, Ingram 116; John 100; Joseph 60, 100; Mary 18, 92; Thomas 2, 3, 18, 22, 26, 35, 41, 67, 89, 100, 117, 128, 129, 144; Thomas, Jr. 100; Thomas, Sr. 100, 101; Wallers 38; Waters 117; William 117, 127
NUNNELY, Edward 107
NUNNS, John 29

OAKES, John 99; Labon 10, 29; James 10, 66, 133, 134, 141; William 65
OAKLEY, James 49; John 137; Richard 140; Thomas 6, 75, 79, 137; William 126
ODELL, Joseph 125
OFFICER, Gilmore 43; James 43, 63, 84; Marget 84; Thomas 84
OFFUTT, Nathaniel 142
OLDHAM, Elizabeth 95; John 1; John, Sr. 1; Mary 1; Mary, Jr. 1; Thomas 1, 2
OLLIVER, William, Jr. 52
O'NEAL, Hugh 138
OSBORNE, John 36, 45
OWEN, Jesse 65

PACE, John 7, 9, 14, 29, 30, 37, 51, 63, 66, 77, 81, 93, 103, 138, 143, 144, 147; John, Jr. 118; Langston 32, 63, 117, 129, 143; Milley 144; Newson 6, 9, 22, 25, 41, 59, 67; Susanna 59, 131; Thomas 63, W. 8, 29, 63; William 59, 63, 79, 144; William, J. 32, 117
PALFREY, Elizabeth 123; John 22, 123; William 10, 11
PANNILE, David 43, 104
PANNILL, David 118, 121
PARBERRY, James 20, 74
PARKER, Thomas 29
PARKERSON, Archibald 117
PARSLEY, John 122
PASSLEY, Hannah 122; John 82
PATTERSON, Jarrett 56; Jarrott 73; John 56; Judith 73
PAYNE Reuben 12, 20, 79, 81, 84, 93, 100, 125, 131, 139, 146; Robert G. 94
PEARSON, Jeremiah 24; Meredith 114, 121; Rhoda 121; Sarah 98; William 16, 23; William, Sr. 23
PEDDECO, Robert, Jr. 8; Robert, Sr. 8
PEDEGO, Henry 57, 92; Robert 67
PEDEGOY, Joseph 62, Robert 62
PEDIGO, Amey 93; Elijah 83, 92, 148; Elisha 82; Henry 57, 92, 116; Joseph 24, 56, 59; Phebe 107, 108; Phebey 84; Robert 52, 53, 59, 68, 70, 83, 84, 92, 115, 116, 125; Robert, Jr. 61, 83; Robert, Senr. 61, 107, 108, 116
PEDIGOE, Joseph 63, Robert 63
PEDIGOY, Robert, Jr. 51, 52; Robert, Sr. 51, 52

PEGRAM, Edward, Jr. 128; George 128
PENN, Abraham 6, 9, 21, 27, 34, 100; Abram 140; George 53, 100; Greensville 116; Sally 53
PELPHREY, John 77
PEREGOY, Amie 120, 121
PEREGUSON, Archibald 134
PERKINS, Constant 65, 69; Nicholas 22, 56, 65; Peter 9, 33, 42, 75, 85, 96, 120, 147, 148
PERSON, ____ 23; Clapton 71; Jeremiah 25; Meredith 129
PERRY, Samuel 36
PHERIS, Archd. 120
PHIFER, Joseph 24, 41, 130, 147
PHILLIPS, Edward 5, 8; James 36; John 6, 65, 77, 140; Roday 8, 13; Thomas 8, 64
PHILPOTT, Charles 75, 101; Charles T. 7, 40, 62, 132; Charles Thomas 9, 14, 51, 74; Edward 45, 123; John 40, 45, 54, 77, 123, 136; Mary Ann 40; Samuel 40, 77, 123; Zachariah 7, 8, 14, 40, 51, 74, 79, 101, 132
PIERSON, William 16
PILSON, Richard 30
PITTMAN, John B. 83
POPE, Warren 121
PORTER, William 68, 101
POSEY, Elizabeth 17, 45; Humphrey 40, 45; Thomas 17; William 119
POSTON, Solloman 82
POTEET, James Sr. 47
POTTS, Richard 71
PRATT, John 124
PREVILLER, John 19
PRICE, John 41, 43, 80, 105, 141, 142
PROCTOR, ____ 117, 118; Charity 118; Joshua 71, 117, 118
PRYOR, John 11, 19, 20
PULLAM, William 134
PURCELL, John 94, 95, 99, 101
PURGASON, Archelus 142
PYRTLE, John 110, 136; John C. 93; John P. 12, 62, 92, 129, 145; Mary 62, 129

QUALLS, ____ 72; John 72
QUARLES, ____ 34; David 6, 23, 25, 32; Drury 59; James 6, 37; John 6, 23, 25, 138; Judith 23, 25; Mary 25; Moses, Jr. 37; Samuel 37; Sterling 37; William 6, 25, 37; William, Jr. 25

RAMEY, Daniel 8, 9, 26, 129, 137, 146; John 21, 50, 132; Mary 9; Sanford 6, 9, 49, 79, 129, 138, 146; Sanford, Senr. 127; William 138
RANDALS, James 110
RANDOLPH, ____ 4, 58, 59, 115, 120; Ben 54; David M. 53, 54, 91, 116; David Meade 91, 92, 116; Mary 53; T. M. 7, 53; Thomas M. 7, 53, 100; Thomas Man 7, 99
REA, ____ 4; Abner 4, 33, 125, 138; Absalom 4; Andrew 4, 33, 36; James 1, 4, 32, 33, 50, 79, 125; James, Sr. 113; John 7, 25, 32, 113, 138, 143; John W. 66; Mary 32; Molly 33; Sally 36; William C. 35, 64, 105; William Collins 6, 28, 55, 76; Winnefred 55
REAMEY, Da. 75; Daniel 77, 79, 131; Elizabeth 98; John 9; Sanford 88, 98

REAMY, Daniel 28, 59, 63, 128, 131, 144; Mary 62, 128; Ramouth 131; Sanford 35, 59, 63, 116, 144
REANY, John 143
REAVES, George 77; Mary 77
REDD, ____ 97, 136; John 3, 8, 9, 14, 16, 31, 39, 40, 47, 53, 54, 56, 57, 66, 77, 80, 83, 84, 85, 91, 103, 104, 106, 109, 119, 130, 136, 138, 139, 142, 143, 144; Mary 3; Waller 92, 104, 106, 109, 130, 139, 144, 145
REED, John 54
REIGER, Jacob, Sr. 104; Richard 104
RENNO, John 9
RENS, Benjamin 21
RENTFRO, Josh. 7
RETHEL, Henry 55
REY, Abner 37, 136
REYNOLDS, Archelaus 4, 26; George 46, 117, 131; Jesse 18; John 133; Moses 18; Richard 28, 117, 119, 120, 121
RICE, Ann 66; Edith 145; John 124; William 66
RICHARDSON, ____ 20, 117; Elijah 22, 130, 142; John 4, 23; Thomas 147, 148
RICKEL, William 22, 40, 56
RICKELS, Frederick 129
RIGG, Charles 12; Peter 133
ROACH, Jesse 6
ROBERSON, Esther 43; Hester 76; Jesse 16; William 33, 43, 76
ROBERT, Alexander W. 54
ROBERTS, ____ 76; James 35, 50, 81, 99, 100; Jeremiah 45, 130, 136, 137; John 148; Joseph 7, 100; William 65, 109, 117
ROBERTSON, ____ 33, 63, 113; Easter 34; Jesse 23; Walter 19; William 4, 34, 43; William, Jr. 35
ROBINSON, Archibald 62; Meredith 106; William 63
ROBISON, William 43, 76
ROCHESTER, Nathaniel 71
ROCK, Winney 138
ROSE, Caroline 102, 142; Caroline M. 102; Hugh 102, 142; John B. 145; Patrick 102, 142; Samuel 102, 142
ROSS, Lewis 110; Robert 124
ROWAN, Robert 4
ROWLAND, ____ 53; Baldwin 85, 92, 131, 140, 146; Gilbert 122, 126, 128, 130, 137; John 3, 14, 20, 35, 41, 45, 55, 67, 74, 81, 85, 93, 97, 125, 131, 137, 138, 139, 146; John, Jr. 44, 76, 101, 105, 109, 122, 123; John, Sr. 131; John H. 78; Michael 1, 101; Robert 145; Washington 99, 101, 109, 130, 131
ROYSTER, Banister 50, 55; Charles 81, 100, 122; Edward 122; Peter 55
RUBLE, Thomas W. 47, 57; Thomas White 47, 85, 103
RUGG, Peter 41
RUNNOLD, George 24, 25, 107
RYAN, Joseph 50; Obedience 58, 117; Philip 36, 52, 58, 67, 94, 117; Philip, Jr. 117; Philip, Sr. 117

ST. WOODSON, John 101
SALMON, ____ 109; Abigail 35; Elizabeth 62, 113; George 11;

SALMON, Continued: H. Jr. 29, 57; Hezekiah 34, 35, 45, 46, 64; John 4, 24, 34, 35, 39, 57, 58, 62, 70, 78, 79, 84, 102, 112, 113, 119, 125, 142; John, Jr. 107, 113, 119; Obadiah 113; Thaddeus 57, 113
SAMES, ____ 137;
SAMON, John 30
SAMS, ____ 140; Elijah 41, 43, 112
SANDS, William 122
SANFORD, Henry 22
SAUNDERS, Peter 14
SCALES, Henry 134; Joseph 65, 106; Nathaniel 65; Peter 106
SCEARCEY, Bennett 31; Robert 31
SCOTT, George 71
SHACKLEFORD, Daniel 133; Henry 80, 92; Henry, Sr. 99; Polly 92; William 129, 139
SHAKLEFORD, Henry 53
SHARP, William 91, 98, 106, 108
SHELTON, ____ 94; Cuthbert 67; James 55, 72, 84, 124, 142; Nathan 100; Nathaniel 46; Nathaniel W. 100; Walter 5, 10; William 2, 10, 12, 34, 55, 64, 69, 72, 75, 78, 88, 142
SHEWMATE, Samuel 40
SHOEMAKE, Samuel 50, 78
SHORT, James 33; John 22
SHORTS, ____ 74
SHOUMATE, Samuel 56, 81
SHUMATE, Samuel 146
SIMMONS, John 20, 39, 62; Nancy 20
SIMMS, Ignatious 61, 130; John 55, 128
SIMPSON, ____ 117; Jesse 140; Patty 142; Presley 115, 118, 129, 142; William 64, 109, 128, 133
SIMSON, Presley 80, 93
SLEATOR, James M. 129
SMITH, ____ 69, 146; Agnes 34, 46; Amey 23; Anthony 32, 34, 46; Bellerophan 3; Beniman 99; Benjamin 31, 139, 143; Caroline 63; Daniel 47, 57, 70, 85, 103, 105, 110; Drury 125; Edward 32, 118; Elijah 17; Henry 43, 74; Jacob 117, 139; James 13, 96, 110, 115, 140, 147; Jesse 23; John 1, 3, 32, 44, 67, 69, 72, 92, 94, 99, 110, 119, 124, 139, 143, 146; Josiah 55; Moses 36, 94; Peter 110; Robert 19, 119, 121, 135, 136, 139; Sally 99; Thomas 3; William 3, 63, 125, 146; William R. 127; Zadock 18
SOLOMON, Drury 32; William 65
SOUTHERLAND, Judith 132, 134, 135; Samuel 87, 134, 135; Samuel D. 132
SPANS, William 50
SPEARS, Nicholas 26
SPENCER, ____ 72, 124; George W. 94; George Washington 46, 78, 124; James 2, 46, 72, 78, 97; James, Jr. 97; John 34, 39, 46, 65, 72, 78; Margaret 78; Patsy 124; Ruth 72; William 46, 65, 72, 78, 94, 145
SPRIGGS, Thomas 71
SPURLOCK, Drury 47; Jesse 47
STANLEY, Ann 111
STAPLES, Edward 145; George J. 72; James 145; James, Jr. 145; John 12, 32, 34, 45-47, 55, 72, 94, 100, 109, 142; Samuel 55, 105

STARK, ____ 2
STARLING, Ann 130; Thomas 68, 89, 90, 95, 103, 110, 144, 145
STEART, Collen 121
STEPHENS, ____ 97; Dudley 81, 114, 119, 127, 138; John 40, 113, 146; Millea 146; Milly 40; Nancy 138; Samuel 35, 45 William 50, 114; William, Jr. 113; William, Sr. 113
STEVENS, James 74; John 40, 81; William 27, 40; William, Jr. 40, 51
STEWARD, Collen 138
STEWART, James 38; Thomas 42, 62, 63, 75, 78, 144; Uselah, 62, 63; Usley 42
STITH, Jesse 4
STOCKTON, ____ 76, 83; Ann 68, 94, Catherine 94; Dorics 94; Elizabeth 28; Richard 12, 28, 37, 136; Robert 3, 9, 20, 21, 25, 38, 61, 82, 94, 95, 98, 99, 101, 116, 117, 136; Robert, Jr. 20
STOKES, ____ 121, 137; Elizabeth 61; Isabell 146; John 14, 28, 60, 61; Polly 61; William 3, 16, 45, 60, 61, 68, 73, 75, 79, 101, 128, 145-147
STONE, Doshe 60; Eeusbus 124; Elizabeth 60; Eusebus 7, 60; Eusebus, Jr. 26, 124, Eusebus, Sr. 22; Jeremiah 41, 88, 89, 97, 126; John 1, 65, 94, 99, 114, 115, 123; Jonathan 13, 93, 94, 114, 135, 136; Littleberry Hurt 92; Stephen 77; Susanah 60; Thomas 60; William 10, 18, 60
STOVALL, ____ 75; Brett 147; Elizabeth 29; Joseph 6, 26, 29, 32, 60; Thomas 11, 29, 111, 146
STRONG, James 83; Robert 115
STUART, Collen 138; James 30, 31; Thomas 27
STULS, Abner 35, 59; Mary 136; Molly 136
STULTS, ____ 71; Abner 44, 104, 133, 134; Adam 102, 136; Gabrie 104; Nancy 133, 134
SUMPTER, ____ 17; Agnes 37; George 30; Henry 14, 15, 24, 30, 37, 65, 114; Henry, Jr. 30
SWAIN, George 11
SWITZLER, George 145

TALBOT, ____ 70; Charles 68
TALMON, Mary 39
TANKERSLEY, Rowland 7
TARBORN, Ellendor 33, 49
TARRANT, Carter 13, 48; Reuben 7; Reuben, Jr. 19; Samuel 18, 91
TATE, Caleb 94
TATUM, Edward 69; Isham Browder 30; Rachel Browder 30
TAYLER, Hughes 40; James 40, 56
TAYLOR, ____ 3; Ann 67; George 26, 41, 56, 83, 99, 115, 125; Ignatious 71; James 3, 11, 13, 18, 23, 35, 41, 67, 97, 115; John 115; Josiah 99, 115, 132; Robert 129; Thomas 133
THOMAS, Augustine 55, 83, 84, 106, 128; Benjamin 13, 15, 20; Joseph 84, 106; Michael 123; Philip 36; William 15
THOMASON, Eleas 118; Fleming 139; Joseph 139
THOMASSON, ____ 15; Arnal 148;

THOMASSON, Continued: Elias 148;
  Fleming 13, 17, 74, 137;
  James 13; William 13
THOMPSON, William 3, 12, 77
TITTLE, Anthony 54; John 55
TOMPKINS, John 32
TOOMBS, ___ 89; Edmond 8; Susan
  127, 128; Susannah 13; William
  8, 13, 71, 112, 127, 128
TORBURN, Eleanor 9
TOWNLIN, Joseph 22, 62, 130;
  Purlla 62
TOWLING, Joseph 62
TRAHORN, John 133
TRAVERS, John 91
TRAVIS, John 45, 63, 104, 105,
  108, 135
TRENT, John B. 142, 145
TUGGLE, Thomas 72
TUNSTALL, Richard 53, William
  53, 83
TURLEY, Leonard 13; Samuel 36
TURNER, Jeremiah 110, 125; John
  123, 125; John, Sr. 103; Jo-
  siah 125; Larkin 123, 125,
  143; Mary 125; Shadrack 47,
  57, 85, 103; Stephen 134; Wil-
  liam 123, 125

UHLES, Frederick 87, 131; Phebey
  131

VAUGHAN, Aris 112; Aristepus
  123; Henry 80, 85; Mary 105
VEANBLE, Richard Nathaniel 18;
  Richard W. 5
VENABLE, Richard N. 18, 19
VERDEL, John A. 145
VERELL, James 61; John 133
VERNON, Tinsley 134

WADE, Agnes 137; Ballenger 26,
  30, 39, 42, 55, 95, 114, 115,
  133, 142, 147; Bartlett 62,
  92, 97, 114, 129, 136, 147;
  Jonadab 35, 43, 56, 97, 110,
  111; Lucy 146; Mary Ann 43;
  Reuben 78, 90, 110, 111, 125,
  131, 132, 146
WALLER, ___ 89; Col. ___ 4;
  Carr 63, 101, 109, 112, 131,
  137, 145; E. 89; Edmond 103;
  Edmund 27, 77, 103; George 3,
  14, 17, 27, 34, 77, 78, 80,
  82, 109, 113, 116, 124, 130,
  147; George, Jr. 3, 13, 17,
  22, 34, 41, 48, 50, 72, 79,
  80, 82, 83, 88, 92, 100, 103,
  107, 109, 111, 112, 116, 119,
  130, 136, 137, 142; George,
  Sr. 17, 142; John 4, 17, 29,
  34, 57, 60, 64, 79, 89, 105,
  109, 113, 127, 134, 145; Joshua 89; Maratha 91; Mary 89;
  Pearce 115; Will. 27; William
  34, 58, 89, 103, 107, 109, 111,
  142
WALTON, George 82
WARREN, William 16, 25, 112, 121
WASH, John 98; Thomas 145
WASHINGTON, Bartlett 24, 30
WATKINS, ___ 42; Edward 28; Stephen 23
WATSON, ___ 45, 59, 88; David 8,
  74, 86; Henry L. 116; Henry S.
  104, 105; J. H. 108; J. W. 31,
  63; John 8, 10 21, 30, 31, 32,
  36, 51, 59, 104, 108, 116,
  129, 140, 144; John W. 104,
  105; Mary Ann 104, 105; Mica-
  hel 118; Phebe 93; Samuel 9,
  68, 93, 120; Sarah 104, 105;
  Thomas H. 63, 104, 105, 108,
  109, 116, 129, 130, 139;

WATSON, Continued: William 5,
  26, 27, 99
WARWICK, William 28
WATTS, Thomas 10
WEATHERFORD, Benjamin 135; David
  27, 33, 98, 127, 131, 135;
  Hardin 98; Mary 27, 33
WEAVER, ___ 89; John 20, 33, 37,
  75, 89, 135, 143
WEBB, Martin 27; Merry 42
WEEKS, John 29
WELLS, ___ 5, 21; Barna 5, 17,
  21, 51, 69, 70, 91, 114, 121,
  131, 135; Barnaba 87, 105;
  Barnaby 21; Barny 132; John
  21, 39, 72-74, 79, 80, 82,
  84, 85, 90; Judith 72, 73,
  90; Mathew 71, 73, 90; Rebek-
  ah 36; Tabithia 73, 90; Wil-
  liam 12, 36
WENIRSE, John 56
WHEELER, ___ 36, 45
WHISETT, William 9
WHITE, Ambrose 55, 75, 114; Dan-
  iel 28; Sally 114
WHITECOTTON, Axton 31
WHITLOCK, Charles 84
WHITTAKER, William 80
WHITTON, ___ 87; William 15
WHITWORTH, Thomas 135
WILBOURN, John 110
WILKERSON, Nathaniel 54
WILKINS, Elizabeth 136, 139;
  Thomas 33, 44, 59, 71, 78,
  81, 86, 91, 115, 117, 136, 139
WILL, Barna 68; Sarah 68
WILLIAMS, ___ 40; Abram 120, 129;
  Angiliche 129; Bennett 117;
  David 108; Elisha 107, 120;
  Elizabeth 129; Ephraim 108;
  Garrott 60, 75, 76, 108; John
  71; Ozburn 23, 76, 138; Per-
  manas 50, 117; R. 5; Robert
  128; Samuel 138; Susanna W.
  129; Tabithia 129; Thomas 23,
  40, 96, 129; Thomas Jr. 105
WILLIAMSON, ___ 5, 86; Nancy 67;
  Robert 3, 4. 119
WILLINGHAM, Jesse 9
WILLIS, Abel 105; David 130; Tho-
  mas 105
WILLS, John 76, 89, 112, 133;
  David 130
WILSON, ___ 146; Aaron 15, 117;
  Daniel 42, 49, 50, 66, 101;
  Ephraim 90, 130; James 15, 27,
  102, 127; John 38, 52; Nathan-
  iel 42; Moses 10, 27, 40, 42,
  43, 51, 81, 102, 134; Thomas
  29, 32, 33, 82, 102, 103;
  Thomas, Jr. 15, 107; Thomas,
  Sr. 141
WINSTON, Dorthea 133; Edmund 132,
  133; George D. 133; George
  Dabney 132, 133
WIRT, William 4
WITT, David 28, 107; Jesse 4, 58,
  64, 69, 115, 134; Jo. 97; Jo-
  el 110; John 24, 30; William
  103
WOMACK, Allen 83
WOODLIFF, Augustine 55, 104
WOODS, Hugh 20, 25; J. 20, 53,
  54; Sarah Ann 20, 25
WOODSON, ___ 45; Benjamin 101;
  John S. 147; John St. 101;
  Samuel 66
WOOLARD, William 135
WORKMAN, George 55; Peter 54, 55
WORSHAM, Richard 11
WYATT, John 20

ZACKERY, Caty 5

___ Betty 17; Brumly 21;
  Jack 21; John 21; John 21;
  Joie 17; Lucy 21; Rachel 21,
  145; Susanah 21

SLAVES

Aaron 66
Agga 32
Aggy 66
Aimy 147
Allet 66
Alse 57
Alsey 105
Amy 103
Andrew 88, 103
Anne 88, 123
Betty 124
Bouzer 103
Bower 88
Brown 88
Cate 98
Ceaser 124
Cele 88
Chaney 98
Charles 103
Charlotte 88, 103
Clementa 66
Daniel 90
Dinah 65
Eady 66
Easter 98
Edmund 105
Elly 66
Feby 118
Franky 66
George 1, 2
Hannah 66
Harry 111
Honor 66
Isham 90
James 95, 147
Jane 147
Jenny 88, 103
Jerey 66, 123
Jinney 66
Joe 88, 103
Judith 123
Kitt 123
Lindy 103
Luce 111
Lucy 66
Major 147
Manec 118
Mary 57, 65
Mourning 66
Ned 88
Nelson 66
Pheen 66
Phill 111
Phillis 90, 111
Plott 98
Polly 98
Rachel 90, 103
Reuben 117
Reubin 98
Ruth 88
Sally 147
Samuel 90
Sarah 124
Sharpes 66
Sinda 88
Squire 66, 124
Starling 118
Stephen 111
Targe 98
Tiller 60
Watt 88
Webb 90
Will 90
William 145
Winiford 2

www.ingramcontent.com/pod-product-compliance
Lightning Source LLC
Chambersburg PA
CBHW031420290426
44110CB00011B/468